Speaking of Profit

Harvard-Yenching Institute Monograph Series 109

Speaking of Profit

Bao Shichen and Reform in Nineteenth-Century China

William T. Rowe

Published by the Harvard University Asia Center
Distributed by Harvard University Press
Cambridge (Massachusetts) and London 2018

Printed in the United States of America

The Harvard-Yenching Institute, founded in 1928, is an independent foundation dedicated to the advancement of higher education in the humanities and social sciences in Asia. Headquartered on the campus of Harvard University, the Institute provides fellowships for advanced research, training, and graduate studies at Harvard by competitively selected faculty and graduate students from Asia. The Institute also supports a range of academic activities at its fifty partner universities and research institutes across Asia. At Harvard, the Institute promotes East Asian studies through annual contributions to the Harvard-Yenching Library and publication of the *Harvard Journal of Asiatic Studies* and the Harvard-Yenching Institute Monograph Series.

Library of Congress Cataloging-in-Publication Data
Names: Rowe, William T., author.
Title: Speaking of profit : Bao Shichen and reform in nineteenth-century China / William T. Rowe.
Other titles: Harvard-Yenching Institute monograph series ; 109.
Description: Cambridge, Massachusetts : Published by the Harvard University Asia Center, 2018. | Series: Harvard-Yenching Institute monograph series ; 109 | Includes bibliographical references and index.
Identifiers: LCCN 2017029362 | ISBN 9780674983809 (hardcover : alk. paper)
Subjects: LCSH: Bao, Shichen, 1775–1855. | Reformers—China—History—19th century. | China—History—1795–1861. | China—Economic conditions—1644–1912. | China—Politics and government—1644–1912.
Classification: LCC DS755 .R69 2018 | DDC 951/.033092—dc23
LC record available at https://lccn.loc.gov/2017029362

Index by Stephen Ullstrom

♾ Printed on acid-free paper

Last figure below indicates year of this printing
27 26 25 24 23 22 21 20 19 18

Contents

Illustrations, Maps, and Table

Illustrations

Maps

Table

Acknowledgments

Over the past several years, I have presented talks and seminars on Bao Shichen at many institutions, including Johns Hopkins University, University of Washington–Seattle, Yale University, Columbia University, University of Pennsylvania, East China Normal University, and the Association for Asian Studies Annual Meeting. In each case, my hosts and audiences were extremely helpful in encouraging me to sort out my ideas. I wish to thank especially Professors Pierre-Étienne Will, Peter C. Perdue, James Scott, Lin Man-houng, Wang Di, Jiang Jin, R. Kent Guy, Richard von Glahn, and Madeleine Dong for their comments and assistance. Two anonymous readers for the Harvard Asia Center Publications Committee offered numerous welcome suggestions for improvement, and Robert Graham of the Center was consistently supportive.

Earlier versions of portions of this book have appeared as the following articles: "Money, Economy, and Polity in the Daoguang-era Paper Currency Debates," *Late Imperial China* 21.2 (December 2010); "Introduction: The Significance of the Qianlong-Jiaqing Transition in Qing History," *Late Imperial China* 22.2 (December 2011); "Rewriting the Qing Constitution: Bao Shichen's 'On Wealth' (*Shuochu*)," *T'oung Pao* 98 (2012); and "Bao Shichen and Agrarian Reform in Early Nineteenth-Century China," *Frontiers of History in China* 9.1 (2014). I am grateful to the editors of these journals and to the publishers—Johns Hopkins University Press and Brill Publishers—for permission to reuse that material here. The maps are by Bill Nelson.

I am extraordinarily fortunate to be a member of the History Department and the East Asian Studies Program at Johns Hopkins University. I thank my Hopkins colleagues and students, and above all my friend Tobie Meyer-Fong, for continued intellectual and moral support throughout the production of this book.

As always, my greatest supporters have been Jill Friedman, Josh Rowe, and Sara Rowe.

INTRODUCTION

The End of the Prosperous Age

Over the past decades, we have learned a great deal about the Qing's "prosperous age" (*shengshi*) of the eighteenth century, and about the first "opening up" (*kaifang*) era of the late nineteenth and early twentieth centuries. But the first half of the nineteenth century—the reigns of the Jiaqing (1796–1820) and Daoguang (1821–50) emperors—has, with the exception of the singular event of the Opium War, attracted much less scholarly attention. The appearance in 1978 of Susan Mann Jones and Philip A. Kuhn's landmark *Cambridge History of China* article on the early nineteenth century, "Dynastic Decline and the Roots of Rebellion," struck like a lightning bolt, precisely because, unlike most of the other articles in that volume, which summarized the well-known work on their topics, Jones and Kuhn were providing remarkably new stuff, since the period they were covering had been so largely ignored in previous English-language studies.[1] Ironically, the magisterial power of their article may have contributed to a prolonged dearth of scholarship after that time, with few scholars feeling they could alter its conclusions very much.[2]

1. Susan Mann Jones and Philip A. Kuhn, "Dynastic Decline and the Roots of Rebellion," in *Cambridge History of China*, vol. 10, *Late Ch'ing, 1800–1911*, part 1, ed. John K. Fairbank (Cambridge: Cambridge University Press, 1978), 107–62.

2. On the dearth of scholarship on early nineteenth-century Chinese history, in Chinese as well as in Western languages, see Seunghyun Han, *After the Prosperous Age: State and Elites in Early Nineteenth-Century Suzhou* (Cambridge, MA: Harvard University Asia Center, 2016), 6–11.

This lacuna is understandable but also rather surprising, since the Jiaqing reign in particular is arguably *the* transition era in modern Chinese history. A recent Chinese biography of the monarch by Guan Wenfa, indeed, characterizes his reign straightforwardly as a turning point "from prosperity to decline" (*cong sheng dao shuai*).[3] There was an immediate and complicated crisis of great severity, but also a more broad-based malaise: things that had seemed easy or routine in the past now were increasingly difficult to do. And what's more, people within and without the administration—pointedly the emperor himself—knew this, were achingly frustrated by it, and fretted over how things might be done better. On the other hand, from a later perspective these men and their world looked positively *good*—post-Taiping political discourse is strewn with nostalgic references to the lost golden age of "Xianfeng *yiqian*" (prior to the mid-century Xianfeng reign). The officials and literati of the Jiaqing reign, again including the monarch himself, impress us generally as capable, knowledgeable, pretty much honest, and energetic, but so very troubled. One particularly influential literatus of this era is the protagonist of this book, Bao Shichen (1775–1855).

From Qianlong to Jiaqing

Several generations of scholarship—at least since Suzuki Chūsei's seminal 1952 *A Study of the Mid-Qing Period*—have outlined for us the myriad ways in which the turn of the nineteenth century signaled the rather sudden and pronounced downturn of Qing dynastic fortunes.[4] Many at the time recognized the existence of a demographic crisis; as early as 1793, Hong Liangji had written that over the previous century the empire's population had increased "ten to twenty times," while the amount of available farmland "has only doubled, or, at the most, increased three to five times." The inevitable outcome would be a Malthusian check of "flood, drought, and plagues," though even this would not be sufficient to alleviate the

3. Guan Wenfa, *Jiaqing di* (The Jiaqing emperor) (Changchun: Jilin wenshi chubanshe, 1993), 30.

4. Suzuki Chūsei, *Shinchō chūkishi kenkyū* (A study of the mid-Qing period) (Toyohashi-shi: Aichi daigaku kokusai mondai kenkyūjo, 1952).

long-term subsistence crisis.[5] A related and very troubling demographic issue was the growing number of unmarried rogue males (*guanggun*), a consequence both of the increasingly skewed sex ratio stemming from the "positive check" of female infanticide and of the inability of downwardly mobile males to support a household.[6] Another, well described by Jones and Kuhn, was the frustration of *upwardly* mobile males to find rewards in the shrinking per capita numbers of examination degrees and official posts—the classic "talent glut" of developing countries in the later post-colonial world.[7]

If the talent glut was a crisis born of extended prosperity, so too was the multifaceted ecological decay widely noted during this period. Generations of encroachment on lakeshores and riverbanks of the middle Yangzi watershed, stimulated by the growing downriver demand for commercial rice, had rendered the Yangzi valley, likely for the first time in imperial history, a source of flooding of equal concern as the Yellow or Huai Rivers to the north. Hillside land, reclaimed over the preceding century, suffered topsoil runoff and progressively declining fertility, contributing to the economic grievances at the root of the White Lotus rebellion.[8] And the failure of Yellow River maintenance during the maladministration of the late Qianlong reign led to silting up of the Grand

5. Hong's famous population essay is translated by K. C. Liu in Wm. Theodore de Bary and Richard Lufrano, *Sources of Chinese Tradition*, 2nd ed. (New York: Columbia University Press, 2000), 2.174–76. For discussion of Hong's ideas and their context, see Guan Wenfa, *Jiaqing di*, 188–94.

6. James Z. Lee and Wang Feng, *One Quarter of Humanity: Malthusian Mythology and Chinese Realities* (Cambridge, MA: Harvard University Press, 1999), 47–51; Ted A. Telford, "Family and State in Qing China: Marriage in the Tongcheng Lineages, 1650–1850," in *Jinshi jiazu yu zhengzhi bijiao lishi lunwen ji* (Modern family and political history) (Taibei: Institute of Modern History, 1992), 921–42; Matthew H. Sommer, *Sex, Law, and Society in Late Imperial China* (Stanford: Stanford University Press, 2000), 12–15 and passim.

7. Jones and Kuhn, "Dynastic Decline," 113–16.

8. Pierre-Étienne Will, "Un cycle hydraulique en Chine: la province du Hubei du 16ème au 19ème siècles," *Bulletin de l'école française d'extrême orient* 68 (1980): 261–87; Peter C. Perdue, "Water Control in the Dongting Lake Region During the Ming and Qing Periods," *Journal of Asian Studies* 41.4 (August 1982): 747–65; Evelyn S. Rawski, "Agricultural Development in the Han River Highlands," *Ch'ing-shih wen-t'i* 3.4 (1975): 63–81.

Canal and the increased difficulty of shipping grain tribute rice to the capital area and the northern frontiers.

Military challenges appeared on many fronts. The White Lotus war was the big one, of course, but there were others. The "Great Miao Uprising" on the Hunan-Guizhou frontier, for example, broke out in 1795, signifying the ultimate failure of decades of vacillating ethnic policy in the region.[9] The White Lotus campaigns themselves were a multifaceted disaster. The sectarian problem was never really suppressed, but merely dispersed, to rise again in 1813 and after.[10] On the other hand, in the course of the campaign the Qing lost, to some degree for all time, control over its own military, as hired mercenary militias unnecessarily protracted the war for years to ensure their continued payment.[11] The extremely costly campaigns wiped out the accumulated surplus from the "prosperous era" in the Board of Revenue, and left the central government ever after having to improvise in unsavory ways to meet its payrolls.[12] Internally, as the young reformer Bao Shichen pointed out in 1801, every office in the bureaucracy was left in arrears on remittances owed to its immediately superior office.[13]

After years of Heshen's administrative racketeering, bureaucratic morale and bureaucratic capacity were manifestly at an all-time low. After assuming his personal rule and arresting and ordering the suicide of Heshen in February 1799, the Jiaqing emperor evoked great literati grumbling for not going farther than he did in purging the bureaucracy of Heshen's clients. In one of the great moments of political theater in all of imperial history, the senior and widely respected Hanlin academician Hong Liangji famously leaked a letter to Prince Cheng lambasting the new

9. Donald S. Sutton, "Ethnicity and the Miao Frontier in the Eighteenth Century," in *Empire at the Margins: Culture, Ethnicity, and Frontier in Early Modern China*, ed. Pamela Kyle Crossley, Helen F. Siu, and Donald S. Sutton (Berkeley: University of California Press, 2006), 190–228.

10. Susan Naquin, *Millenarian Rebellion in China: The Eight Trigrams Uprising of 1813* (New Haven: Yale University Press, 1976).

11. Yingcong Dai, "Civilians Go into Battle: Hired Militias in the White Lotus Wars, 1795–1805," *Asia Major*, 3rd ser., 22.2 (December 2009): 145–78.

12. Elisabeth Kaske, "Fund-Raising Wars: Office Selling and Interprovincial Finance in Nineteenth-Century China," *Harvard Journal of Asiatic Studies* 71.1 (June 2011): 69–141.

13. See chapter 2, below.

monarch for his timidity, inviting first a death sentence and ultimately banishment upon himself, but becoming a hero to the younger generation of disillusioned literati, frustrated in their career aspirations, who emerged at about this time.[14] And Hong was far from alone: the young scholar Bao Shichen, while agreeing with the emperor's decision to pardon lesser wrongdoers in the civil service, called for a fundamental overhaul of the dynasty's administrative structure, a call which was ignored by the throne but influenced a generation of reformers over the succeeding decades. The scholarly literature as a whole, it seems fair to say, views the Jiaqing emperor's seeming failure of nerve in cleaning out his administration at the turn of the century as the original sin that eventually spelled doom for the Qing empire.

Not least, in the long term, the Jiaqing reign is seen by some as a key moment in the major process of late Qing history: the devolution of political control from the central imperial administration into the hands of extrabureaucratic local elites. In his epochal 1970 work on local and regional militarization, Philip Kuhn identified this "boundary of modern [Chinese] history" as occurring during the Taiping and Nian rebellions of the 1850 and 60s, but in a reflective preface to his book written ten years later he acknowledged that the major turning point—not yet militarization, but already significant local elite incursion into the tax collection process—may have come a half century earlier, during the Jiaqing reign.[15] More recently, Kuhn's student Seunghyun Han argues for the retreat of the central state and concomitant rise of local elite power in the early Jiaqing reign, with, in most cases, deliberate governmental prompting, or at least concurrence. Han finds this exemplified in three phenomena. First was the greater elite funding of local public causes, stimulated

14. Hong's letter is translated in de Bary and Lufrano, *Sources of Chinese Tradition*, 172–74. For studies of the affair, see David S. Nivison, "Ho-shen and His Accusers: Ideology and Political Behavior in the Eighteenth Century," in *Confucianism in Action*, ed. David S. Nivison and Arthur S. Wright (Stanford: Stanford University Press, 1959), 209–43; Susan Mann Jones, "Hung Liang-chi (1746–1809): The Perception and Articulation of Political Problems in Late Eighteenth-Century China," Ph.D. dissertation, Stanford University, 1971. For the younger literati influenced by Hong, see James M. Polachek, *The Inner Opium War* (Cambridge, MA: Harvard University Council on East Asian Studies, 1992).

15. Philip A. Kuhn, *Rebellion and Its Enemies in Late Imperial China: Militarization and Social Structure: 1796–1864* (Cambridge, MA: Harvard University Press, 1970).

by the state via campaigns to sell brevet ranks and offices (*juanna*) and other means. Second was the relaxation of central controls over the enshrinement of local worthies in local temples (*minghuan* and *xiangxian*)—individuals whose worthiness was defined in connection to local rather than central government interests. And third was the revived production of local literature—for example, publication of market town gazetteers, which rose dramatically in this era—in response to the administration's relaxation of the censorship campaigns of the *Siku quanshu* "literary inquisition" of the 1770s and 80s.[16]

Court-Centered Reform: A Jiaqing Restoration?

A wave of recent scholarship has put forward a newly positive view of the Jiaqing reign, emphasizing signs of dynastic renewal that actually worked, at least a for few decades, perhaps until the Daoguang depression and the Opium War presented wholly new kinds of threats. (The Daoguang emperor, by contrast, is usually still seen today as rash and indecisive.)[17] Jiaqing's modern biographer, Guan Wenfa, with seemingly deliberate resonance intended to the century-later "late Qing reforms," terms the emperor's package of reformist legislation the "*Jiaqing* xinzheng" (Jiaqing new policies).[18] In a brief but powerful article, Zhang Yufen summarizes the policy shifts of the first years of Jiaqing's personal rule as the *xianyu weixin* (comprehensive reform), a phrase that Daniel McMahon boldly translates as the "Jiaqing Restoration." The phrase had its origins in the discourse of the day itself. The new emperor, of course, had out of the dictates of filiality to avoid distancing himself too publicly from the

16. Seunghyun Han, "Changing Roles of Local Elites from the 1730s to the 1820s," in *Cambridge History of China*, vol. 9, *The Ch'ing Dynasty to 1800*, part 2, ed. Willard J. Peterson (Cambridge: Cambridge University Press, 2016), 606–48. On the Jiaqing reign as a turning point in the escalation and decentralization of office selling, see also Kaske, "Fund-Raising Wars," 90–92.

17. See, for example, Mao Haijian, *Tianchao de pengkui: Yaian zhanzheng cai yanjiu* (Imperial collapse: a revisionist study of the Opium War) (Beijing: Sanlian shudian, 2005).

18. Guan Wenfa, *Jiaqing di*, 113–14.

policies and practice of his late father. Thus, when on New Year's day of Jiaqing fourth year (1799), the first new year after the Qianlong emperor's death, the libationer of the Imperial College, Mongol bannerman Fashishan (1753–1813), included in his New Year's greeting to the monarch congratulations on his implementation of a *xinzheng weixin*, Jiaqing took exception to this formulation, insisted that he was simply continuing his father's good work, and cashiered Fashishan for his boldness. But others of the time, including the young prince Zhaolian (1780–1833), were similarly flushed with the excitement of political reform and wrote privately of the *weixin* (restoration) they saw going on around them.[19]

The new scholarship emphasizes several components of this restoration agenda. Most basic was a concerted, protracted, and largely successful propaganda campaign organized by the emperor himself to demonize Heshen as the "primal evil" (*yuan'e*), and isolate him as the "one man" responsible for decades of corruption and maladministration. (The success of this campaign is such that conventional historiography today still bears its influence!) The implication, of course, was that Heshen's personal removal would lead in and of itself to reformed governance. But the new monarch also consistently promoted himself as the antithesis of Heshen, the man who would personally restore "substantive administration" (*shizheng*), diligent and attentive governance (*qinzheng*), and, most emphatically, "enlightened rule" (*minzheng*).[20] *Shi*, *qin*, and *min* became staples of imperial discourse in these years, the new emperor having devoted detailed study to the historical meanings of these terms during his long tenure as heir apparent. "Regardless of how good the laws [*liangfa*] and how well thought-out the policies [*meiyi*]," the emperor wrote, "none will succeed unless you have selected persons to carry them out who embody *qin* and *min*."[21]

19. Zhang Yufen, "Lun Jiaqing chunian de 'Xianyu weixin'" (On the "comprehensive reforms" of the early Jiaqing reign), *Qingshi yanjiu* 1992.4: 49–54; Daniel McMahon, "Dynastic Decline, Heshen, and the Ideology of the Xianyu Reforms," *Tsing Hua Journal of Chinese Studies*, new ser., 38.2 (June 2008): 231–55. On Zhaolian, see also R. Kent Guy, *Qing Governors and Their Provinces: The Evolution of Territorial Administration in China, 1644–1796* (Seattle: University of Washington Press, 2010), 139.

20. McMahon, "Xianyu Reforms."

21. Guan Wenfa, *Jiaqing di*, 103.

Guided by his newly recalled childhood tutor Zhu Gui (1731–1807), scion of a powerful family of metropolitan officials and intellectuals who had been banished to the provinces by the Heshen faction (where, incidentally, he had discovered and patronized the young Bao Shichen), Jiaqing began just a few weeks after his father's death "to dismantle the provincial power structure Heshen had built." In the four years 1799–1802, he made forty-three new gubernatorial and viceregal appointments, touching every quarter of the empire. In many of these cases, the previous incumbent was simply dismissed by the new emperor.[22]

The new emperor implemented a strict prohibition on gift giving within the bureaucracy (*jincheng baowu*), and launched a campaign for personal frugality on the part of officials (*chongjian chushe*). He promoted himself as a model of such frugality, in such ways as conspicuously avoiding the southern tours much favored by his father. He also minimized his visits to the summer palaces, and issued a prohibition on the erection of stages for performances of opera within the gates of the imperial city.

In quest of "attentive" and "enlightened" governance, and in stated pursuit of "promoting the beneficial and eliminating abuses" (*xingli chubi*), the new emperor in the first month of the first year of his personal rule proclaimed the broadest possible opening (*guangkai*, *dakai*) of the "pathways of words" (*yanlu*), input from below outside the normally sanctioned communications hierarchy, on any issue of popular concern. This too became something of a propaganda campaign, with the emperor repeatedly insisting that he "actively sought out truthful speech" (*zhaoqiu zhenyan*). And in fact, the new scholarship suggests, Jiaqing in the early years of his personal rule did prove an unusually tolerant emperor for remonstrance and open discussion. He also ostentatiously rehabilitated several prominent whistle-blowers (*ganyan zhi chen*) who had been cashiered under his late father, including the censor Cao Xibao (1719–92), dismissed in 1786 for having impeached one of Heshen's henchmen, and the Board of Rites president Yin Zhuangtu (1738–1808), who had charged in 1790 that provincial treasuries throughout the empire were running on empty, with the people suffering as a consequence.

As a stated corollary of his opening the *yanlu*, the Jiaqing emperor sought to revive the institution of capital appeals (*jingkong*), the presen-

22. Guy, *Qing Governors*, 141–42.

tation of cases that had been resolved unsatisfactorily, in the plaintiffs' view, at the local and provincial levels, to either the Censorate or the Capital Gendarmerie at Beijing. The number of such cases had begun to rise during the late Qianlong era, prompting that emperor to tighten restrictions on those that might be heard and, in 1784, to impose strict punishments on appellants (the great majority) whose cases were decided to be without merit. In 1801, his successor reversed these decisions. Jiaqing tied the need to hear more appeals with that to clean up the evils of the Heshen era—he noted that he was especially interested in cases that dealt with official malfeasance and with imposition of burdensome taxes at the local level—and he explicitly connected the restriction of this channel of expression of grievances in the recent past with the outbreak of violent rebellion. The emperor succeeded beyond all expectation in soliciting greater numbers of capital appeals, which multiplied enormously during the first few decades of the nineteenth century, creating huge backlogs and prompting central authorities to return the bulk of appeals to the provincial level for rehearing. After protracted experimentation, a new provincial-level institution was developed, an auxiliary court attached to the office of the provincial judge and staffed by head prefects, known as the *fashenju*. Recent scholarship has argued that this was a painfully expensive innovation for the cash-strapped imperial administration, but that it seems to at least correlate with a decline in violent protest (as the emperor had projected), and that it was an important step toward the development of an independent judiciary in late imperial China.[23]

Seunghyun Han offers further support for the view of an unusual tolerance of dissent in the early Jiaqing reign. Han centers on the issue of examination strikes (*bakao*) by students, which in late Qianlong commonly came to be punished by "elevated punishments" (*congzhong*) imposed on the perpetrators, a hard-line policy that the Jiaqing emperor actively reversed. This same tolerance was extended toward participants in market

23. The classic study of the appeals process is Jonathan K. Ocko, "I'll Take It All the Way to Beijing: Capital Appeals in the Qing," *Journal of Asian Studies* 47.2 (May 1988): 291–315. See also Zhang Shiming and Feng Yongming, "Bao Shichen zhengyi de chengben" (The cost of Bao Shichen justice), *Qingshi yanjiu* 75.4 (November 2009): 1–34; Qiang Fang, "Hot Potatoes: Chinese Complaint Systems from Early Times to the Late Qing (1898)," *Journal of Asian Studies* 8.4 (November 2009): 1105–36.

strikes (*bashi*) by merchants and in tax resistance protests. It was also seen in Jiaqing's tendency to sanction officials who had engaged in "arbitrary" flogging of literati. Han's statistical analysis concludes that, across the board, "various forms of collective action that would very likely have been punished with capital punishment during the Qianlong reign were penalized one degree less severely during the Jiaqing period."[24]

In a provocative and controversial recent book, Wensheng Wang explores the Jiaqing emperor's attempts to "soften the distinction between the inner and outer courts."[25] Having determined that the major vehicles of Heshen's racketeering were the Grand Council and the Imperial Household Department, Jiaqing quickly went about reforming their procedures. In the case of the Imperial Household Department, he sought to end the pattern of having its personnel effectively selecting their own colleagues, instead asserting his right to make appointments to that body personally, normally for limited three-year terms. He also imposed restrictions on the practice that had led to the Household Department's outsized growth during the late Qianlong reign, the collection of "self-assessed fines" (*yizui yin*) on officials for alleged administrative offenses.[26] With regard to the Grand Council, Jiaqing disregarded literati calls for its abolition, instead seeking to bureaucratize, standardize, and regulate its activities. He began with a major personnel reshuffle. He made it at least in part subject to the normal bureaucratic law of avoidance—no family members would be allowed to serve simultaneously on the council—and he prohibited council members from holding certain other collateral posts. He abolished the practice of board superintendency (*zongli*) by grand councilors, limited the number of council clerks, reformed the council's paperwork procedures and communications channels, and ordered it in the future to submit for his consideration multiple opinions on a pending decision rather than the single one the council had already selected. He placed the council for the first time under formal censorial surveillance,

24. Seunghyun Han, "The Punishment of Examination Riots in the Early to Mid-Qing Period," *Late Imperial China* 32.2 (December 2011): 133–65.

25. Wensheng Wang, *White Lotus Rebels and South China Pirates: Crisis and Reform in the Qing Empire* (Cambridge, MA: Harvard University Press, 2014).

26. On the growth of "self-assessed fines" in the later eighteenth century, see Ting Zhang, "Penitence Silver and the Politics of Punishment in the Qianlong Reign, 1736–1796," *Late Imperial China* 31.2 (December 2010): 34–68.

ordering one censor to sit in on each of its meetings. And he revived the old consultative body the "nine ministers" (*jiuqing*) to serve as an institutional counterweight to council power. All of these new regulations were spelled out in the new Jiaqing edition of the *Da Qing huidian shili* (Institutes of the Qing empire), published in 1818 but begun already at the turn of the century, in which the council's existence was legally acknowledged for the first time.[27]

Almost everyone seems to agree that the reforms of the early Jiaqing reign, genuine and efficacious as they may have been in the short term, did not prevent the further long-term decay of the Qing empire. The larger question would appear to be: did they have a more subtle impact that *was* relatively long-lasting? In other words, assuming as we do that the significance of the crisis at the turn of the nineteenth century was secular as well as cyclical, was there also a secular impact on China's longer modern history of the Jiaqing court's energetic attempt at solutions? Did the activist new emperor inadvertently let the genie out of the bottle? For example, did the early Jiaqing reforms contribute to the long-term empowerment of local elites at bureaucratic expense? Did they enable a lasting more open political discourse? Did they help spawn the rise of Han nationalism?

Both Ho-fung Hung and Wensheng Wang invoke Jack Goldstone's concept of "state breakdown" as an aid to putting the Qianlong-Jiaqing transition into comparative historical perspective. Goldstone identifies the late eighteenth century as a moment in which several Eurasian *anciens régimes* confronted comparable crises: the French monarchy, for example, failed to meet these crises and collapsed, while the Qing did meet these crises and survived.[28] Doing so required the Jiaqing emperor to initiate what Wang calls a "pragmatic retreat" from the late Qianlong state, which was "overloaded" and "ungovernable" under the cost limitations of premodern technology, and to restore the "balance" between state and societal managerial responsibilities. In Hung's scenario, this bought the Qing merely a few more decades of effective governance, an era of what

27. On this last point, see also Guy, *Qing Governors*, 142. For Bao Shichen's view on abolition of the council, see chapter 2, below.

28. Jack A. Goldstone, *Revolution and Rebellion in the Early Modern World* (Berkeley: University of California Press, 1991), 4–5.

he calls "delayed state breakdown."[29] Wang goes considerably further, and, drawing upon the notion of "preserving achievements" (*shoucheng*) in the Jiaqing court's own discourse, celebrates the reentry of the Qing into an era of "sustainable political development."

Bao Shichen and Literati Reformism

In this study I propose to explore the complexities and anxieties of China's early nineteenth-century crisis through a detailed examination of the role of a single well-placed observer, Bao Shichen. Bao was part of a cohort of self-conscious reformers of the Jiaqing and Daoguang reigns, both within and outside of government, a cohort I sketch in the table below. Some of these men—Hong Liangji, Gong Zizhen, Wei Yuan, Tao Zhu, He Changling—are better known, and certainly better studied, than Bao.[30] And yet I will argue that in many ways it was Bao who served as the preeminent policy "expert" of the era, an individual not often seen in the limelight, but nevertheless deeply influential on the period's more visible political actors and administrators.[31]

29. Ho-feng Hong, "Cultural Legitimacy, Capital Appeal, and Delayed State Breakdown in Qing China, 1805–1839," unpublished paper, cited with permission.

30. Amid a large literature, see Liu Guangjing (K. C. Liu), "Wei Yuan zhi zhexue yu jingshi sixiang" (Wei Yuan's philosophy and statecraft thought); Sun Guangde, "Gong Zizhen de jingshi sixiang" (Gong Zizhen's statecraft thought); Judith Whitbeck, "From K'ao-cheng to Ching-shih: Kung Tzu-chen and the Redirections of Literati Commitment in Early Nineteenth Century China"; Zhou Qirong, "Cong 'kuangyan' dao 'weiyan': lun Gong Zizhen de jingshi sixiang yu jingjin wenxue" (From "crazy words" to "trifling words": Gong Zizhen's statecraft thought and literature); and Wei Xiumei, "He Changling de jingshi sixiang" (He Changling's statecraft thought); all in *Jindai Zhongguo jingshi sixiang yantaohui lunwen ji* (Papers from the conference on modern Chinese statecraft), comp. Institute of Modern History (Taibei: Academia Sinica, 1984). Also Jane Kate Leonard, *Wei Yuan and China's Rediscovery of the Maritime World* (Cambridge, MA: Council on East Asian Studies, 1984); Duan Zhao, *Tao Zhu yu Jia-Dao jingshi sixiang yanjiu* (Tao Zhu and Jiaqing-Daoguang statecraft thought) (Beijing: Zhongguo shehui kexue chubanshe, 2001).

31. A similar observation is made in Zheng Dahua, "Bao Shichen yu Jia-Dao nianjian de xuefeng juanbian" (Bao Shichen and intellectual transition in the Jiaqing-Daoguang period), *Anhui shixue* 2006.4.

Table 1
Some Reformist Scholar-Officials of the
Jiaqing-Daoguang Reigns (1796–1850)

	Native Place	Age in 1820
Lower Yangzi		
Hong Liangji (d. 1809)	Changzhou, Jiangsu	–
Ruan Yuan	Yangzhou, Jiangsu	56
Li Zhaoluo	Yangzhou, Jiangsu	51
Fang Dongshu	Tongcheng, Anhui	48
Bao Shichen	Jingxian, Anhui	45
Liu Fenglu	Changzhou, Jiangsu	44
Wang Fengsheng	Qiantang, Zhejiang	44
Gong Zizhen	Hangzhou, Zhejiang	28
Hunan		
Yan Ruyi	Xupu	61
Tang Jian	Shanhua	44
Tao Zhu	Anhua	41
He Changling	Shanhua	35
Wei Yuan	Shaoyang	26
Zeng Guofan	Xiangxiang	9
Hu Linyi	Yiyang	8
Other Localities		
Jiang Youxian	Liaoyang (Hanjun)	54
Lin Zexu	Houguan, Fujian	35

As we shall see, Bao had virtually no official career, serving only one term as a county magistrate, a position granted only relatively late in his life and largely for honorary reasons. He spent much of his late teens and early twenties as private secretary (*muyou*) to officials on the frontlines of the White Lotus campaign, but thereafter his advisory role was less formal and more sporadic, occasionally serving as special investigator of problem areas either on official commission or on his own behalf. He was, in effect, something relatively new to the early nineteenth century: a recognized "expert," consulted in a broad but defined range of policy areas.[32]

32. The institution of the "expert" seems to have been an early nineteenth-century innovation in the West as well. Although "expert" as an adjective had a long previous history in both English and French usage, the first nominal use of the word in reference to an individual of respected specialist knowledge, as recorded by the *Oxford English Dictionary*, came only in 1825; www.oed.com.proxy1.library.jhu.edu.

Not blessed with significant family or landed wealth, Bao (see fig. 1) claimed that he derived most of his income from his writing, but he was not widely published during much of his lifetime. His youthful magnum opus *Shuochu* (On wealth) did not appear in print until a half century after his death. He published a collection of essays on political economy, *Zhongqu yishao*, in 1825,[33] the year before Wei Yuan and He Changling's bestseller *Huangchao jingshi wenbian* (Collected essays on statecraft from the reigning dynasty), in which Bao was represented, but only by a small handful of contributions. In 1844, at age seventy, Bao republished *Zhongqu yishao* in his collected works, *Anwu sizhong* (Four books by Bao Anwu), which was well received and which he revised and republished seven years later.[34] But it seems clear that Bao's income from writing came far less from his policy essays than from his writings on calligraphy—his much-admired critical work *Yizhou shuangji* (Two oars for the boat of art) was in print at least by 1851, and a collection of his own brushwork, *Xiao Juanyouge caoshu* (Small collection of calligraphy from the Juanyou Studio) survives from 1833.[35] Almost certainly, when Bao says he lived by the sale of his writing he was referring not to published work at all, but to individual calligraphic works produced on commission.[36]

By far, however, Bao's influence was an outgrowth less of his written work than of his interpersonal relations with the most powerful men in the empire. He was an energetic correspondent, and his collected works bulge with letters he wrote, not only to other advisor-types such as Wei Yuan, but even more to high-ranking central and provincial officials, offering usually unsolicited but often appreciated advice on a wide range of policy issues; as Arthur Waley noted, Bao "was regarded as a great authority on current affairs."[37] These letters were often passed around and

33. Hu Pu'an, *Bao Zhenbo xiansheng nianpu* (Chronological biography of Mr. Bao Shichen) (hereafter *Nianpu*), in Bao Shichen, *Bao Shichen quanji* (Complete works of Bao Shichen) (hereafter *Quanji*) (Hefei: Huangshan shushe, 1991), 231.

34. Hu Pu'an, *Nianpu*, 239–40.

35. WorldCat.

36. Bao suggests this himself in an 1846 letter to Board President Xu Taichang, in Bao Shichen, *Bao Shichen quanji* (Complete works of Bao Shichen) (Hefei: Huangshan shushe, 1997), 237–39.

37. Arthur Waley, *The Opium War through Chinese Eyes* (Stanford: Stanford University Press, 1958), 137.

FIGURE 1. Portrait of Bao Shichen by his student Wu Xizai (1799–1870). Courtesy of the Tokyo National Museum.

read eagerly by officials at court.[38] Personal interviews were arguably a yet more important means than textual communication for Bao to dispense advice. Over the five decades of the Jiaqing and Daoguang reigns, Bao never stayed in one place too long. He rotated among major intellectual centers in the lower Yangzi region—Suzhou, Yangzhou, Nanjing, Changzhou—sometimes buying or renting a residence for a year or two but more commonly staying as a guest with friends. (Susan Mann has written sensitively about the tender relations of "Uncle Bao" with one such host family, the Zhangs of Changzhou.)[39] He also spent shorter sojourns in Beijing, on his repeated attempts to pass the metropolitan examination

38. Hu Pu'an, *Nianpu*, 224.

39. Susan Mann, *The Talented Women of the Zhang Family* (Berkeley: University of California Press, 2007), passim.

(ironically, although he never did pass this exam, while in Beijing it was not unusual for him to be welcomed by, or even visited by, officials of grand secretary or other exalted rank seeking his policy advice);[40] in Guangzhou, where he worked briefly in the Maritime Customs Office in 1826 and hobnobbed with the scholars at Ruan Yuan's Xuehai Tang Academy; and in Nanchang in the late 1830s and early 40s, in conjunction with his brief stint as magistrate of Jiangxi's Xinyu county. It was at Nanchang where Bao was visited by Lin Zexu in February 1839, to seek counsel prior to taking up his post as special commissioner in charge of opium suppression at Guangzhou, and again in May 1841, as Lin was leaving Guangzhou in disgrace. General Yang Feng and others involved in the war effort and in the antiopium campaigns did likewise.[41] Bao's biography in the *Qing shi gao* (Draft history of the Qing) notes that "all of the great officials of the southeast, when faced with great policy decisions regarding warfare, famine, river conservancy, grain tribute, or salt administration, never failed to come to him humbly for advice, and he would expound his views with vigor."[42]

Probably because he acted so discreetly behind the scenes, historians of the Qing have been slow to recognize Bao Shichen's central importance. In his pioneering intellectual history of the era, *Qingdai xueshu gailun* (1920), Liang Qichao does not mention Bao at all, though he devotes considerable space to Bao's younger contemporary and sometime associate Wei Yuan. Bao is similarly omitted in Xiao Gongchuan's monumental 1945 history of Chinese political thought, *Zhongguo zhengzhi sixuang shi.* Bao did merit an individual entry in Arthur Hummel's *Eminent Chinese of the Ch'ing Period*, published in the same year. But the first truly sustained study of Bao's thought and career I have seen is a magnificent 1969 article by the Japanese sinologist Ōtani Toshio.[43] In Chinese, among the earliest articles focused on Bao is a parallel study of Bao and Wei Yuan by the Chinese-American scholar Liu Guangjing

40. *Nianpu*, 720–21, 731–32.

41. Waley, *The Opium War*, 16–17, 137–38, 153; *Nianpu*, 237.

42. Zhao Erxun, ed., *Qing shi gao lie zhuan* (Draft history of the Qing dynasty: biographies) (Taipei: Mingwen shuju, 1983), 486:13417.

43. Ōtani Toshio, "Hō Seishin no jitsugaku shisō ni tsuite" (On Bao Shichen's "substantive studies" thought), *Tōyōshi kenkyū* 28.3 (December 1969): 162–95.

(K. C. Liu) from 1980.[44] There have been an increasing number of article-length investigations of aspects of Bao's career in Chinese since that time, but, other than my own preliminary efforts, none specifically focused on him in English or other Western languages. Remarkably, given the fact that most scholars now more or less acknowledge Bao Shichen's influential role in the thought and policy of his day, he seems not to have been the subject of a monograph-length study in any language.

Past scholarship on Bao reads his significance in a variety of ways. Treatments in the post-Mao People's Republic, both standard textbooks and specialized studies, begin by identifying him as a representative thinker of the "landlord ruling class," usually adding that he epitomized the response of this class to a perception of crisis to its continued hegemony.[45] One such analysis is that of the prominent cultural historian Feng Tianyu, who sees Bao as articulating the long-standing complaints of the *shidafu* elite, including overtaxation, imperial absolutism, and a demand for broadening the base of power among the landed literati; noting that in this time of epochal change this amounted to a call for restoration of the old order, Feng sees Bao as participating in "the last stand of Chinese feudalism."[46]

Identification of Bao Shichen with an agrarian elite tends to place his thought in tension with two other forces: rising commercial-manufacturing interests, and the rural commoner population. Nearly all scholars see him as espousing a traditional faith in agriculture as the true

44. Liu Guangjing, "Shijiu shiji chuye Zhongguo zhishifenzi: Bao Shichen yu Wei Yuan" (Two early nineteenth-century Chinese intellectuals: Bao Shichen and Wei Yuan), *Zhongyang yanjiuyuan guoji Hanxue huiyi lunwenji* (Taibei: Academia Sinica, History and Archeology Section, 1980), 995–1030.

45. For standard textbook or handbook accounts, see the entries on Bao in Shao Jing and Yi Menghong, *Zhongguo jindai jingji sixiang shi* (History of modern Chinese economic thought) (Beijing: Zhonghua shuju, 1980), 61–79, and Hu Qizhuang, *Zhongguo jingji sixiang shi* (History of Chinese economic thought) (Shanghai: Caijing Daxue chubanshe, 1998), 3:584–90. Judgments in these works are echoed in articles on Bao in local scholarly journals from his native Anhui, such as Chen Wenyu, "Aiguo chenmin, lichang gaige de Bao Shichen" (Bao Shichen, a patriotic and populist reform leader), *Anhui shixue* 1994.1: 48–49; and Zheng Dahua, "Bao Shichen yu Jia-Dao nianjian de xuefeng zhuanbian."

46. Feng Tianyu, "Daoguang Xianfeng nianjian jingshi shixue" (Statecraft and substantive learning in the Daoguang and Xianfeng eras), *Lishi yanjiu* 1987.4: 138–51.

basis of the economy, but most also acknowledge that his conventional call for "encouragement of farming" (*quannong*) was accompanied by one for "solicitation for commerce" (*xushang*).[47] Many studies take note of Bao's recurrent formula *benmo xifu* (the root and the branch are both forms of wealth); the "root" is agriculture of course, most specifically grain, but what is the branch? In some of Bao's own usages it clearly refers to currency, to monetized wealth, but scholars differ on whether or not it includes commerce and manufacture more generally. The historian of economic thought Hu Qizhuang, for example, observes that although Bao appears comfortable with, and supportive of, a monetized commercial agriculture, his economic prescriptions tend to ignore nonfood commodities altogether. That said, he adds, Bao was among the first thinkers to recognize the de facto emergence of an independent merchant entrepreneurial class, and sought to make creative use of them in his reform programs for the grain tribute and salt administration. In so doing, Bao anticipated the fuller government reliance on merchant forces in the latter half of the nineteenth century.[48]

What about the rural poor? Ōtani pointed out years ago that Bao was deeply committed to the improvement of the life of farmers (*nongmin shenghuo*), and also that he had great faith in them as the salvation of the society and polity. But was he, as the liberal historian K. C. Liu and some Chinese Marxist sources insist, a thorough populist, sympathetic to and willing to redress the exploitative levels of both taxes and rents? Was he, as Feng Tianyu claims, sensitive to the rising tide of class conflict, or was he, as Hu Qizhuang argues, nearly totally oblivious to class contradictions?[49] Was he, as a member of the landlord class, implacably hostile to popular uprisings (*minbian*), or did he sympathize with their cause even while he strove for pacification? Nearly all scholars agree that Bao did not question the existing land regime of strong landed property rights and widespread tenancy and agrarian hired labor, but to what extent was he supportive of equitable redistribution of food and other goods?

47. In light of this, Shao Jing and Yi Menghong, *Zhongguo jindai jingji sixiang shi*, assign Bao's thought to that of a distinctively "modern" landlord class.

48. Hu Qizhuang, *Zhongguo jingji sixiang shi*, 587.

49. Liu, "Bao Shichen," 995; Hu Qizhuang, *Zhongguo jingji sixiang shi*, 587.

Many scholars observe that Bao was unusually concerned about the financial stability of the state (*guojia*). His concern for popular livelihoods (*minsheng*) was paired with that for state finances (*guoji*), and he repeatedly insisted that these goals were not necessarily in contradiction. His frank advocacy of pursuit of profit/benefit (*li*)—one of his most striking and unconventional themes—was equally applicable for the people and for the state.[50] Bao was not afraid to admit that he sought wealth and power (*fuqiang*) for the imperial state, and answered his critics by arguing that these goals were not in tension with adherence to the "kingly way" (*wangdao*), but indeed were essential to that pursuit.[51] In this way, it is suggested, Bao paved the way for later generations of "self-strengthening" reformers, by whom "wealth and power" were openly celebrated as political goals.[52]

At the same time, Bao is seen as deeply opposed to excessive bureaucratization, which leeches off resources from both society and state (*zhongbao*).[53] As noted, he is comfortable with utilizing private commercial forces to achieve administrative ends, at times seeming to "privatize" state operations.[54] Does this suggest that Bao was a precocious Chinese advocate of free-market, laissez-faire economic liberalism? This notion, implicit in much other scholarship, is most energetically articulated by the Harvard-trained Taiwanese scholar Lin Man-houng. In a series of articles from 1991, and in somewhat modified form in an important 2006 book, Lin argues that a school of Chinese economic thought emerged in the early nineteenth century with ideas about the value of commerce and the virtues of free trade and laissez-faire policies, that were similar to those of Adam Smith and which she feels comfortable calling "economic liberalism." Lin identifies Bao Shichen, along with Wei Yuan, Gong Zizhen,

50. Zheng Dahua, "Bao Shichen yu Jia-Dao nianjian de xuefeng zhuanbian," 134–35; Hu Qizhuang, *Zhongguo jingji sixiang shi*.

51. Ōtani, "Hō Seishin no jitsugaku shisō ni tsuite," 168.

52. Liu Guangjing, "Jingshi ziqiang, xinxing qiye—Zhongguo xiandaihua de kaishi" (Statecraft, self-strengthening, and modern enterprise—the beginnings of China's modernization), in *Jingshi sixiang yu xinxing qiye* (Statecraft thought and modern enterprise) (Taibei: Lianjing, 1990), 1–22.

53. Shao Jing and Yi Menghong, *Zhongguo jindai jingji sixiang shi*, 62–63.

54. For example, Zheng Dahua, "Bao Shichen yu Jia-Dao nianjian de xuefeng zhuanbian."

and others, as representative of this school, and cites the reforms of the salt monopoly, the grain tribute administration, and the currency system—with all of which, as we shall see, Bao was directly associated—as prime examples of this school's thinking.[55] Lin alternatively dubs these same "liberals" as "realists" (versus "moralists"), that is, believers in the "intractability" of autonomous market laws, the counterproductivity of state attempts to intervene and contravene these, the possibility of economic growth, acceptance of the importance of private acquisitiveness as contributing to the economic well-being of all, a concept of strong private property (similar, she argues, to that of John Locke), and "the superiority of private enterprise."[56]

Most Chinese scholarship on Bao, even when decrying his landlord bias and willful ignorance of class-based exploitation, celebrates his precocious, frequently sabre-rattling patriotism. His concern for the polity (*guojia*), fiscal and otherwise, was linked to an early awareness of the Western threat, and not merely in a military sense. As Ōtani observes, Bao was one of the earliest literati to recognize that the empire had now become heavily immersed in an emerging world economy and, when scholars commend his "anti-imperialism," this clearly involves an economic as well as a strategic dimension.

Despite his deep, and clearly painful, awareness of the multifaceted crisis wracking the empire in the Jiaqing and Daoguang reigns, Bao remained, as several scholars correctly observe, a consistently optimistic voice. He was, among his contemporaries, unusually steadfast in his faith in the continuing potential of the empire's resource endowment and its population to produce wealth and abundance. And he was equally confident in the capacity of his own literati class to eventually find creative

55. Lin Man-houng, "A Time in Which the Grandsons Beat the Grandfathers: The Rise of Liberal Political-Economic Ideologies in China's Monetary Crisis, 1808–1854," *American-Asian Review* 9.4 (December 1991): 1–28, esp. 10 and 13.

56. Lin Man-houng, "Two Social Theories Revealed: Statecraft Controversies over China's Monetary Crisis, 1808–1854," *Late Imperial China* 12.2 (December 1991): 1–35, esp. 14 and 27. In her later book, *China Upside Down: Currency, Society, and Ideologies, 1808–1856* (Cambridge, MA: Harvard University Asia Center, 2006), Lin replaces the "realist"/"moralist" dichotomy with "accomodationist"/"interventionist," and downplays, though does not eliminate, comparison to the free-trade ideas of Adam Smith.

and innovative solutions to the multitude of institutional and situational problems with which the empire was confronted. In the view of K. C. Liu, this places him squarely in the mainstream of the Chinese intellectual tradition.[57]

How original, how "modern," is Bao Shichen's thought? The liberal historian K. C. Liu is most impressed with Bao's consistently "creative" and "innovative" solutions to practical problems, whereas the Marxist Hu Qizhuang stresses instead his "accomodationist" adherence to fundamentals of the existing political and economic system.[58] Somewhere in between is the view of Feng Tianyu, who assigns Bao to a distinctive "transitional" strain of Chinese political economy thought. Substantively, according to Feng, Bao and others of his cohort were vaguely aware that they were responding to new forces in the world economy, but were not yet able to comprehend them fully. Methodologically—and independent of Western influence—Bao came to employ new analytic techniques, including the quantitative analysis with which he was deeply infatuated, but had not yet arrived at a "modern" disciplinary social science. In both substance and style, then, he was precisely "early modern."[59]

A major task of this study of Bao Shichen will be to assess the validity of many of these claims and characterizations. We will concentrate on Bao's writings and activities in the area of political economy, for the most part leaving aside his often equally influential work on military strategy, hydraulic engineering, and calligraphy. My primary purpose is to contribute to an evaluation of the early nineteenth century as a milestone era in late imperial history, and of the collective project to rescue the empire from its manifest decline. In the process, I will suggest that Bao, by unabashedly professing an interest in the pursuit of "profit" (*li*) for the people, and economic security and power for the state, anticipated themes in reformist discourse throughout the remainder of the Qing era, and participated in another (less self-conscious) project to reconfigure the Qing empire (Da Qing) into an essentially Chinese nation (Zhongguo).

57. Liu Guangjing, "Shijiu shiji chuye Zhongguo zhishifenzi," 995. See also Hu Qizhuang, *Zhongguo jingji sixiang shi*, 587.

58. Hu Qizhuang, *Zhongguo jingji sixiang shi*, 587

59. Feng Tianyu, "Daoguang Xianfeng nianjian jingshi shixue," 148–50.

CHAPTER 1

Orientations

Bao Shichen was born in 1775 in Jingxian, a mountainous and heavily forested county in eastern Anhui of no particular distinction, other than its artisanal production of fine writing paper.[1] Jingxian was not too far removed from other places of greater significance, but it was not exactly near to them either (see map 1). Within Anhui province, it lay less than a hundred miles north of Huizhou, the native place of the mid-Qing's greatest mercantile diaspora, and a slightly greater distance east of Tongcheng, home of eminent Qing ministers and a celebrated scholarly tradition. Jingxian's social and cultural link with either of these places seems, however, next to nonexistent. More compelling by far was its relationship with the great cities of the lower Yangzi, arrayed in an arc to the county's northeast—Nanjing was roughly a hundred miles due north of the county, Hangzhou a slightly greater distance due east, and in the quadrant between and beyond them lay Yangzhou, Suzhou, and the emerging Shanghai. Jingxian itself had no prominence remotely approaching any of these places, but, though it was certainly hinterland, it seems unfair to call it a backwater. Hu Pu'an, Bao Shichen's earliest biographer and a proud Jingxian native himself, noted that in the same year as Bao's birth the county also spawned three eventual metropolitan degree

1. According to the 1996 county gazetteer, Jingxian's "Xuan paper" had been famous throughout the empire since the Tang; *Jingxian zhi* (Beijing: Fangzhi chubanshe, 1996), 215–16.

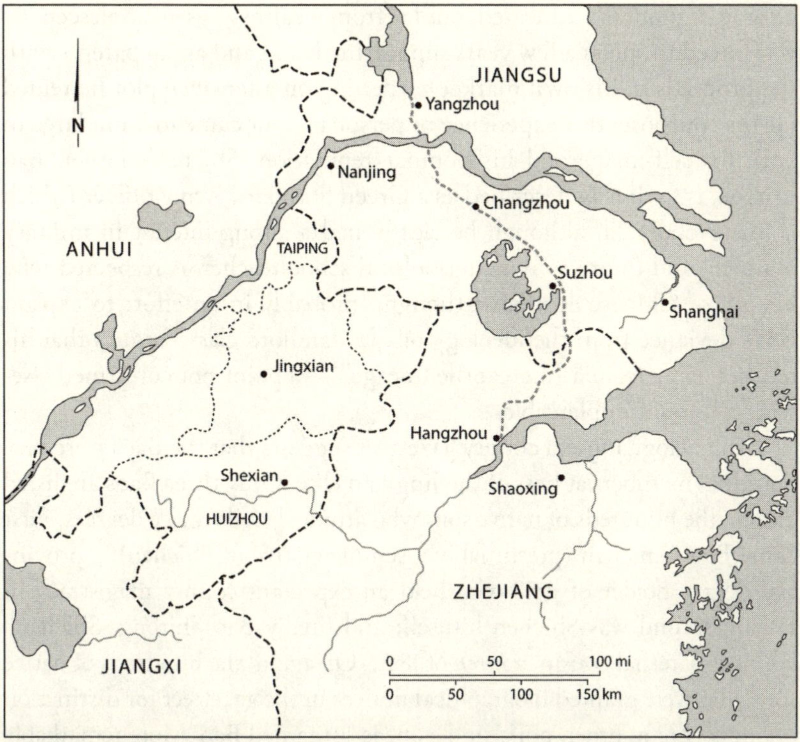

MAP 1. Bao Shichen's native place (Jingxian), in relation to other lower Yangzi localities.

winners, two of whom had the honor of appointment to the Hanlin Academy.

Bao's own family background was not especially distinguished. He is generally described today as hailing from "a landlord-literati family in decline," and this seems fair. The family surname forms part of the name of the village he was born in (Bao cun), so he likely came from a patriline of some local pedigree.[2] Growing up, he was sufficiently comfortable to

2. The only "Bao" recorded in the 1996 county gazetteer who predates Shichen himself is the eleventh-century Bao Zheng, who is credited with having carved out an expanse of irrigated land and amassed an impressive personal library, but there is no clear evidence of any familial connection between this man and the Baos of the mid- and late Qing. *Jingxian zhi*, 900.

be at least modestly educated, but far from wealthy—as an adolescent he was forced to spend a few years supporting his ill and aging parents with the proceeds of his own market gardening on a ten-*mou* plot he rented for that purpose; this experience of personal labor came to loom large in both his self-image and his popular reputation. Shichen's father, Bao Junxue, is variously described as a Green Standard Army officer (which is uncorroborated, although he clearly had a strong interest in military matters), and (more convincing) a local schoolteacher. A respected 1980 history of Chinese economic thought, probably in an effort to explain Bao's deviance from the ideology of the "landlord class," argues that his mother came from a "mercantile lineage"[3]—a point not confirmed elsewhere, but not implausible.

The Daoguang-era county gazetteer suggests that the Baos were very marginal members at best of the Jingxian elite. Only three Baos are listed among the hundreds of native sons who attained civil service degrees. First came Bao Ganchen (presumably a senior relative of Shichen), a provincial degree holder of 1788 who held an expectant county magistracy in Fujian; second was Shichen himself; and finally Bao Shirong, Shichen's younger paternal cousin, a *juren* of 1821.[4] Of, again, the hundreds of native sons who were granted biographical notices in the gazetteer for distinction of one sort or another, not a single one is surnamed Bao. More remarkably still, no Bao man was credited among the thousands who contributed even the smallest sum to the 1825 edition of the gazetteer itself.[5] After launching himself into his career, and eminence of a sort, Bao Shichen seems to have left Jingxian behind him and never looked back.

Bao's childhood education, at the hands of his father and in the county school, was based on the hope of examination success and official appointment.[6] Between the ages of five and eight *sui*, he worked his way through the core of the exam curriculum, the Four Books; reportedly he was most fond of *Mencius*, but was troubled by the fact that such lofty

3. Shao and Yi, *Zhongguo jindai jingji sixiang shi*, 62.

4. Bao Shirong, like his famous cousin, grew up in poverty. His education only began in earnest when the somewhat established Shichen took him along to Yangzhou for study. He died young, at age forty-two. *Jingxian zhi*, 928.

5. *Jingxian xu zhi* (1825). The Bao family is similarly almost totally absent among the hundreds of local sons whose biographies are recorded in the 1996 county gazetteer.

6. Bao, preface to *Anwu sizhong*, in *Quanji* (1993), 1–3; Hu Pu'an, *Nianpu*; *Jingxian zhi*, 927.

prescriptions for social and political ordering had never really been put into effective practice. At eight he went with his father to Nanjing, where he began intensive training in the composition of eight-legged essays (*bagu wen*), the routinized format for examination answers, and in 1790, at the respectably young age of fifteen *sui*, this paid off with his passing of the licentiate (*shengyuan*) examination. Six years later he was admitted to the Zhongjiang Academy at Wuhu, under headmaster Cheng Shishun. But it took him another eighteen years to pass the provincial (*juren*) examination, at age thirty-three *sui* in 1808, and he famously never passed the metropolitan (*jinshi*) examination at all, despite attempting it more than a dozen times.

This was hardly the result of inherent incapacity, but reflected instead a serious distraction of his interests. At eighteen *sui* he temporarily abandoned study of the examination curriculum, in part out of economic exigency but also out of frustration with the formalism of the exams—in his 1801 treatise *On Wealth* (Shuochu) he joined others of his generation (most notably Gong Zizhen) in proposing abolition of the *bagu wen* format[7]—and the idealism and impracticality of the Four Books. From early childhood Bao had loved poetry, especially the sixth-century collection *Wenxuan*, from which his father taught him to recite, and he remained an active poet all his life.[8] At least by his twenties he had also developed an intense interest in calligraphy (see fig. 2), an art of which he would become both an esteemed practitioner and an authoritative historian. Calligraphy for Bao and his contemporaries was hardly innocent of politics, and his adamant preference for the bold, unfussy Northern Wei (386–535 CE) style was a political statement, signifying a quest for national strength.[9]

7. See Nivison, "Ho-shen and His Accusers," 198–200; Sun Guangde, "Gong Zizhen de jingshi sixiang."

8. The first of the four volumes that make up Bao's self-collected works, *Anwu sizhong* (1844), is an eight-*juan* collection of his verse entitled "Three Styles of Harnessing the Emotions" (*Guanqing sanyi*), the three styles being the poetic forms of *fu*, *shi*, and *ce*. On the *Wenxuan*, see Bao, preface to *Anwu sizhong* in *Quanji* (1993), and Arthur Hummel, ed., *Eminent Chinese of the Ch'ing Period* (Washington, DC: Government Printing Office, 1943), 856.

9. Hu Pu'an, *Nianpu*, 217; Hua Rende, "The History and Revival of Northern Wei Stele-Style Calligraphy," in *Character and Context in Chinese Calligraphy* ed. Cary Y. Liu et al. (Princeton: Princeton University Art Museum, 1999); Yuehping Yen, *Calligraphy and Power in Contemporary Chinese Society* (London: Routledge, 2005), 88–89; and Mann, *Talented Women*, 51–54.

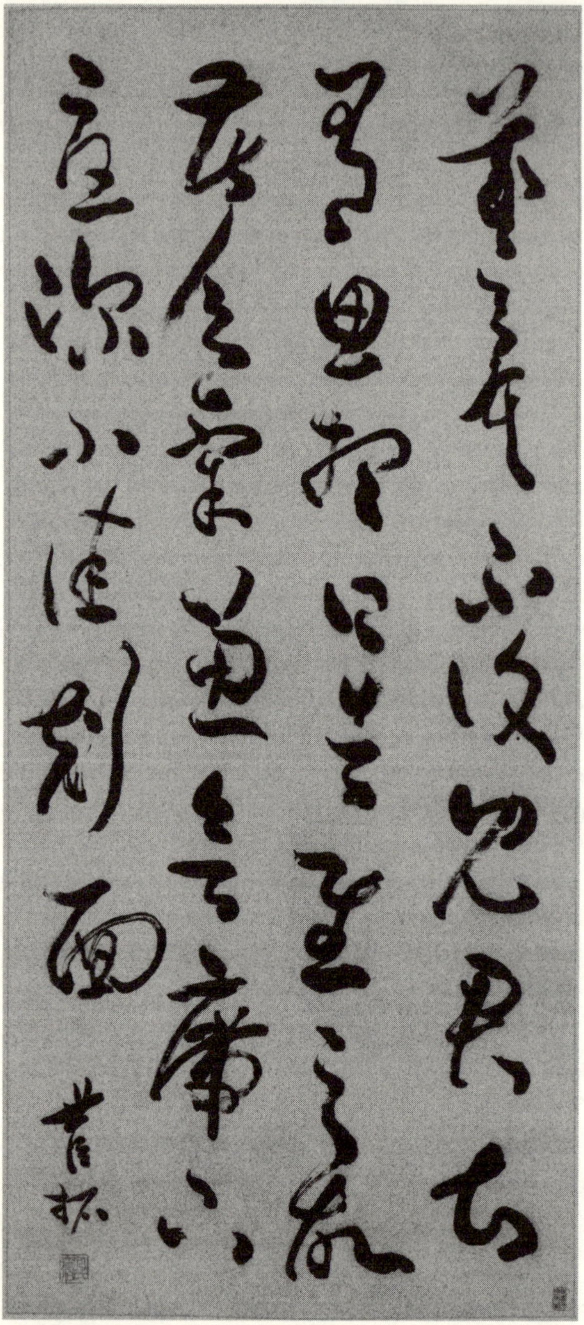

FIGURE 2. Sample of Bao Shichen's calligraphy, in the style of Wang Xizhi (303–361). Courtesy of the Tokyo National Museum.

But already by age twelve, according to his own later testimony, the major focus of Bao's scholarship had shifted away from the examination curriculum and aesthetic pursuits to more "useful studies" (*youyong zhi xue*): hard-headed works of history, policy, and military strategy.[10] At age fifteen—inspired in part by seeing local troops grandly marching off to combat the Lin Shuangwen rebellion in Taiwan—he began an intensive study of Sunzi's *Art of War*, and moved on to the *Spring and Autumn Annals*, Xunzi, Sima Qian, and histories of the Warring States, with special attention to their treatment of military affairs.

Based on this reading, he produced in 1793 (at age eighteen) his first book, a sixteen-chapter analysis of the fundamentals of military leadership, entitled *Liangyuan* (Two refuges).[11] In it, he argued that mastery of the military arts were necessary to proper manhood (*nanzi suo you shi*), and that, in the present day, anyone who conceives himself a gentleman (*shidafu*) cannot shirk military education. The treatise's title is a bit cryptic. *Yuan* can mean "deep" or "profound," and in the work's opening pages Bao claims that it refers to an essential personal quality comprising a perceptive character (*xingming*) and a tranquil disposition (*qijing*). But *yuan* can also mean a forest refuge for wild animals, a meaning that he underscores by entitling the first section of the work "Ciyuan" (a refuge for female birds) and the second section "Xiongyuan" (a refuge for male birds). The *ci* and the *xiong*, he adds, refer to the inner and the outer, and the two sections mirror this, concentrating respectively on inner qualities of command and on matters of strategy.

Study of Xunzi also prompted Bao's reflection on the social utility of ritual to maintain stability in a world less sanguine than Mencius had imagined; in this, his interests paralleled those of Gong Zizhen and many others of those who would be leading reformist thinkers of the Jiaqing and Daoguang reigns. As Ōtani Toshio pointed out, Bao found Xunzi's pessimistic view of human nature, and his sense of deepening crisis, more appropriate to his own day. For Mencius and those who followed him, the key to the world was *li* (principle); for Xunzi it was a quite different *li* (ritual). This, argues Ōtani, was a useful step toward

10. Zheng Dahua, "Bao Shichen yu Jia-Dao nianjian de xuefeng quanbian."

11. Bao seems not to have published this work at the time, but included it in his 1844 collected works, *Anwu sizhong*; it is available today in *Quanji* (1997), 425–37.

the third *li* that Bao himself sought: advantage, benefit, profit, or simply "what works."[12]

As an older man, Bao poignantly summarized his intellectual odyssey in a letter to a friend, Yang Jizi.[13] He wrote in part:

> I was born in the Qianlong reign, and by the time I was a young student everything was falling apart [*baiwei feishi*]. Bribery was pervasive and open, the administration was contaminated and vile, and the people's energy was taut like a string, as if there might be a rebellion. I thought then of how to prevent violence and ward off chaos, so I studied the works of the military strategists [*bingjia*].
>
> When I observed that the people's livelihood [*minsheng*] had grown so precarious that with a single drought they were reduced to starving on the roadsides, I wondered how to restore our economy and enrich their lives, and I turned to the writings of the agronomists [*nongjia*].
>
> Then I noticed that, while most people trod innocently through life, villains preyed on them as if they were ducks, and came away with immense profits. Wondering how to punish wrongdoing and eliminate crime, I turned to study the Legalists [*fajia*].[14]

This taxonomy is largely followed in the organization of Bao's own major collection of his reformist writings, *Four Strategies to Relieve the People* (Qimin sishu, 1844), a twelve-chapter work arranged into four sections on agriculture (*nong*), ritual (*li*—conceived rather broadly to encompass many aspects of local social organization, educational practice, and so on), criminal punishments (*xing*), and warfare (*bing*).

12. Ōtani, "Hō Seishin no jitsugaku shisō ni tsuite," 168.

13. I have been unable to locate this letter in Bao's published works. It is reproduced at length in Chen Weizhao, *Daixue de wange: Qingdai wenren de xintai shi* (Bloody requiem: the history of Qing literati mentality) (Shijiazhuang: Hebei jiaoyu chubanshe, 2001), 199. Based on Chen's version, Susan Mann translates this letter in *Talented Women*, 251. The translation here follows Mann with only slight modifications.

14. In summarizing the major influences on his intellectual development in 1844, Bao mentioned the Legalist Han Fei, along with Sunzi, Mencius, and Xunzi, as the most important "philosophers" (*zi*). He also notes that he had made an intensive comparative study of imperial legal codes from Han to Ming, and their interaction with customary law (*renxin sufeng*). Preface to *Anwu sizhong*, in *Quanji* (1993). As an adult, Bao's expertise on the details of the *Qing Code* was "world-famous" (*youming yu shi*); Hu Pu'an, *Nianpu*, 229.

At the Front

Bao's early scholarship, then, and his initial reputation, was as a specialist in military affairs. Based in part perhaps on the private circulation of his *Liangyuan*, the young Bao was hired as military advisor to a succession of important officials. In 1797 he worked in this capacity for the Anhui governor Zhu Gui, and the following year for the Hubei governor Chen Jijiu. In the summer of 1799, Mingliang was appointed overall commander of the antirebel campaigns in Sichuan and Hubei, and invited Bao to come serve with him in the pacification of Sichuan. This brought the young man to the very frontline of the war.[15]

Bao's general notions about warfare lie outside the concerns of this study, but certain of his ideas in this area foreshadow themes of his political-economic thought that we will obseve in subsequent chapters. Already in the first chapter of his 1793 *Liangyuan*, he argued that the single most basic quality of military command was an understanding of agriculture (*mingnong*), which in turn comprised cherishing the people (*aimin*) and valuing their land (*zhongdi*). In other words, an informed knowledge of the local agrarian economy and a respect for local people's labor (*minli*) and property (*mincai*) was necessary not only to winning their support, but also to provisioning one's own troops.[16]

In each of his White Lotus postings, Bao's specialty seems to have been this effort to win the hearts and minds of the local population—as he put it, "getting close to the people's feelings" (*jin renqing*). More specifically, he concentrated on local militarization. When Zhu Gui wanted to raise militia in Anhui to combat potential spillover of hostilities from neighboring Hubei and Henan, Bao cautioned above all that any militiamen recruited must be men of great ability and personal character; this meant paying them well, which in turn required raising adequate funds by subscription from local elites. In Hubei, Bao found the problem to be not too few militiamen, but rather too many; they had deteriorated into renegades, pillaging the local people and turning them against the state.[17]

15. Hu Pu'an, *Nianpu*, 206–14.
16. Bao, *Quanji* (1991), 427.
17. For uncontrolled militia as a wider problem in this era, see Yingcong Dai, "Civilians Go into Battle."

He proposed tasking the prosperous ironmongers of Wuhan with manufacture of farm tools and levying a large contribution on Hankou salt merchants. Equipped with tools and start-up cash, the excess militiamen might then be demobilized and resettled to their native place.

After returning from the front to Jiangnan in 1801, Bao set down on paper his general thoughts on the rebellion, which he characterized as the greatest single threat confronting the empire at the time. Again, the problem of local militarization was central to his concerns. The population of the war zone, he argued, had been exploited by corrupt officials for so many years that, despite the Jiaqing emperor's welcome proclamation of leniency in pacification (*zhaofu*), it was extremely difficult to restore peace. In the five provinces of Hubei, Henan, Sichuan, Shaanxi, and Gansu, there were as many as four hundred thousand men under arms—all of them underpaid and undisciplined. Worst of all were the thirty thousand to forty thousand militiamen recruited from the area, who in peacetime were nothing but "rustic roughnecks" (*caomang yingxiong*). Some seventeen thousand of these had already been formally demobilized—for the most part simply returning to their prewar hooliganism—while the remainder were completely outside the control of their commanders. Bao's proposed solution—laid out in considerable detail and anticipating policy options that he would advance periodically throughout his career, was resettlement of all combatants in military-agricultural colonies (*tuntian*), financed largely with revenues from the government salt monopoly.[18]

Changzhou and Classical Scholarship

Given the heavy emphasis on classical hermeneutics that dominated the intellectual world of Bao's youth, it seems fair to ask how scholarship on the Classics (*jingxue*) fit into Bao's educational development. The answer is, not very much. As a youth he studied the *Book of Odes* and the *Book of Rites*, but I know of none of his writings that engage significantly with

18. Bao, *Quanji* (1991), 182–84.

classical exegesis, and, as K. C. Liu has argued, Bao "never became a serious classicist."[19]

This was not, however, a product of lack of exposure. In the mid-1790s, Bao had met Zhang Qi (1765–1833), who was then teaching in Shexian, Huizhou. Sharing a passion for Northern Wei calligraphy, the two men became lifelong friends. Though hailing originally from Wujin county (Jiangsu), Zhang was a partisan of the school of classical scholarship centered on Changzhou (Zhejiang), and he introduced Bao to its leading figures and their ideas. In 1802, after returning from the White Lotus campaigns, Bao spent seven months in Changzhou itself as a houseguest of Li Zhaoluo (1769–1841). They went over Bao's recently completed manuscript *Shuochu* (see chapter 2), with the celebrated stylist Li making several edits to trim Bao's verbosity. Bao met numerous other Changzhou luminaries and discussed a wide range of topics, most intensively calligraphy, in which they all had deep interest.[20]

During the Jiaqing and Daoguang reigns, most scholars agree, there was an epochal shift in the focus of Chinese elite scholarship. The detailed philological, phonological, and textual study (*kaozheng*) that had dominated intellectual life throughout much of the eighteenth century was displaced by a heightened interest in "practical learning" (*shixue*) and the sociopolitical policy analysis (*jingshi*), usually (and somewhat misleadingly) translated as "statecraft." Feng Tianyu has depicted this entire, complex movement as characteristic of "early modern" Chinese thought, and as a "bridge" to later, Western-influenced scholarly movements.[21] But the scholarly and factional divides within those groups of literati who separately pioneered the shift to *shixue* and *jingshi* were arguably as great as the urge to practical policy study that united them. The two schools

19. Liu Guangjing, "Shijiu shiji chuye Zhongguo zhishifenzi," 996.

20. Hu Pu'an, *Nianpu*, 217; Xu Liwang, "Shiyi shibian: lun Bao Shichen yu Changzhou shiren de jiaowang ji jingshi sixiang de shanbian" (Conditions change over time: on Bao Shichen's interaction with Changzhou scholars and the evolution of statecraft thought), *Anhui shixue* 2005.5; Shi Liye, "Bao Shichen 'Shuochu' chutan" (A preliminary investigation of Bao Shichen's *Shuochu*) *Anhui daxue xuebao*, Philosophy and Social Science ed., 1997.6: 67–70. On Zhang Qi see also Hummel, *Eminent Chinese*, 25–26.

21. Feng Tianyu, "Daoguang Xianfeng nianjian jingshi shixue," 148–50. See also Jones and Kuhn, "Dynastic Decline."

usually seen as most influential in the new alignment were those identified with the prefectures of Tongcheng and Changzhou.

The Tongcheng school had included some of the great ministers of the high Qing era, notably Zhang Tingyu (1672–1755) and Fang Bao (1668–1749), and in the early nineteenth century was represented by such eminent scholars as Yao Nai (1732–1815) and Bao Shichen's contemporary Fang Dongshu (1772–1851). Throughout the Qing, Tongcheng scholarship had been distinguished by its dogged insistence that the teachings of Zhu Xi and other Neo-Confucian (*lixue*) scholars remained the authentic line of transmission of the teachings of Confucius and also provided workable models of social organization for the present day. This identified Tongcheng affiliates among their contemporaries as adherents of "Song learning" (*Songxue*). They derided as pedantic literati games the philological exegesis of the Five Classics practiced by other scholars, dubbed in contradistinction "Han learning" (*Hanxue*); as late as 1824 Fang Dongshu published a work, *Hanxue shangdui* (An assessment of Han learning), which systematically dismissed any advances in understanding of the Classics that this opposition movement might claim to have achieved. The Tongcheng school also actively clung to their faith in the authenticity of works written in the "old text" (*guwen*), a style of orthography supposedly dominant in the classical era of the Zhou dynasty, but more confidently associated with the Latter Han (25–221 CE). Most significantly this meant their acceptance of the Zuo commentary (*Zuozhuan*), which depicted Confucius as a modest editor of inherited texts, as the authoritative commentary on the fountainhead work *Spring and Autumn Annals* (*Chunqiu*). The distinctive Tongcheng merger of Cheng-Zhu moral and ritual orthodoxy with the search for pragmatic solutions to pressing social, economic, and political issues was also exported into the literati culture of Hunan's Xiang River valley and the academy scene of Changsha, where it underpinned the thought of Hu Linyi, Zeng Guofan, and several generations of activist Hunanese scholar-officials.[22]

The alternative Changzhou school, into which Bao Shichen waded somewhat cautiously in 1802, was generally acknowledged as descending

22. Hellmut Wilhelm, "The Background of Tseng Kuo-fan's Ideology," *Asiatisch Studien* 3–4 (1949): 90–100; McMahon, "Dynastic Decline"; William T. Rowe, *Saving the World: Chen Hongmou and Elite Consciousness in Eighteenth-Century China* (Stanford: Stanford University Press, 2001), 123–24.

from the teachings of Zhuang Cunyu (1719–88). In the nineteenth century this school was rather slower than that of Tongcheng to distance itself from *kaozheng* philology and from "Han learning," but from the start it had dismissed "Song learning" as a mere product of a bygone era, with no transcendent claim to authority as interpreter of the Classics. Zhuang's signal scholarly contribution had been to assert the superior authenticity of versions of the Classics written in the "new text" (*jinwen*) orthography employed in the former Han (206 BCE–25 CE), and by extension the greater authority of the Gongyang commentary to the *Spring and Autumn Annals*, written in that script, over the Zuo commentary favored by the Tongcheng school and the mainstream of late imperial thought; for Zhuang, the Zuo commentary was likely a forgery of the Han usurper Liu Xin, and was a cynical prescription for passive acceptance of imperial authority. The picture of Confucius that Changzhou scholars reconstructed from the Gongyang commentary was not that of a modest editor and transmitter, but rather that of a charismatic radical reformer and the "uncrowned king" (*suwang*) of the late Zhou era. As Benjamin Elman points out, this intellectual move was from the start deeply politicized: it had its origins in the reformist opposition of Zhuang Cunyu and others to the ascendency of the Heshen clique in the 1780s, and it prominently included the Changzhou native, Hanlin academician, and heroic dissident of 1799, Hong Liangji.[23] New text scholarship would also, famously, be inherited and seized upon as a mandate for change by Kang Youwei and other radical reformers of the Qing's final decades.

In the early nineteenth century, however, the Changzhou school was itself loosely divided into two subsets, a "Gongyang school" represented by Liu Fenglu (1776–1829) and a "Yanghu school" led by Bao Shichen's host Li Zhaoluo.[24] Liu and Li were in fact close friends, and were known collectively as the "two Shen of Changzhou"—their courtesy names shared the character *shen*. They were also both committed to reform and literati political engagement, but their intellectual groundings for reform, while overlapping considerably, were a bit different. Liu was the grandson

23. Benjamin A. Elman, *Classicism, Politics, and Kinship: The Ch'ang-chou School of New Text Confucianism in Late Imperial China* (Berkeley: University of California Press, 1990), xxii.

24. Zheng Dahua, "Bao Shichen yu Jia-Dao nianjian de xuefeng zhuanbian"; Ōtani, "Hō Seishin no jitsugaku shisō ni tsuite," 164. See also the respective biographies of Li and Liu in Hummel, *Eminent Chinese*, 448–50 and 518–20.

on his mother's side of Zhuang Cunyu, and devoted himself to explicating the hidden messages for political activism of the Gongyang commentary. Both Wei Yuan and Gong Zizhen studied for a time with Liu, coming away with the belief that historical conditions change, and consequently that institutions must likewise by transformed, dramatically if necessary, to accord with them.[25] Wei moreover was prompted by his study with Liu to come up with a cyclical model of human history that depicted his own age as one of "degeneration" (*moshi*), demanding epochal transformation.[26]

Li Zhaoluo was more cautious theoretically than Liu Fenglu. Li was a good Changzhou partisan in his distaste for old text and Song-learning scholarship, and attacked the Tongcheng luminary Yao Nai for Yao's devotion to this. He also helped edit the works of the Changzhou pioneer Zhuang Cunyu, which meant that he could not but be conversant with the more radical reinterpretations offered by new text and Gongyang scholarship. But his personal tastes clearly ran to other, more empirical elements of the Changzhou "practical studies" curriculum: mathematics, natural science, history, and geography. Li produced a study guide to Sima Guang's great history of the early and middle empire, *Zizhi tongjian* (Comprehensive mirror for aid in governance, 1090), as well as a historical atlas with an accompanying dictionary of place names, and, late in life, two works on the geography of the "maritime countries" (*haiguo*) based on interviews with a Chinese sailor who had worked on Western ships and visited Western countries.[27] Bao Shichen met Liu Fenglu, and, in a poem, acknowledged the attractiveness of Liu's Gongyang studies.[28] Far more than Liu Fenglu's new text radicalism, however, it was the empirical *shidi xue* (historical and geographical study) of Li Zhaoluo and the

25. Sun Guangde, "Gong Zizhen de jingshi sixiang," 276.

26. Jones and Kuhn, "Dynastic Decline,"153; Leonard, *Wei Yuan and China's Rediscovery*, 13–17.

27. Ōtani, "Hō Seishin no jitsugaku shisō ni tsuite," 164; Hummel, ed., *Eminent Chinese of the Ch'ing Period*, 448–50; Elman, *Classicism, Politics, and Kinship*, 95, 119–20, and 294–95.

28. Liu Guangjing, "Bao Shichen, yu Wei Yuan," 1003.

"Yanghu school" that left a mark on Bao from his seven months in Changzhou.[29]

It is instructive in this context, I believe, briefly to compare these two Changzhou-influenced scholars, Bao and Wei Yuan, with their sometime patron Tao Zhu (1779–1839). Tao served first as Jiangsu governor and then as Liang-Jiang governor-general for altogether some fifteen years, 1825 to 1839, during which time he regularly consulted both Bao and Wei on matters relating to his reforms of the grain tribute and salt administrations, overhaul of the regional hydraulic infrastructure, and other matters. Tao was a native of Anhua, Hunan, and a product of the Tongcheng-influenced academy scene of his home province, with its twin commitments to Song-learning moral and ritual propriety and empirically based "practical studies." For this reason, as we are told by Tao's biographer, while he was suitably impressed with the Gongyang-devotee Wei Yuan's overarching vision and zeal for innovation, he found far more useful as a guide to his reforms the detailed field investigations and pragmatic policy recommendations of Bao Shichen. Bao's view accorded more closely with Tao's own conviction that, while historical change was real and must be adjusted to, there was actually more constancy in the world than epochal shift. Reformism, thus, must be predicated above all on workability or serviceability; there was no reason to validate it by invocation of the Classics.[30]

Though Bao Shichen rarely personalized his attacks on those whose writings he disparaged, he did not mince his words. He deplored the vacuousness (*gongshu*) and abstruseness (*yufu*) of Han-learning scholarship, ridiculing its philology and phonology as "mistaking parsing characters for study, and chopping up sounds for cultural attainment" (*yi piaozi wei*

29. Bao's eldest son, Bao Cheng (1800–71), also followed Yanghu teachings, but specifically those of the medical authority Zhang Wanling. After a brief experience in local administration, Bao Cheng went on to become an important medical scholar himself; his book of prescriptions, *Shiji biao* (Beijing: Zhongyi guji chubanshe), was republished as late as 1982. *Jingxian zhi*, 928–29.

30. Duan Zhao, *Tao Zhu*, 122. See also Hummel, *Eminent Chinese*, 710–11. Man-houng Lin identifies Tongcheng thought with state "interventionism" and Changzhou thought (under which she lumps both Wei and Bao) as "accomodationist"—that is, adapting to market and societal realities without undue state interference; *China Upside Down*, 250–52. My own view, as seen above and throughout this study, differs significantly from hers.

xue, yi jiaosheng wei wen).[31] He dismissed those whom we might term armchair scholars as "petty" or "degenerate" Confucians (*xiaoru, louru*), and the arguments based on conventional wisdom (*wen er de*) as "idle chatter of those with book-learning only" (*shusheng yutan*).[32]

Bao has retrospectively been identified as an exemplar of Jiaqing-Daoguang *jingshi* (usually translated "statecraft"), and correctly so, but he himself rarely used this term, for the most part preferring *zhiyong* or *youyong* (scholarship "of real utility"). This applied both to the proper subject of scholarship and its appropriate methodology. Condemning the frivolous exercise of literary skill (*wen*) on abstract speculation on the Dao, he contended that the only valid use of *wen* was in description and analysis of "human affairs" (*renshi*)—human affairs indeed *were* the Dao.[33] The proper subjects of literati output, he endlessly repeated, were "state finances and popular livelihoods" (*guoji minsheng*)—the relative balance of these would be a continual theme of his writings. Following his own inclination, but reinforced by his studies with Li Zhaoluo, Bao held that the most effective way to comprehend "human affairs" was through the study of history and geography, and through personal field observation.

Though he shared to some extent the Gongyang emphasis on historical relativism,[34] Bao nevertheless found study of the past critically important. Reasoning by historical analogy was valid, because "ancient and modern run on the same track" (*gujin yiche*)—that is, they behave according to similar historical rules. Though he read heavily in the history of the Warring States and the early imperial era, he was cautious about the specific relevance of the ancient world to present conditions, but was more confident that Tang and Song history was worth knowing

31. Zheng Dahua, "Bao Shichen."

32. Bao, "Gengchen zazhu, er," in *Quanji* (1993), 209; Ōtani, "Hō Seishin no jitsugaku shisō ni tsuite," 168; Zhang Yan, "Bao Shichen yu jindai qianyue de 'haiyun nancao' gaige" (Bao Shichen and the sea transport of grain tribute on the eve of modernity), *Jindaishi yanjiu* 2000.1: 133.

33. Bao, "Yu Tang Jizi lunwen shu" (Letter to Tang Jizi discussing *wen*), cited in Zheng Dahua, "Bao Shichen."

34. See especially Xu Liwang, "Shiyi shibian."

well.[35] In 1801—during or just after his period of study at the Zhongjiang Academy in Wuhu—Bao had been engaged as tutor to the son of the local prefect Yao Fengnian. Very likely to his father's consternation, Bao made the central text of the young man's education the Song-era history (and Li Zhaoluo favorite) *Zizhi tongjian*; it was on the basis of his lectures drawn from this work that Bao went on to compose his own radical reformist tract *On Wealth*.[36] Like others of the reformist literati, Bao also valued especially study of the history of the Qing empire itself.

The necessary complement to historical study was field observation, allowing one to "fully grasp" (*qiu er de*) conditions on the ground. Bao's career was punctuated by lengthy trips into the field to understand local topographies and how they affected the operation of institutions such as hydraulic flows and market organization; his policy papers are astonishing (and astonished his superiors) by how much he knew about how things worked on the ground. This meant not simply geographical factors, but also local popular mentalities: when asked by one of his superiors in the White Lotus wars what the secret was to mounting a successful pacification campaign, Bao replied simply "get close to the people's feelings" (*jin renqing*).[37] Based on his own ethnographic investigations of village society, culture, and lifestyles, he produced a manuscript with the working title "Rural Rituals" (*Xiangren li*), which he revised several times but ultimately decided not to publish.[38]

Given these tastes, it is hardly surprising that Bao Shichen was deeply attracted to the work of the great early Qing scholar Gu Yanwu (1613–82). Deeply influential among succeeding generations of scholars, first for his contributions to classical studies and later for his political economy writings, Gu's reputation was never higher than in the Daoguang reign; in Wei Yuan and He Changling's 1826 *Statecraft Compendium* (*Huangchao jingshi wenbian*), he is by far the most represented individual, with well over a hundred of his writings included. Bao's interest in Gu long predated this, but deepened over the course of his life. He first encountered Gu's seminal work *Rizhilu* (Record of accumulated knowledge) in a bookstore

35. Bao, "*Shuochu* shangpian qianxu" (preface to *On Wealth*, part 1), cited in Shi Liye, "Bao Shichen," 71.

36. Hu Pu'an, *Nianpu*, 215–16.

37. Hu Pu'an, *Nianpu*, 214.

38. Bao, preface to *Anwu sizhong*, in *Quanji* (1993), 1–3.

in 1792, while caring for his aged father at home in Jingxian; he managed to read a chapter or two, but could not afford to buy a copy. A decade later, while living in Changzhou with Li Zhaoluo, his host lent him the complete work, flatteringly pointing out the similarity of Gu's thinking on several points with that of his young guest. At the same time, Bao read Gu's geographical work *Tianxia junguo libing shu* (Treatise on the assets and liabilities of various localities throughout the empire), and in consequence abandoned work on a similar project he had himself been pursuing. Finally in 1819, as an established scholar of forty-four, he was able to purchase a copy of Gu's complete works (*Tinglin yishu*) and devoured it all, including the poetry.[39]

Toward the end of his life, Bao wrote an essay discussing the impact Gu Yanwu's work had made on his own life and thought. Gu, he judged, was the greatest writer of the past several centuries, unmatched in the breadth and boldness of his vision. Bao indicated his personal identification with the master: though Gu came from a relatively privileged background, which allowed him in his younger days to engage in the textually rich comparative philology that Bao himself was not able to afford, both men had left home at a relatively early age and spent most of their life traversing the empire and observing the conditions of its various localities. What was most inspiring about Gu was his overriding sense of mission, his recognition of the need for personal heroism (*yinghao*) in order to meet the challenges of the time. It was the duty of "we literati" (*wuru*) to pull the world out of its current state of crisis (*zhiluan*) and usher in an era of peace and prosperity (*kai taiping*). Bao describes this process as *jingshi* (ordering the world), but also as *jingguo* (ordering the state). As we shall see, the state, even the nation, was a powerful concept in Bao's thought. But in this essay, he also cites approvingly Gu's famous differentiation between the state or dynasty (*guo*) and the realm of civilized society (*tianxia*): whereas it is the task of state officials to look to the salvation of the former, it is the duty of all literate men to save the latter. (Depending on how one reads this, it may be one of Bao's few hints that he believes the Qing regime may be endangered beyond salvation.) Gu has shown that in this quest it is necessary to utilize study of the past to effectively plan for the present (*yingu choujin*), but he also recognized the facts of

39. Bao, preface to *Anwu sizhong*; Hu Pu'an, *Nianpu*, 207, 217, and 229.

temporal and geographical specificity, even relativism. Achievement of successful policies demands close attention to local popular attitudes and preferences (*renqing, minxin*), but these may also be molded through moral instruction (*jiaohua*). Popular opinion may in fact turn against you, but, as Gu has shown, saving the world requires steadfast faith in your own abilities.[40]

In other ways as well, Bao's intellectual formation interlinked with the Changzhou school. One of these was his fraught relationship with Hong Liangji. Hong (1746–1809) was thirty years older than Bao, and I have found no evidence that they ever personally met. But the two men shared several elements of education and personal patronage, making it especially striking that their views clashed so dramatically on critical policy matters.

In the summer of 1796, while studying at Wuhu's Zhongjiang Academy, the academy's headmaster Cheng Shishun recommended Bao for service on the staff of the Huining Circuit intendent Song Rong. The following year the area experienced a drought, and Song asked Bao to compose a prayer for rain. He did, and the rain came. Mightily impressed, the intendant recommended Bao to Anhui Governor Zhu Gui, who immediately hired the young man for his staff. Zhu, who served as Anhui governor for eight years in the 1790s, had a special reputation for his efforts at water conservancy and suppression of sectarian unrest. He found many occasions to employ the young man's own fledgling expertise in just these areas, until, as we have seen, Bao found posts as strategic advisor to commanders more directly at the front of the White Lotus wars.[41]

Zhu Gui was no ordinary patron.[42] A Beijing native who had received his *jinshi* at the precocious age of eighteen *sui*, Zhu was also a master of partisan politics. He was a leader of what James Polachek has called the "northern scholar faction," which got its start in opposition to the Tongcheng clique in the 1740s but by the last decades of the Qianlong reign had rallied to organize clandestine literati opposition to the rise of

40. Bao, "Du Tinglin yishu" (Reading Gu Yanwu's works), in *Yizhou shuangji* (Two oars for the boat of art), 6 *juan* (Beijing: Zhonghua shudian, 1983), 2:1–4.

41. Hu Pu'an, *Nianpu*, 209.

42. On Zhu, see variously Hummel, *Eminent Chinese*, 185–86; Polachek, *The Inner Opium War*, 37–38 and 294–97; Elman, *Classicism, Politics, and Kinship*, 283–84; Wensheng Wang, *White Lotus Rebels*.

the Heshen mafia. In the 1780s as well Zhu Gui had served as tutor to the imperial heir—the future Jiaqing emperor—and when the Qianlong emperor died and Jiaqing forced Heshen's suicide in 1799, Zhu was recalled from Anhui to Beijing and for nearly a decade, until his own death, he was probably the most powerful Han Chinese official in the empire. During this time he made repeated efforts to invite Bao Shichen to serve on his staff in Beijing, but for reasons that are unclear each time Bao declined.[43]

As he showed with Bao, Zhu Gui was a master at cultivating brilliant protégés. Polachek credits him with being the "teacher" of several members of the young literati movement institutionalized as the "Xuannan Poetry Club" in Beijing after 1814, including at times Lin Zexu and Wei Yuan.[44] But none could have been closer to him, at least initially, than Hong Liangji. Hong was a product of the Changzhou school—like Li Zhaoluo he was a native of Yanghu county, his family had several times intermarried with that of Changzhou patriarch Zhuang Cunyu, and he had attended the Longcheng Academy, run by successive generations of Zhuang headmasters, where he imbibed revisionist new text classicism.[45] But he was also very much in the Zhu Gui entourage. He had served in 1771 as an assistant to Zhu Gui's elder brother Zhu Yun (1729–81), a guiding spirit behind the Imperial Library [Siku Quanshu] project under Emperor Qianlong. Moreover, as a member of the metropolitan examination "class of 1790" and subsequently as a Hanlin compiler, Hong had been assiduously cultivated by Zhu Gui himself.

But the policy views of Zhu and his protégé had gradually grown apart. Things reached a head when Hong in 1799 wrote his celebrated letter condemning the timidity of the Jiaqing emperor for not going nearly far enough in his purge of the Heshen faction. Hong sent the letter to several senior statesmen whom he hoped would deliver it to the emperor, one of whom was his patron Zhu Gui. Zhu, however, had come to favor a more cautious minimalist purge in order to keep the empire operating, and declined to pass along Hong's letter to the throne.[46]

43. Hu Pu'an, *Nianpu*, 218.
44. Polachek, *The Inner Opium War*, 42.
45. Elman, *Classicism, Politics, and Kinship*, xxii and 58.
46. Among other sources see Jones, "Hung Liang-chi."

On this issue, the most salient and divisive of its time, we shall see that Bao Shichen aligned himself on the side of Zhu Gui, not that of Hong Liangji. On a second urgent matter as well, the capacity of the empire's agriculture to support its manifestly booming population, Hong and Bao also came to opposite conclusions (see chapter 3). Clearly, similar scholarly and patronage backgrounds could lead to dramatically differing policy stances.

To sum up, Bao Shichen hailed from a modest rural background, on the far fringe of the empire's cultural and economic heartland, Jiangnan. His education was primarily at home, with his father, and in local schools, but this was rigorous and not notably inferior. After early success in the lower civil service examinations, he opted to eschew both the examination curriculum and classical scholarship in favor of studying nonorthodox texts that he saw as offering more "useful learning." He continued to sit for the highest level examination without success, seemingly because he felt it was simply the appropriate thing to do—and it gave him an opportunity to maintain his contacts in the imperial capital—but he does not appear to have been unduly damaged either psychologically or professionally by his repeated failures. Bao seems to have been personally quite affable, and he was demonstrably good throughout his life at securing influential patrons. Rather than in examination study he received his "higher" education in the field, in the White Lotus campaigns, and in the intellectual center of Changzhou, both experiences strengthening his faith in the value of empirical field observation and the quest for pragmatic solutions for real-world problems. In the remainder of this book we will look at how this translated into practice in a variety of policy areas; first, however, we turn to examination of Bao's one systematic—some might say "utopian"—treatise on imperial political-economic reform: the *Shuochu* of 1801.

CHAPTER 2

Governance

In 1906 at Shanghai the notorious twenty-three-year-old radical Liu Shipei oversaw the first-ever publication of a book-length political treatise by Bao Shichen, a manuscript then already more than a century old.[1] Liu (1884–1919) was a chameleon-like figure in early twentieth-century Chinese politics. He has been seen variously by historians as an anarchist, a "Confucian populist," a rabidly antiforeign Han chauvinist, a champion of "natural rights" (*tianfu quanli*) theory, and a propagandist of the notion of "social contract." Liu's 1903 book, *Zhongguo minyue jingyi* (Essentials of the social contract in China) laid out what he claimed to be antecedents of the recently translated ideas of Rousseau in ancient Chinese statecraft. At the time he published Bao's century-old manuscript, Liu was a famous and virulent anti-Qing agitator—he was heir to a familial and local tradition of extreme anti-Manchuism in his native Yangzhou—but the very next year (1907) he underwent a public and dramatic conversion to the Qing imperial cause, and in the early Republic he became a front man for President Yuan Shikai's monarchical restoration attempt.[2]

Liu Shipei was a leader, along with Zhang Binglin (1868–1936) and others, of the "National Essence" movement (*guocui yundong*), a well-

1. Bao Shichen, *Bao Shenbo Shuochu* (Shanghai: Guoxue baocun hui, 1906).

2. Hao Chang, *Chinese Intellectuals in Crisis: Search for Order and Meaning, 1900–1911* (Berkeley: University of California Press, 1987), chap. 5; Peter Zarrow, "Anti-Despotism and 'Rights Talk': The Intellectual Origins of Modern Human Rights Thinking in the Late Qing," *Modern China* 34.2 (April 2008): esp. 189–91.

funded campaign to rescue the authentic Han Chinese heritage from centuries of, first, repression by the Manchu barbarian conquerors, and then the corrupting influence of the West. In conscious imitation of eighteenth-century German *volksgeist* and later Japanese "national learning" (*kokugaku*) movements, Liu and his colleagues sought to rediscover China's "national soul" (*guohun*) through its suppressed literary and aesthetic tradition. As part of this project, they published the *National Essence Journal* (*Guocui xuebao*) and a series of National Essence Books (*Guocui congshu*) in order to recover texts banned by the Qing or otherwise lost. The series included records of atrocities (such as that at Yangzhou) committed during the seventeenth-century conquest, works by the graphically racist anti-Manchu Wang Fuzhi (1619–92), and writings of other politically outspoken Ming loyalists like Huang Zongxi (1610–95)—all identified by Liu and his associates as Han "family heirlooms." National Essence Books were published in several series; it was in the first series that Liu's publication of Bao Shichen's book appeared.[3]

To contemporaries of Liu Shipei, encountering Bao's treatise for the first time in 1906, its author would have been recognized first and foremost as a historian of calligraphy. His 1844 book *Yizhou shuangji* (Two oars for the boat of art) had been lionized by no less a reformist hero than Kang Youwei himself, in his own 1893 *Guang yizhou shuangji* (Two oars for the boat of art, expanded). Bao would also have been known as a rabid antiforeign patriot, an extreme hardliner in the opium debates and the First Anglo-Chinese War of 1839–42.

But why was this particular youthful work by Bao, having nothing to do with either calligraphy or foreign relations, included, and so prominently, in a series of works on China's "national essence"? In a postscript to his edition, Liu Shipei called its author a prophetic visionary, who, in the mid-Qing era of political stagnation, had devised a way to simultaneously "strengthen the state and empower the people," in a fashion that anticipated uncannily several of the radical plans of Kang Youwei and

3. Lawrence A. Schneider, "National Essence and the New Intelligentsia," in *The Limits of Change: Essays on Conservative Alternatives in Republican China*, ed. Charlotte Furth (Cambridge, MA: Harvard University Press, 1976), 90–112; Martin Bernal, "Liu Shih-p'ei and National Essence," in Furth, *Limits of Change*, 57–87; Shimada Kenji, *Pioneer of the Chinese Revolution: Zhang Binglin and Confucianism*, trans. Joshua A. Fogel (Stanford: Stanford University Press, 1990).

his confederates during the aborted court reforms of 1898, and of the more enduring New Policies (*xinzheng*) of the early twentieth century. Liu also saw in this text "some resemblance to Western systems of constitutional governance."[4] That may be a stretch, but there is nevertheless no doubt that the newly rediscovered work did propose systematic institutional reform (*bianfa*) of the basic structure of the Qing state apparatus (*dazhi*), a rewriting, if you will, of what we might term the "Qing constitution."

"Shuochu": A Textual History

Remarkably, apart from a few pages here or there in articles by scholars in China or Taiwan, Bao's treatise seems to have attracted remarkably little scholarly attention.[5] He wrote the work when he was twenty-six years of age (twenty-seven *sui*), but he was then by no means an inexperienced youth. As we have seen, Bao in 1797 had been hired as a staff member by the Anhui governor Zhu Gui. He then enjoyed a rapid succession of appointments as personal advisor (*muyou*) to a series of midranking civil and military officials, eventually seeing frontline service in the White Lotus campaigns in northwestern Hubei and Sichuan. This experience had a deep impact on Bao, and he was not reticent about telling his employers how the war could better be prosecuted and the areas peaceably resettled.[6] In 1801 he removed himself from the campaign, accepting a post in the household of the Taiping prefecture (Anhui) subprefect, Yao Fengnian, as tutor for Yao's thirteen-year-old son Chengqian. Bao was

4. Liu Shipei, "Ba" (Postscript), in Bao, *Bao Shenbo Shuochu.*

5. The most extensive—albeit brief—discussions of the work appear in Liu Guangjing, "Shijiu shiji chuye Zhongguo zhishifenzi Bao Shichen yu Wei Yuan" (The early nineteenth-century Chinese intellectuals Bao Shichen and Wei Yuan), in *Zhongyang yanjiuyuan guoji Hanxue huiyi lunwenji* (Proceedings of the Academia Sinica International Conference on Chinese Studies) (Taipei: Academia Sinica, 1980), 997–99, and Shi Liye, "Bao Shichen 'Shuochu'" chutan," *Anhui daxue xuebao* 1997.6: 67–70. Yet briefer references appear in Feng Tianyu, "Daoguang Xianfeng nianjian jingshi shixue," and Zheng Dahua, "Bao Shichen yu Jiaqing nianjian de xuefeng zhuanbian," *Anhui shixue* 2006.4.

6. Hu Pu'an, *Nianpu,* 204–16; see also Hiromu Momose, "Pao Shih-ch'en," in Hummel, *Eminent Chinese,* 610–11.

delighted with his young charge, whom he believed brilliant, and for Chengqian's benefit devised a series of lectures that deliberately strayed from the examination curriculum, emphasizing non-Confucian as well as classical and orthodox texts, and especially study of historical works. It was these lectures that formed the basis of the *Shuochu.* As Bao wrote in the work's preface, young Chengqian had inquired of him what were the most critical things that needed to be done in order to "rescue our times" (*jiushi*), and this was his extended answer.[7]

What does the title mean? Bao, neither in his text itself nor elsewhere that I have seen, ever tells us. The first character, *shuo* may refer to an established literary genre of discursive essay, often on a complex topic. The second, *chu* means to collect or to accumulate. An identically titled work by the late-Ming literatus Chen Yumo, with a preface dated 1609, is essentially a set of unconnected reading notes, embellished by the author's own wide-ranging theories.[8] This precedent (referred to in the published index to the *Siku quanshu* and so quite possibly known to Bao) suggests a rather limp reading for the title as a generic "collection of essays." But Bao's own work is much more integrated and focused than that of Chen Yumo. This suggests an alternative reading of the title as "an essay on accumulation," "on [state] finance," or "on wealth," which is in fact what the work is generally about. This is the reading which, all things considered, seems the most likely.[9]

But there is yet an alternative reading, which, though perhaps a bit of a stretch, offers an intriguing possibility about Bao's intentions for his work. A secondary meaning of *chu*, especially but not necessarily in the combination *chujun*, is "heir apparent." (The first character, then, normally read *shuo*, to speak, might in this usage be read *shui*, to admonish or advise.) But who is the young heir whom Bao is advising? A conceivable candidate would be his wealthy and talented pupil, Yao Chengqian, but this would require an extremely loose reading of "heir apparent" that

7. Bao Shichen, preface to *Shuochu*, 133. Bao's original text is undivided into chapters and unpaginated. Except where noted, my page references to *Shuochu* are to the reprint version in *Bao Shichen quanji* (1991).

8. Pierre-Étienne Will, personal communication.

9. In a brief reference to Bao's work, Judith Whitbeck offers the translation of its title as "An Explanation of Wealth," which seems to me to effectively capture the intent; Whitbeck, "From K'ao-cheng to Ching-shih," 332.

I'm not sure the language of the day would have allowed. Another possible addressee would be the Jiaqing emperor, who only two years earlier in 1799 had assumed personal rule, but who had been formally and publicly identified as his father's *chujun* throughout the final two decades of the Qianlong reign.[10] Yet a third possibility is Jiaqing's son, Aisin Gioro Minning, who, also in 1799, at age seventeen, had been installed as heir, and who eventually did succeed to the throne as the Daoguang emperor in 1820. Although Bao Shichen much later wrote an epitaph for the court official Dai Junyuan, who had played a central role in Minning's selection as *chujun* in 1799, I have seen no evidence that Bao at the time knew anything about the selection, which was not, like Jiaqing's installation two decades earlier, revealed to the public at large.[11] I suspect that the most likely addressee of all, should this title be read as "Advice to the Prince," would simply be an imagined ideal future ruler, of the sort invoked by early Qing writers in the tradition of political commentary upon which Bao drew. Huang Zongxi's *Mingyi daifang lu* (Waiting for the dawn), for instance, was addressed to an imaginary "prince"; Huang's early Qing contemporary Gu Yanwu had begun his famous essay "Junxian lun" (On bureaucratic local administration) with the hope that a future sage-ruler would arise and take his prescriptions seriously, and had prefaced his major work, *Rizhi lu* (Record of daily-acquired knowledge) with the stated hope that it would await rediscovery by "a true king."[12] Indeed, Bao himself, on the first page of his treatise, expresses the hope that in the future "some gentleman in a position of authority [*danglu junzi*]" may wish to follow the detailed advice he there presents.

Bao wrote in his preface that he could not publish the work at the time he wrote it, because there was no way his ideas would be imple-

10. This possibility is strengthened by Bao's experience as an assistant to Zhu Gui, who had previously served as the future Jiaqing emperor's tutor during his time as heir apparent. See Hummel, *Eminent Chinese*, 185–86; R. Kent Guy, *Qing Governors and Their Provinces: The Evolution of Territorial Administration in China, 1644–1796* (Seattle: University of Washington Press, 2010), 141.

11. Hummel, *Eminent Chinese*, 574.

12. Gu Yanwu, "Junxian lun," in *Gu Tinglin shiwen ji* (Beijing: Zhonghua shuju, 1959); Wm. Theodore de Bary and Richard Lufrano, comps., *Sources of Chinese Tradition*, 2nd ed. (New York: Columbia University Press, 2000), 2.6 and 2.39; John Patrick Delury, "Despotism Above and Below: Gu Yanwu's *Record of Daily Learning* on Money, Power, and Mores," Ph.D. dissertation, Yale University, 2007, 126.

mented: "People of our time simply discard such things." Moreover, the first few years of Jiaqing's personal rule were an inviting time to speak out boldly, but also a potentially perilous one. The White Lotus rebellion was at its height, Grand Councilor Heshen had just recently been deposed, and a hunt was under way to identify his corrupt followers within the bureaucracy. One response had been Hong Liangji's remonstrance letter of 1799, which brought a death sentence (later commuted to banishment) upon its author. Hong thereupon became a hero and model for a generation of younger reformist literati, including very likely Bao Shichen. But, lacking a comparable taste for martyrdom, for reasons of prudence, cost, or simply lack of patronage, Bao chose to withhold publication of *On Wealth*, although he allowed the making of manuscript copies, such as one made by Bao's friend and teacher Li Zhaoluo in Changzhou in 1802.[13]

Nearly half a century later, in 1844, the elderly Bao oversaw the publication of his collected works, *Anwu sizhong*. This was not a timid book; most of its contents were pointed and politically outspoken. Included within it were five essays on aspects of local administration—*baojia* public security systems, agricultural and educational administration, local militia, and the evaluation of territorial officials' performance—that espoused genuinely radical ideas, as we shall see. In the preface to the overall collection, Bao noted that these essays also dated from 1801, and had been written as supplements to the *Shuochu*, which he felt had not effectively addressed the current crisis at the village and county level. Nevertheless, the main text of the *Shuochu*—designated by Bao as "Part One" (*shangpian*) with the five local administration essays as "Part Two" (*xiapian*)—was *not* included in Bao's collected works. He suggested that it was too large and cohesive a treatise to be broken up and distributed in this essay collection. In reality, he may also have felt that its moment had passed—the dithering post–Opium War Daoguang court was quite different from the heady atmosphere of the Jiaqing emperor's early personal rule, when the new emperor repeatedly declared the broad opening of communications to the throne (*guangkai yanlu*) and his eagerness to consider "comprehensive reforms" (*xianyu weixin*) and lifted in practice much of the censorship restrictions of the late

13. Bao, preface to *Shuochu*, 133; Pierre-Étienne Will, personal communication.

Qianlong reign.[14] Nevertheless, Bao noted that he still had the manuscript in his household, and added that interested scholars might visit him and consult it there.[15] Based on a survey of Bao's correspondence, one modern scholar has concluded that a great many did in fact take advantage of this invitation, and discussed the work's contents with its author, and that Bao continued to circulate the manuscript to friends as well.[16]

In 1872, Shichen's son Bao Cheng published a new edition of his father's collected works. In the preface he noted that the *Shuochu* was still filed away at home, available for scholarly consultation. He promised to introduce it to the wider world at some later time, as a "supplementary publication" (*xukan*), but for whatever reason he never did so. Neither was the work included in a still later and widely read expanded edition of the *Anwu sizhong* in 1888.[17]

The treatise thus awaited its first publication with Liu Shipei's "national essence" edition of 1906. Liu tells us he found the manuscript, in the author's own hand, in his family library (the reference leaves unclear whether this was Bao's—the more likely in my view—or Liu's own family). Twenty years later, however, a bibliophile named Wu Weizu came upon a manuscript in the hands of a Nanjing bookseller. Believing he had found a copy of Bao's *Shuochu*, he took the text to the historian and director of the Jiangsu Guoxue Library, Liu Yizheng (1879–1956), who validated the find and arranged its publication by his library in photo-offset in 1936. At least a portion of this text is in Bao Shichen's celebrated Northern Wei calligraphy, although Liu Yizheng suspected that most of it was in the hand of one of Bao's secretaries. As with the manuscript discovered by Liu Shipei thirty years earlier, the 1936 edition bears not only the complete text of *Shuochu*, part 1, but also numerous marginal notes by two of Bao's friends, Shen Qinhan (1775–1832) and Zhou Baoxu (*jinshi* 1805)—Liu Shipei had considered them superfluous and omitted them

14. Zhang Yufen, "Lun Jiaqing chunian de 'xianyu weixin,'" *Qingshi yanjiu* 1992.4: 49–54. On censorship relaxation in the early Jiaqing reign, see, for example, Seunghun Han, *After the Prosperous Age*.

15. Bao, general preface to *Anwu sizhong*, dated Daoguang 24/9/26, in *Quanji* (1993).

16. Zheng Dahua, "Bao Shichen."

17. Liu Yizheng, "Shuochu ba," dated winter 1936, in Bao, *Quanji* (1991), 199–201.

from his published edition.[18] The modern edition of *Shuochu*, part 1, published in Bao's collected works in Hefei in 1991, is based primarily on Liu Shipei's 1906 edition, but restores Shen's and Zhou's marginal comments in the form of endnotes.

Bao Shichen's "On Wealth"

Shuochu proceeds from an analysis of the current situation, which Bao emphatically identifies as a crisis of the first magnitude, and makes many specific recommendations for immediate remedies. More basically, though, it offers a detailed blueprint for reorganizing the state apparatus. The greatest problem, in the wake of the Heshen ascendancy, is pervasive official corruption and acquisitiveness; it is this, above all, that has predicated the current crisis. Bao details two general ways to attack this. First, set up better personnel procedures: selection, review, promotion, and disciplining state functionaries against corruption and misgovernment. Second, basically reconceive existing approaches to state finance, on both the revenue and expenditure sides. In the process of laying out in great detail his ideas on these fundamental issues, the *Shuochu* comments briefly but tellingly on a range of other matters, including the economy (population, agricultural productivity, commerce), management of the *san da zheng*,[19] foreign relations, rebel suppression, and military affairs (a great deal on these subjects), and reform of the social order.

He opens with some general reflections on dynastic legitimacy. According to Bao, establishing a state/dynasty (*liguo*) demands three things: *de* (the ruler's virtue, prowess, or will), *wei* (the ruler's charisma, ability to inspire awe, or simply military force), and *cai* (economic resources). Bao insists that all three of these things must be available, but his emphasis is on the pragmatic recognition that virtue and coercive force are of little

18. For a biography of Shen Qinhan, who was noted in his lifetime for providing just such marginal comments as he did for the *Shuochu*, see Hummel, *Eminent Chinese*, 640–41.

19. Bao's recommendations regarding the grain tribute and Yellow River administrations appear in *Shuochu*, 186–88. His ideas on the grain tribute and salt administration will be discussed in chapters 4 and 5, below.

import without a sound economic base. He then moves into a distinction famously drawn by Gu Yanwu, that between "above" (*shang*) and "below" (*xia*). As John Delury has argued, for Gu these are shifting, relational categories, that can refer to throne versus bureaucracy, upper versus lower officialdom, state versus society, or private elites versus the mass of poor commoners.[20] Here, it is the first relationship to which Bao refers. Like Gu in his *Junxian lun*, Bao argues that excessive concentration of economic resources in the ruler's hands alone in fact enfeebles him by isolating him at the top (*gu li yu shang*), inevitably leading to state/dynastic collapse (*wangguo*).[21]

In this general discussion, Bao discreetly makes no direct reference to the legitimacy of the current ruling house. Although, as we shall see, there is much throughout his work that the Qing court might have found offensive, anti-Manchuism per se does not seem to have been on Bao's agenda, nor to have been the reason he declined to publish his book. Only one of his recommendations, in my view, could easily be construed as ethnically charged, that being his suggestion that the constitutional principle of dyarchy (balancing a Chinese official with a Manchu or Mongol bannerman in central government posts) be dispensed with, in favor of recruiting the best available talent regardless of national origin.[22] Obviously, this undercut a basic instrument of Qing control, and would in practice, though not in theory, have increased the number of Chinese officials in controlling positions in the imperial administration.

Bao argues, however, that as of 1801 the Qing *guo* is confronting imminent collapse: we are faced, he says, with an immediate need to "rescue our times." To deny that crisis is upon us, when it so evidently is, is simply irresponsible ministerial conduct. He identifies three aspects to the current crisis: (1) the military situation precipitated by the White Lotus (but compounded by renegade militia and imperial troops), which is totally out of control; (2) the widespread immiseration facing the empire, because the *shang* have systematically expropriated resources from the *xia*—the rich live extravagantly, while the poor suffer from lack of morale

20. Delury, "Despotism Above and Below," 261.

21. Bao, *Shuochu*, 133.

22. Bao, *Shuochu*, 141–42.

and productivity; and (3) the huge deficits facing official budgets, at all levels, virtually *necessitating* extortion and squeeze at all levels of administration.[23]

Crisis, however, also spells opportunity, Bao notes. Wise policies can reverse losses of productivity, and can restore the "wealth of the state" (*guofu*)—he is not reticent about stating as his goal the restoration of the financial assets of the "*guojia*." We need to demonstrate our willingness to work with the people to make a fresh start (*yu min geng shi*). Somewhat surprisingly, Bao proposes as a first step the declaration of a general amnesty (*dashe*): release all government prisoners (except those guilty of crimes calling for decapitation, for example, incest), pardon all disgraced officials (except those guilty of offenses calling for death by slicing, for example, desertion of their posts), and forgive all private debts to the government. A yet greater problem than personal venality, he says, is that, after decades of superior officials' having systematically expropriated "gifts" or other resources from their subordinates, every single office in the bureaucratic structure is saddled with shortfalls (*kuikong*) in its accounts, which it is legally responsible to make up (*mibu*); Bao recommends as his "priority number one" that these intragovernmental debts be forgiven across the board by imperial mandate.[24] Having done this, new regulations can be instituted, and stricter punishments for future offences. The government can also systematically reconstitute the state apparatus. Bao then proposes, very near the outset of his work, the key institutional innovation that he will elaborate upon later, an Office of Personnel Evaluation (Shenguanyuan). This, it turns out, is far more than what its title claims: it is a central clearing house for input from below—from officials, literati, and even commoners—on all matters of government performance and policy.[25] We will return to this below.

23. *Shuochu*, 133–34; for Bao's extended analysis of the White Lotus situation, see *Shuochu*, 182–84. For a recent historical analysis, largely agreeing with Bao that the military crisis after ca. 1800 was essentially one of supposedly "loyalist" forces' own making, see Yingcong Dai, "Civilians Go into Battle."

24. *Shuochu*, 189.

25. *Shuochu*, 134–35.

Central and Provincial Government

The largest single portion of Bao's text is devoted to laying out in detail his recommendations for a revised structure of the imperial administration. His table of offices eclectically incorporates elements from various historical eras he has studied. It exactly replicates the administrative structure of no particular dynasty, but, to my eye, most closely resembles that of the early Ming. Let us consider but a few elements of Bao's table; as we shall see, it systematically undoes several of the most significant innovations introduced by the Qing over the preceding century and a half.

Bao's central administration is headed by two officials, the chancellors (*chengxiang*) of the Left and the Right, sole bearers in the civil bureaucracy of rank 1A (*zheng yipin*). These two officials, he says, "control the affairs of state" (*zhi guozheng*); they are the leaders of the Grand Secretariat (*neige*), have responsibility over both civil and military matters, and authority over eunuchs and other palace functionaries as well. Throughout imperial history, officials bearing this title had commonly functioned as the head of the bureaucratic administration, and so they had in the early Ming. But, he continues, since the abolition of this post in 1380 by Ming Taizu, jealous of its power, there had been no such position, neither in title nor in function. The relatively numerous "grand secretaries" (*da xueshi*) under the later Ming and throughout the Qing enjoyed considerably reduced authority.[26] Subsequent commentators, including Gu Yanwu, had tended to see the abolition of the chancellorship as something of an original sin in the history of late imperial governance, enhancing the autocracy of the throne while isolating it further from the real affairs of the empire; Bao Shichen does not make this point explicitly, but he seems to have agreed.

Bao surrounds his chancellors at the central level with presidents and vice presidents of the Six Boards, and a host of more specialized central posts, most of them familiar from the contemporary practice of his own

26. *Shuochu*, 143 and 154. On the historic post of *chengxiang*, see Charles O. Hucker, *A Dictionary of Official Titles in Imperial China* (Stanford: Stanford University Press, 1985), 126–27.

day. He argues, however, that his table of capital officials in fact streamlines administration, eliminating various posts that have grown up over imperial history since the Han, in the process both cutting costs (see below) and reducing the redundancy that impedes efficient responsiveness to societal needs.[27]

Most conspicuously absent in Bao's restructuring is the preeminent central government post of the era, grand councilor (*junji dachen*) and the collective body of such officials, the Grand Council (*junji chu*). Over the course of the late Kangxi and Yongzheng reigns, this institution, with its privileged access to the new state-of-the-art tool of government communication, the palace memorial (*zouzhe*), had gradually supplanted the policy-making powers of the Grand Secretariat. By comparison to the more bureaucratized Secretariat, the Grand Council was a personal tool of monarchical rule, a privy council of sorts, and, though an occasional Chinese joined its ranks, its tightly restricted membership was dominated by members of the imperial clan and other bannermen of non-Han origin.[28] It remained an extraconstitutional organ, however, inasmuch as it was not mentioned, and its powers defined, in the list of state organs in the then-current Qianlong edition of the *Da Qing huidian* (Institutions of the Qing empire). Bao Shichen does not explicitly announce his intention to abolish the post of grand councilor in the *Shuochu*, but his cavalier nonmention of it in his systematic list of official posts was a radical act. According to Liu Guangjing, coupled with the restoration of the post of chancellor, this was part of Bao's general desire to eliminate bottlenecks in the relationship between the center and the localities, the throne and the people.[29]

At the time Bao wrote, in 1801, there was in fact widespread discomfort with the powers the Grand Council had appropriated to itself, especially under the tenure of the abominated Heshen. In the two years since his assumption of personal rule, the Jiaqing emperor himself had initiated several reforms, including "opening widely the pathways of communications" (*guangkai yanlu*), in order to curb its abuses. As we saw in the

27. *Shuochu*, 141–42.

28. For a magisterial history of this institution, see Beatrice S. Bartlett, *Monarchs and Ministers: The Grand Council in Mid-Ch'ing China, 1723–1820* (Berkeley: University of California Press, 1991).

29. Liu Guangjing, "Shijiu shiji chuye Zhongguo zhishifenzi," 998–99.

introduction to this volume, the new ruler imposed a series of far stricter regulations on the council, including for the first time formalizing its existence in a new edition of the *Da Qing huidian*.[30] Bao Shichen and his monarch, in other words, both identified the Grand Council as a dysfunctional institution of governance, but sought to remedy the problem in different ways: Bao by abolishing it altogether, and the emperor by constitutionalizing it and restricting its powers.

Bao's central military structure is complex and frankly a bit bewildering.[31] What is striking, however, is that he downgrades the commanders of the Eight Banners (*dutong*) from their actual Qing rank of 1B to 2A, and places them under the control (*ling*) of a single commander in chief (*tidu*), rank 1A, whose job also includes "deliberating state governance" (*yi guozheng*). There was during the Qing no single military official comparable to Bao's commander in chief; the military title *tidu* was a provincial-level post only, rank 1B. In other words, it seems that Bao Shichen has cheekily proposed something of a newly unified command structure for the empire, within which the Banners—the engines of the Qing conquest, no less—are firmly subordinated to a single bureaucratized commander.[32]

Bao is even bolder in his table of field officials, where he eliminates at a stroke the principal existing posts of regional administration, the governor general (*zongdu*) and the provincial governor (*xunfu*). Bao proposes that governance at this level, between the center and the localities, be left entirely in the hands of two functionaries. The *fansi* (often today translated as "provincial treasurer") is an omnicompetent official of rank 2A, assigned one to each province, responsible for administering education

30. Wensheng Wang, *White Lotus Rebels*; Guy, *Qing Governors and Their Provinces*, 142.

31. Bao divided his list of military officials (*wuguan*) into three categories: *suwei*, *zhengzhi* (regular posts), and *muzhi* (adjunct posts?). The first category is clearly intended to be preeminent, but the usual meaning of *suwei* in Qing military parlance was "night guard," the relevance of which to these high officials I cannot determine. See E-tu Zen Sun, *Ch'ing Administrative Terms: A Translation of the Terminology of the Six Boards with Explanatory Notes* (Cambridge, MA: Harvard University Press, 1961), 235.

32. *Shuochu*, 148 and 155; compare Hucker, *Dictionary of Official Titles*, 498 and 545, and William Frederick Mayers, *The Chinese Government* (Shanghai: Kelly and Walsh, 1897), 56 and 65. Mayers says that under the Qing, while *dutong* were usually Manchu, *tidu* were "almost always Chinese."

and examinations, enforcing public security, commanding a significant military force, overseeing military colonies (*tuntian*)—a favorite institution of Bao Shichen—collecting taxes and other revenues, provisioning the population, and maintaining the hydraulic infrastructure, among other matters. He is aided by the *niesi* (commonly, "provincial judge"), a lesser 3B official in charge more narrowly of criminal and judicial matters and the postal system.[33] In relying on these two functionaries and eliminating their provincial superiors, Bao was proposing reversing a wave of innovations in regional administration of the late Ming and early Qing. The antecedents of the *fansi* and *niesi* had originally been deployed in 1376 by Ming Taizu as his first line of provincial administration. Later in the dynasty a grand coordinator (*xunfu*) was added, to mediate and coordinate their activities, and still later a supreme commander (*zongdu*) was dispatched, to take charge of regional military duties. Neither of these latter officials, however, was really a multifunctional field administrator, and neither had a permanent staff; rather, they were seen as *central* government commissioners on temporary assignment. It was in the early Qing (1661) that these latter two posts were gradually regularized into the governors and governors general familiar from eighteenth- and nineteenth-century practice.[34]

For Bao Shichen, this was superfluous and counterproductive. Lying behind his move was an ideology of opposition to overregulation and excessive surveillance that went back at least to Gu Yanwu, and likely much earlier. In Gu's famous treatise on local governance, the "Junxian lun," he had proposed eliminating regular provincial administrators altogether, leaving only a roving regional inspector (*yushi xunfang*) who toured on an annual basis. Gu argued that the imposition of an additional stratum of officials essentially for surveillance purposes was self-defeating: it emasculated local officials, without comparably strengthening the center. It took powers out of the hands of competent and trustworthy local magistrates, in the process further strengthening their competitors for power at the local level: subbureaucratic petty clerks, and extrabureaucratic local bullies. In the reading of John Delury, Gu argues that

33. *Shuochu*, 173–75.

34. Guy, *Qing Governors and Their Provinces*, chap. 2; Hucker, *Dictionary of Official Titles*, 127, 208, 355, 495–96; Delury, "Despotism Above and Below," 174–75.

"simply put, empowerment [of local officials] magnifies [imperial] authority. Surveillance diminishes it."[35]

Whether or not Bao Shichen was deliberately echoing Gu Yanwu on this question, he was clearly thinking along the same lines. Bao writes:

> If there are too many supervisors, if the salaries offered are too low, and if there are too many underlings brought along, the result will be that people with plans will be unable to develop them and that [officials] will be unable to get by financially without engaging in corruption. Officials are assigned to govern the population; if instead they end up harming the population, this suggests that the system is bad. The county magistrate is subordinate to the prefect, and the prefect to the provincial treasurer and provincial judge. Why then is there any need for a governor general, governor, or circuit intendant [*daotai*]? You may say that they are needed to check up on the provincial treasurer and provincial judge, who are not trustworthy, but if so what makes you think that the governor general or the governor will themselves be trustworthy?
>
> The Board [of Civil Office] appoints local officials to their posts, but as their competence cannot be fully ascertained at that point, the provincial officials, arguing that they need to have the man fit the post, arbitrarily transfer them around, entailing considerable expenses in welcoming and sending-off [ceremonies]. All kinds of abuses accumulate, such as provincial officials using the pretext of determining the simplicity or difficulty of a [local] post to solicit bribes.
>
> As for the circuit intendants, they are inserted between the provincial commissioners and the prefects, but their inspection tours and [efforts at] military preparedness exist in name only.
>
> Thus it is obvious that the posts of governor general, governor, and circuit intendant ought to be abolished.[36]

For a man with a deep anathema to overregulation, however, Bao imposes a great many laws and stipulations, not only on his various administrative personnel, but also on the society at large. He proposes a detailed and fussy code of sumptuary legislation, for both government employees and commoners (all commoners must wear solid-colored cotton clothing,

35. Gu Yanwu, "Junxian lun," 13; Delury, "Despotism Above and Below," 128.
36. *Shuochu*, 141–42.

blue for artisans and merchants, any color *other* than blue for farmers, etc.).[37] Scores of varieties of official misconduct are identified, along with appropriate strict punishments for each offense.[38] The key would seem to be effectiveness. Any law must remain "the ruler's law" (*wangzhe zhi fa*) under the secure control of the throne, rather than be left to be opportunistically manipulated by petty functionaries at the bottom of the administrative order. Moreover, any worthwhile law must be demonstrably enforceable; if it is not, abolish it.[39] With these caveats, Bao is fine with lawmaking; he admits that in his youth he read and was inspired by the Legalist classics, and has systematically studied the legal codes of past dynasties all his life.[40] In the *Shuochu*, Bao effectively quotes the Legalist master Han Fei's dictum that laws must be simple and clearly understandable, while their enforcement must be certain and severe.

Local Administration

Bao Shichen's thoroughly innovative ideas about local administration are contained to some extent in his manuscript *Shuochu*, part 1, but are yet more developed in the several contemporaneous (1801) essays he referred to as "*Shuochu*, Part Two," and dared to publish in his 1844 collected works, especially the remarkable "Essay on *Baojia*" (*Shuo baojia shiyi*). The innovation is less at the level of the local officials themselves than at the level of subbureaucratic infrastructure.

Though, as we have seen, Bao dispensed with the higher-level local official the circuit intendent (*daotai*), he did retain as the core of his local administration the posts of prefect (*zhifu*)—some 185 of these bearing rank 4A—and county magistrate (*zhixian*)—1,511 of these at rank 5A. He also allowed for some 1,513 assistant magistrates, at rank 7A, and a number of lesser local posts. He proposed that the alternative local administrative units then in existence (*zhou* and *ting*) be uniformly standardized

37. *Shuochu*, 139–40.
38. *Shuochu*, 177–78, 189.
39. *Shuochu*, 133 and 137.
40. Bao, preface to *Anwu sizhong*, in *Quanji* (1993).

to county (*xian*) status. His discussions of the magistrate's duties could have been drawn from the writings of "statecraft" (*jingshi*) officials of the previous century: make regularly scheduled tours of your district, talk with as many local people as possible, prepare detailed maps of your jurisdiction, prepare detailed annual performance evaluations on each of your subordinates, preside over proper ritual performances and select model local residents for bestowal of ritual honors, and govern your district "in collaboration with public-minded local notables" (*yu difang xianshi dafu gongzhi*)—almost a mantra among Qing critics of creeping bureaucratism. But a closer look at Bao's actual proposals for subcounty administration makes it clear that his is no simple model for the style of local-elite autonomy that sometimes went under the rubric of *fengjian* (literally: feudal) political thought.[41]

Perhaps Bao's most striking and emphatic proposal is for the total elimination of private secretaries (*muyou*) to local officials—surprising because this was a position that Bao himself held periodically throughout his career. Our conventional understanding of the role of private secretary is that, faced with an army of notoriously corrupt petty clerks who were entrenched in local society prior to his rotation into a post, as well as an array of local elites whose commitment to public causes was unreliable, prudent officials brought with them an entourage of trusted friends who specialized in aspects of local administration (legal issues, financial management, bureaucratic communications), paying them out of their own pockets to protect their service records from scandal. An unfortunate byproduct of the basic problem of Qing local governance—the paucity of regular officials on the ground—the number of *muyou* escalated and their functions multiplied, especially over the last century of the dynasty.[42] According to Bao Shichen, the system was already well

41. *Shuochu*, 143–44, 175–81. For eighteenth-century takes on this problem, see William T. Rowe, *Saving the World: Chen Hongmou and Elite Consciousness in Eighteenth-Century China* (Stanford: Stanford University Press, 2001), and numerous studies by Pierre-Étienne Will, including "The 1744 Annual Audits of Magistrate Activity and Their Fate," *Late Imperial China* 18.2 (December 1997): 1–50.

42. T'ung-tsu Ch'u, *Local Government in China under the Ch'ing* (Stanford: Stanford University Press, 1962), chap. 6; Kenneth E. Folsom, *Friends, Guests, and Colleagues: The Mu-fu System in the Late Ch'ing Period* (Berkeley: University of California Press, 1968).

out of control by his time of writing in 1801, and in fact had been a major contributor to the rampant corruption and maladministration of recent decades.

The basic problem, for Bao, is that these "friends" are nonregulated persons usurping functions that are properly those of the state. They oppress the local population, and more often control the official than are controlled by him. It is *muyou* who have been the principal facilitators of the bureaucracy's degeneration, presenting on the official's behalf "red envelopes" (*hongbao*) containing monetary gifts to superiors on birthdays and other ceremonial occasions. While the cost of these retainers is supposedly borne by the official himself, in practice it is passed along to the local population—to the tune, Bao estimates, of an average of 2,500 taels per year for each county. Bao argues that the necessary functions now served by *muyou* should be assumed instead by subordinate officials (*muliao*) and by clerks, both groups regularized and salaried by the state. Of course, he notes, many of the existing *muyou* are highly talented men, and even honest ones; those should be encouraged to sit for evaluation and assignment in a regularized capacity once the position of *muyou* has been universally eliminated.[43]

As for the clerks (*shuli*), for centuries the conventional whipping boys for every failure of local administration, they should be treated, says Bao, by the magistrate with the same respect he currently treats his *muyou*, not as if they were his household slaves (*jianu*). Indeed, Bao wants clerks to be regarded and administered as ordinary low-ranking officials (*shi*): tested, graded, and assessed on an annual basis, in an examination system administered directly by the official one level above the jurisdiction in which they work (that is, county clerks by the prefect, prefectural clerks by the provincial treasurer), but designed and overseen at the central level. Clerks who fail will be dismissed and repatriated to their native county.[44]

With his considerable experience on the front lines during the White Lotus campaigns, Bao unsurprisingly is a strong proponent of local

43. *Shuochu*, 178–79.

44. The proposal that clerks should at least be granted the possibility of advancement by examination into low-ranking officialdom had antecedents in the eighteenth century (see Rowe, *Saving the World*, 342–44), but Bao here goes considerably farther than earlier proposals I have seen.

militarization. A corps of militiamen, he advises, should be recruited in each county, and paid, drilled, and commanded by local officials themselves. Recruits should be selected not on the basis of their social origins, nor of their preexisting military skill level, but according to the simple measure of how much weight of stone they can lift. Once organized, they can be used not only for local defense, but also for water conservancy and other civil construction projects. Moreover, the magistrate is to identify critical spots of territory (*yaodi*) in his jurisdiction in special need of defense. As near to these spots as possible, he is to clear a tract of land for occupation by special militia units. (If the tract is too large, or the defense need too critical, this can be turned over to higher authority for formal designation as a *tuntian* military colony; if only 2,000 *mou* or less, the county should manage it itself.) Militiamen and their families should be recruited (again, on the basis of personal strength), and granted parcels of land and draft animals in return for tax and military service obligations. The men are to be organized into five, twenty-five, and seventy-five men groups, given distinctive banners, and trained in arms under the magistrate's supervision. In essence, Bao is calling for a "strategic hamlet" system as a counterinsurgency measure during these troubled times.[45]

Bao was also preoccupied with the issue of selecting local social leadership. As a first step, he insisted that the government practice of offering gentry and brevet official ranks for sale be completely eliminated; this ran counter to the pragmatic advice of many eighteenth-century "statecraft" officials, as well as to the fact that the government had long been deeply dependent for revenue on such sales. Men currently holding purchased ranks would have their honors revoked, although they might still be eligible for the new types of local honors that Bao prescribed. There were essentially two such honors, both awarded by the local magistrate directly. The first, which Bao called *gongshi* (graduate), was reserved for youths of exceptional filiality and obedience (*xiaodi*), and for local elders who had displayed a history of paternalistic family leadership and of community mediation. Males of all walks of life, merchants and artisans included, might qualify. But the second honorific title, *shengyuan* (licentiate), was

45. *Shuochu*, 135; Bao, "Junxian rongzheng," in *Quanji* (1997), 460–67.

reserved for those who actively worked in the fields (*litian*), and in doing so had demonstrated a record of avoiding tax resistance, feuding, or litigation—they were essentially model farmers. Strikingly, neither of these ranks, normally associated with the Chinese "literati," demanded classical education or even literacy as a prerequisite. Bao did, however, also maintain the system of literary examinations, albeit with his own idiosyncratic curriculum (see below), to meet the needs of official recruitment. These exams began at the county level, and his *gongshi* and *shengyuan* were eligible to sit for them, but others might as well. Local social leadership and education for bureaucratic recruitment, in other words, were treated as separate matters altogether.[46]

The cornerstone of Bao's local governance reforms was a revivified *baojia* system, the hoary concept of regimenting households into nested decimal units primarily for purposes of mutual public security.[47] Bao of course was hardly alone among late imperial policy writers in fixing upon this system, in constant need of reinvigoration, as a focus of reform efforts, but his ideas were much more far-reaching than most.[48] (The most radical aspect of Bao's proposed system is its role in economic redistribution, discussion of which we will defer to chapter 3.) Bao prescribed four levels of *baojia* regimentation: a ten-household *jia*, a ten-*jia* unit known as the *li*, a ten-*li bao*, and a ten-*bao xiang*. As much as possible, these decimal units should follow the natural terrain, and reflect natural residence communities; lower-level units would be numbered, but larger ones would be named. Each level would be headed by a community leader or leaders selected through some negotiated process involving both popular selection (*jumin xuanju*) and appointment by the magistrate, who would assidu-

46. *Shuochu*, 135–36; Bao, "Shuo xuezheng shiyi," in *Quanji* (1997), 282–85. See also Liu Guangjing, "Shijiu shiji chuye Zhongguo zhishifenzi," 998–99.

47. Bao, "Shuo baojia shiyi," in *Quanji* (1997), 271–82.

48. See Kung-chuan Hsiao, *Rural China: Imperial Control in the Nineteenth Century* (Seattle: University of Washington Press, 1960), chap. 3, which argues that in most times and places during the Qing *baojia* was simply a dead letter. I, and many others, have shown that Hsiao's dismissive view is grossly overstated; William T. Rowe, "Urban Control in Late Imperial China: The *Pao-chia* System in Hankow," in *Perspectives on a Changing China*, ed. Joshua A. Fogel and Rowe (Boulder: Westview Press, 1979), 89–112.

ously check local archives on the candidate's past behavior, and broadly interview residents in the affected district during his annual tours. Bao does not say whether holders of literati degrees were eligible for such positions (in existing Qing statutes they were not), but he does disqualify merchants or artisans or their descendents—not an unusual position for a reformer with a strong agrarian bias, but striking in a man like Bao so often identified as a commercial-leaning economic liberal.

Bao would have his *baojia* headmen engage in the usual public security, conflict resolution, and community ritual leadership tasks, and also in the somewhat more ambitious—but common to the Qing statecraft tradition—project of aiding the magistrate in drawing up detailed local maps. Echoing a particularly utopian effort of the mid-eighteenth century, he hoped to use his system in a campaign of local behavioral modification, the headmen drawing up annual lists of customs in their jurisdictions to be either encouraged or expunged (*quanjie gaoshi*) during the following year; households who performed exceptionally well or poorly in meeting these expectations would have their names posted on the headman's door, with the least compliant threatened with expulsion from the community.[49]

The Economy and State Finance

Very clearly, Bao's revised state structure would be an expensive proposition, most especially at the local level, with many more clerks, militiamen, and other functionaries put directly on state payrolls. To his credit, he was aware of this, and presented detailed calculations about how his reforms might be financed. It all tied in with his views on the mid-Qing economy as a whole, which he insists can quickly be brought back to good health. As we shall see in the next chapter, Bao deployed elaborate mathematical calculations to demonstrate that, even given likely population growth, the empire's resource base was adequate to ensure steady or even

49. The eighteenth-century effort referred to occured in Shaanxi in 1744–45, under the rubric *xingli chubi* (promote the functional and expunge the dysfunctional); see Rowe, *Saving the World*, 356–62, and Will, "Annual Audits."

improving standards of living; more labor input, properly husbanded, would yield greater output.[50]

Bao acknowledges that he lives in a multisectoral economy—signified by the term *simin* (the four branches of popular livelihood)—and recognizes that merchants and artisans make invaluable contributions, but he insists that staple agriculture represents the basis (*ben*) of the economy and the true productive wealth (*shengcai*) of the empire. The task of official policy should thus be to lead people as much as possible back into farming, rather than making it unprofitable, as recent tax policy has done. Like others before him, he wants to outlaw superfluous crops such as tobacco, and to limit alcohol production from otherwise edible food grain to that controlled by the government monopoly.[51] In a lengthy disquisition on the salt monopoly (foreshadowing his salt reform recommendations of the 1820s and 30s), Bao argues that salt represents "nature's bounty" (*tiandi zhi cang*) to all humanity. He then extends this to other natural resources such as copper, lead, and timber, which have less commonly been treated in the past as state monopolies. They, like salt, belong to no single private individual (*fei minjia siye*), and should be managed by the state in the collective interest.[52] Private entrepreneurs and merchants have a legitimate role to play in all these trades, but only under supervision of the state, acting as steward for the public—for example by rooting out private monopolies. This, it seems to me, is hardly a "liberal" position. Bao does however recognize, at the same time, that specific managerial decisions (such as the most efficient routes to be followed by commercial salt distributors) are often best made by profit-minded businessmen, rather than by government fiat.

An even more striking illiberalism—a radical protectionism—emerges in Bao's discussion of foreign trade. He allows the need for some officially regulated intercultural exchange with Central Asia. However, all overseas trade (*chuyang maoyi*), as well as all maritime navigation to Southeast Asia and beyond (*dongnan kaiyang*), is to be absolutely prohibited. All "foreign devil merchants" (*gewai yanghang guizi*) are to be

50. One Marxist economic historian, somewhat hopefully, deduces from this that Bao precociously advanced a labor theory of value; Hu Qizhuang, *Zhongguo jingji sixiang shi*, 587.

51. *Shuochu*, 133, 186.

52. *Shuochu*, 184–86.

immediately expelled from the empire. Foreign-made textiles are prohibited to Qing subjects, as are foreign contrivances such as cuckoo clocks (*ziming zhongbiao*), mechanical men (*zixingren*), self-propelling vehicles (*zixingche*), and all products of foreign ingenuity using steam or mechanical power. (So much for technology transfer!) Qing subjects found in possession of such novelties will be subject to beatings of one hundred strokes, while Chinese craftsmen involved in making them will be summarily beheaded.[53] This, recall, is 1801. Bao's strident antiforeignism thus long predates the Opium War, though his attitude toward foreign trade in general will actually soften by that time.

With the economy restored to prosperity, we can return to the question of state finance. Bao, we remember, argued at the very outset of his treatise for the necessity of adequate state financing. Like Gu Yanwu and others before him, he insisted that the empire's wealth should not be greedily monopolized by the throne versus the bureaucracy, nor by the state versus the private economy, which is the basis of all productivity. Yet at the same time, writing in an era of growing government incapacity, Bao seems to me far more concerned than Gu and others of the need to put his state on a strong financial footing. As the lessons of the recent past suggested, an underfunded state necessarily becomes a predatory one, and invites popular rebellion.[54]

In no one place in his text does Bao tally up the revenues and expenses of his ideal state, the way he does for his revived agrarian economy. But we can attempt to put together scraps of what he says to see if

53. *Shuochu*, 141. Bao's inclusion in this list of foreign novelties of *zixingche*, the usual translation today for "bicycle," poses a special problem, inasmuch as the forerunner of the bicycle is conventionally understood to have been invented only in 1817, in Germany. For some this may raise suspicion that Bao's 1801 text was subsequently tampered with prior to its initial 1906 publication. However, the term *zixingche* was indeed available in the vocabulary of Bao's time. For example, in the widely read 1634 catalog of Western engineering marvels, *Yuanxi qiqi tushuo*, translated into Chinese by Wang Zheng from an original text by the Jesuit Joannes Terentius, the term is invoked, along with others such as *zimingzhong* (self-chiming clocks) to illustrate the principle of "natural" (*tianran*) motion. Terentius does not define further the nature of the machine to which he refers; it was almost certainly not a bicycle. *Yuanxi qiqi tushou* (reprinted Shanghai: Shangwu yinshuguan, 1936), 1:14. I am indebted to Victor Mair and Paul Golden for their inputs on this question.

54. *Shuochu*, 189.

his prescriptions make at least rough sense. He expects to save money for the people by imposing frugal measures on his officials: each office in his bureaucratic table is assigned a strict expense budget, and many currently tolerated practices, such as housing great numbers of the official's family members at government expense, are prohibited.[55] He does not total up the savings he anticipates from this overall, but clearly it is substantial. He claims that by outlawing the extension of gifts-cum-bribes by officials to their superiors, he will save the taxpayer over 1 million taels per year. His blanket elimination of *muyou* will save on average 2,500 taels per year per county, or some 3,750,000 empire-wide. He wants to radically trim the personnel of the domestic and maritime customs administrations, for a savings of 1,600,000 taels per year. And by essentially privatizing the operations of the salt administration, he can cut surplus state employees to the tune of 4,600,000 taels per year. Altogether, Bao estimates that his economies will result in an annual savings to the taxpayer of over 10 million taels worth of silver and grain; especially in straitened economic times, such as the present, leaving these additional financial resources in the hands of producers is indeed "the great way of producing wealth" (*shengcai zhi dadao*).[56]

This sounds like a "liberal" formulation, but Bao is in fact hardly trimming the size of government. Alongside these "remitted" (*juan*) state revenues are the considerable new expenditures proposed in Bao's scheme. He calculates, for example, the additional cost of county government operations (*gongfei*), including the newly regularized salaries of clerks and local militiamen, at a nationwide total of some 4 to 5 million taels, plus another 800,000 to 900,000 piculs (*dan*) of grain in kind.[57]

So where does Bao expect to generate compensating government revenue? He outlines several new sources of state finance. He claims, for example, that by turning over salt distribution to the private commercial market he will not only vastly cut government payrolls, but also, by claiming a share of the merchants' profits, raise an additional 10 million taels per year; engaging in some very detailed calculations, he argues that his new scheme will yield eight times the average annual revenue from salt

55. *Shuochu*, 175–76 and passim.

56. *Shuochu*, 182.

57. *Shuochu*, 182.

taxes as they now stand. (To a considerable extent, the salt administration is the cash cow of Bao's reconstructed imperial state.) More broadly, Bao proposes imposing a commercial tax on *all* merchants and artisans at the local level, pegged to their individual levels of capitalization. He claims that on average this new shop tax will yield some 3,600 taels for each county, for an empire-wide total of 5,400,000 taels per year. He will allow 1,600,000 of this to be retained for local use, while the remaining 3,800,000 is remitted upward for provincial or central purposes.[58]

Altogether, it seems that Bao is doing two things. He is shifting the weight of government finance downward in the administrative scale, funding the localities more generously at the cost of trimming expenses at higher levels. (In Gu Yanwu's terms, this would be redressing the balance between *shang* and *xia*.) At the same time, he is shifting the burden of government finance from the agrarian to the commercial sector. This by no means suggests, I hasten to add, an anachronistic anticommercial, agrarian bias; Bao in fact expected that he was opening many new opportunities for private commercial entrepreneurs, and he anticipated that this would stimulate the economy overall. He understood, however, that the commercial sector in mid-Qing China was in fact undertaxed, and he was by no means laissez-faire about leaving this as it was.

Toting up his proposed gains and losses to state finances overall, to the extent his sometimes fuzzy figures allow us to do this, leaves the impression that his new calculus might have been viable—there are more savings and new revenues in aggregate than lost revenues and new expenditures. This presupposes, however—and this is a gargantuan supposition—that all or even *any* of his individual economic schemes would have worked.

Personnel Management

If, as we have said, one-half of Bao Shichen's solution for restoring good government in his crisis-stricken times is to set the state on a sound financial footing, the other half is to establish procedures for recruiting,

58. *Shuochu*, 184–86.

assessing, and getting in place the best possible personnel. This is the function of Bao's capstone institutional innovation, a broadly powerful central administrative organ that he calls the "Shenguanyuan," the Office of Personnel Evaluation. Though this office does not rank highest in his new government apparatus (it is headed by an official whose rank, 2A, is equivalent only to that of a board vice president), Bao introduces his entire plan for constitutional reform with a discussion of this new creation, and a claim for the regenerative role it will play in imperial governance. There was no such office in the Qing bureaucratic structure as Bao found it; indeed, an institution of this name had existed only briefly in imperial history, in the Song, between 995 and 1080 CE.[59] In Bao's scheme, the Shenguanyuan works closely with the Board of Civil Office, the Board of Rites, the Imperial Academy (Guozi jian), and the Hanlin Academy, but it is clearly the controlling node for all of these.[60]

The Shenguanyuan will systematically review the credentials of central government employees—personnel of the Grand Secretariat, the Boards, the Hanlin Academy, and the Censorate—stripping the undeserving of their ranks, but examining them for possible reassignment elsewhere. It will organize a new, three-tier system of qualifying examinations, beginning at the local level. Bao's somewhat idiosyncratic curriculum will center on the *Spring and Autumn Annals* and its various supplements, the "old text" *Zuozhuan*, as well as the "new text" *Gongyang*, which would come to inspire Kang Youwei in leading the 1898 Reforms, and also the *Hu Commentary* of Hu Anguo (1073–1138), something of a cult classic that had fired up radical reformers since the late Ming dynasty.[61] The *Elementary Learning* (*Xiaoxue*) and *Classic of Filial Piety* (*Xiaojing*) will also be tested; the other classics only peripherally. Eight-legged essays are explicitly abolished. The best students will be reexamined on the *Zizhi tongjian* (Comprehensive mirror for aid in governance), and the dynastic histories. At all levels, students will have to demonstrate the applications of their reading to current events. In all, it is a curriculum tightly focused on practical administration. Those who pass the highest

59. Hucker, *Dictionary of Official Titles*, 418.

60. *Shuochu*, 134–35.

61. On the reformist appeal of the *Hu Commentary*, and of the *Spring and Autumn Annals* itself, see William T. Rowe, *Crimson Rain: Seven Centuries of Violence in a Chinese County* (Stanford: Stanford University Press, 2007), 116–17.

level examination will be awarded *jinshi* degrees, and their qualities examined by the Shenguanyuan for consideration to be posted as officials.[62]

Another major task entrusted to the Shenguanyuan, along with its support staff in the Hanlin and Imperial Academies, is the systematic and exhaustive review of fitness reports submitted annually for every single government functionary in the empire, down to the newly bureaucratized county clerks. Bao provides extremely detailed prescriptions for the criteria that each superior official must use, first to assess his subordinates, then to compile an annotated list ranking them numerically in terms of performance. Such reports are passed up through the chain of command, read closely at each stage and acted upon in terms of promotion and demotion of the individuals on the list. Within the Shenguanyuan, a detailed survey of every post in the empire and its specific difficulties and requirements is also to be compiled and routinely maintained, so as to allow the precise placement of the best qualified incumbent to the most appropriate post.[63]

Important as is this official evaluation function, it is not the Shenguanyuan's most basic task, Bao explains. Its prime task is to solicit and deliberate upon written comment from all Qing subjects—"officials, gentry, government secretaries, clerks, ordinary farmers"—on all matters of basic statecraft (*jingguo*), including frontier policy, water conservancy, military colonies, agricultural improvement, military training, the strengths and weaknesses of the current administration (*lizhi libi*), proposed revisions of existing laws, and things that should be promoted or prohibited (*dangxing dangchu*) in local society. Proposals from the people may be written in informal style, and submitted in sealed envelopes to the local official, who will send them upward to the Shenguanyuan via the postal service. The Shenguanyuan will sort and give due consideration to any proposal it receives; if it seems unworthy it will be returned to the sender (without recrimination), but if it has merit its author will be brought to the capital (transportation and housing at government expense), questioned on the proposal, and possibly assigned to a central government post.[64]

62. *Shuochu*, 135–37 and 155; Bao, "Shuo xuezheng shiyi," in *Quanji* (1997), 282–85.
63. Bao, "Shuo keji shiyi," in *Quanji* (1997), 317–19.
64. *Shuochu*, 134–35.

If the Jiaqing emperor had opened the *yanlu* (pathways of words) two years earlier on the specific matter of rooting out Heshen-linked bureaucratic corruption, Bao Shichen was proposing a far broader and more routinized opening of communications, both within the government and between the government and the populace. It is no wonder that Bao's 1906 publisher, Liu Shipei, saw him as a forerunner of Kang Youwei, who set up a remarkably similar mechanism to solicit private suggestions for government reform in September 1898.

Rewriting the Qing Constitution

Although the explicit language of "constitutionalism" only appeared in the Qing empire in its very last decades, imported from the West and Japan, it is clear that late imperial China did nevertheless operate under a widely assumed set of constitutional principles which defined and constrained the activities of the organs of state, including the throne itself. As Pierre-Étienne Will has suggested, this "dynastic constitution" was embodied in three forms: (1) ancestral practices, as revealed in the Classics, (2) the descriptions and regulations of government organs laid out in the recurrently updated edition of the *Institutes* (*Da Ming huidian* and *Da Qing huidian*), and (3) the entire accumulated body of administrative and criminal law and precedents of the ruling dynasty.[65] It was this unwritten Qing constitution that Bao Shichen's *Shuochu* boldly sought to rewrite.

A generation of scholarship has left us with the tentative understanding that a persistent constitutional debate existed in the political thought of the Qing empire. Central to this debate were three features that most historians today would likely consider to be among the most fundamental provisions of the Qing constitution: (1) a universal empire (*tianxia*), with specific privileges and duties assigned to various ethnic constituencies, but no inherent right to national self-determination on the part of "Han Chinese" or any other national group; (2) absolute power of the dynastic monarch,

65. Pierre-Étienne Will, "Le contrôle de l'excès de pouvoir sous la dynastie des Ming," in *La Chine et la démocratie*, ed. Mireille Delmas-Marty and Pierre-Étienne Will (Paris: Fayard, 2007), 116–25.

ruling by the equivalent of divine right (*tianming*); and (3) a centralized bureaucratic state, claiming monopolistic authority through its depersonalized field administration (*junxian*) over such functions as fiscal collection, exercise of military force, and administration of justice.

Already in the seventeenth century, however, at the very outset of Qing rule, a number of important political writers had already proposed, at least incipiently, challenges to these constitutional assumptions. Wang Fuzhi and Lü Liuliang, for example, had suggested that the Chinese patria rightly belonged to Chinese alone; Huang Zongxi had intimated that the powers of the throne were at least in part conditional; and Gu Yanwu had offered a model of territorial administration in which bureaucratic centralization was qualified, and the principle of local self-rule under indigenous elites (*fengjian*) cautiously advanced.

A number of scholars have suggested intellectual lineages by means of which these ideas may have been kept alive and developed through the remaining centuries of the imperial era, and even beyond. Philip Kuhn, for example, has famously traced the origins of local self-government (*difang zizhi*) programs under the Republic to the proposals of Gu Yanwu; Wm. Theodore de Bary has controversially argued for the continuity of a "liberal tradition in China," building upon the ideas of Huang Zongxi, Lü Liuliang, and others; and more recently Stephen Platt has shown how, in the later nineteenth century, the racial-nationalist arguments of Wang Fuzhi were recalled and elaborated into a theory of Chinese national self-rule.[66] How, we may ask, was Bao Shichen's unpublished 1801 treatise, *On Wealth*, situated within this persistent constitutional debate?

In certain key ways, it is not very radical. Its treatment of the Manchu racial question is, as we have seen, very mild: Bao is certainly no Wang Fuzhi. It shies away from any hint of critique of the imperial institution per se, in the manner of Huang Zongxi (though its generalized discussions of principles of dynastic legitimacy might have been read in a way that was politically dangerous). Bao's book is extraordinarily frank in its identification of systemic dysfunction, and of the rampant bureaucratic

66. Philip A. Kuhn, "Local Self-Government under the Republic: Problems of Control, Autonomy, and Mobilization," in *Conflict and Control in Late Imperial China*, ed. Frederic Wakeman Jr. and Carolyn Grant (Berkeley: University of California Press, 1975), 257–98; Wm. Theodore de Bary, *The Liberal Tradition in China* (New York: Columbia University Press, 1983); Stephen R. Platt, *Provincial Patriots: The Hunanese and Modern China* (Cambridge, MA: Harvard University Press, 2007).

corruption that the current Jiaqing emperor had inherited, but which he had not since his succession managed to redress; unlike Hong Liangji, however, who had taken the emperor to task for this and suffered the consequences, Bao proposes a general amnesty for the offenders, which is in practice what Jiaqing had himself done.[67]

Bao's book never mentions or specifically echoes Wang Fuzhi or Huang Zongxi, but it is strongly reminiscent in several aspects of Gu Yanwu. Liu Shipei in his 1906 edition says that the *Shuochu* is basically derived from Gu's late seventeenth-century *Rizhilu* (Record of daily-acquired knowledge). But is he right? We know that Gu Yanwu was not part of the curriculum that Bao's father laid out for his early education. When in 1792, at age seventeen, Shichen first discovered the *Rizhilu* in a bookstore, he had never heard of its author; unable to afford the new edition, moreover, he managed only to skim the first chapter. It was only in 1802 when he had completed his own book and gone to study with Li Zhaoluo in Changzhou, that Li compared for Bao the similarities and differences of his ideas with those of Gu, and gave him his own version of the *Rizhilu* to read in its entirely. According to Bao, he was both enlightened and heartened; the fact that his own thoughts echoed Gu's on several points gave him even greater confidence in their correctness. But at the time of writing the *Shuochu* his knowledge of Gu was still highly fragmentary.[68]

In fact, Bao's overlap with Gu was far from complete. Gu's concern that both power and economic resources not be monopolized by the throne or others in a position of superiority (*shang*), but rather be shared with those below (*xia*), is very deeply reflected in the *Shuochu*. Gu's general

67. Although I do not concentrate on this here, the similarities of the reformist agendas of Bao and the Jiaqing emperor at the turn of the century are worthy of investigation. Bao's elaborate stipulations for personal frugality at every level of administration, for example, dovetailed neatly with the Jiaqing emperor's concerted campaign against official waste and extravagance, and his ostentatious attempt to serve as a personal exemplar of such behavior; see Zhang Yufen, "Lun Jiaqing chunian de 'Xianyu weixin,'" 49–54. The overlap in agendas is unsurprising given the importance in shaping the thinking of both men of Zhu Gui, Jiaqing's childhood tutor and Bao's early patron. During the first years of his personal rule, Jiaqing recalled Zhu to serve as president of the Boards of Revenue and Civil Office, and the latter had a key influence on his policy choices. See Guy, *Qing Governors and Their Provinces*, 141.

68. Bao, "Du Tinglin yishu," in *Yizhou shuangji*, in *Quanji* (1993), 2:1–4. See also Bao, general preface to *Anwu sizhong*, in *Quanji* (1993), and Liu Guangjing, "Shijiu shiji chuye Zhongguo zhishifenzi," 1000.

critique of excessive surveillance and oversight as sapping the initiative of lower officials, and his specific recommendation to abolish the position of provincial governor, are both picked up by Bao. But, though Bao's ideas for the reform of local administration are, in their own way, as radical as Gu's, they are very different. As Philip Kuhn has shown, Gu Yanwu's recommendation that county magistrates not be short-term sojourners deployed by the central state but instead be drawn from the highest ranks of the indigenous elite was picked up by Bao Shichen's younger contemporary Wei Yuan, and passed down for further refinement at the hands of Feng Guifen, Kang Youwei, and other pioneering advocates of local self-governance and popular representation.[69]

There is nothing like this in Bao Shichen. Bao lived in very different times than Gu: whereas the latter had been deeply concerned about the excessive power of the central state over private literati and local interests, Bao, faced with massive internal disorder and an emerging Western challenge (represented in the *Shuochu*, for example, by the foreign contrivances to which Bao so objects) was instead more concerned about restoring effective state control, wealth, and power. Rather than the stateless "ordering the world" (*jingshi*) that served as the project of many of his reformist contemporaries, he preferred to think of "ordering the state" (*jingguo*). He discourses at length over state finance (*guoji*) and state administration (*guozheng*). Rather precociously (and illiberally), he admits to state/government/national wealth (*guofu*) as a worthy and indeed essential goal of policy.[70]

At the same time, we may see Bao Shichen's *Shuochu* as a founding document in what Kuhn has termed the late Qing "constitutional agenda." According to Kuhn, this agenda had its origins in the alarmed response of literati to the perceived general crisis of the turn-of the-century era—he cites Hong Liangji's 1799 criticism of the Jiaqing reforms as one of its earliest statements. The gist of this constitutional agenda was to legitimate and stimulate greater literati participation in government decision making ("literati" defined as upper gentry out of office), *while simultaneously* strengthening the authority of the central imperial state, to make it more capable of responding to the growing threats, both domestic and international. Kuhn concentrates his analysis on the thought of Bao

69. Kuhn, "Local Self-Government."
70. *Shuochu*, 133.

Shichen's younger contemporary Wei Yuan, but concedes that "we search Wei's writings in vain for any institutions through which literati participation might be exercised."[71]

It is here, at the very outset of articulation of a constitutional agenda, that Bao had already supplied a possible answer. His Shenguanyuan, the newly conceived agency to which he gave pride of place in his text, was precisely a means to institutionalize literati input into the policy-making process, while still strengthening the state. In this, Bao closely anticipated the institutional innovations of Kang Youwei (a great admirer of Bao) nearly a century later during the 1898 Reforms. Still more striking is the way that Bao further broadened the base of the constituency to be listened to, well beyond the narrowly conceived "literati" of Wei Yuan, explicitly in order to incorporate the opinions of the common people. This, indeed, anticipates the "transformation of the constitutional agenda" that Kuhn finds only as the empire neared its end. Ultimately, it is not difficult to see why an angry young man like Liu Shipei, infused with heady new ideas of natural rights and social contract, would find the *Shuochu* a suppressed milestone along the way to a modern Chinese political form.

In the context of Bao Shichen's own life and work, *On Wealth* clearly stands somewhat apart for its scope and youthful exuberance. Some have argued, not inappropriately, that Bao's career may be divided into two phases: the idealistic first phase of *On Wealth,* and the subsequent more pragmatic and mature period of concrete policy recommendations, addressed for the most part to officials in an actual position to consider their implementation.[72] At the same time, however, *On Wealth* remained throughout his life Bao's most systematic overview of his thinking on the broad range of political economy issues. In the following four chapters, I will deal in turn with four such issue areas—agricultural production, grain tribute, the salt administration, and currency management. In each of these, we can take Bao's youthful views expressed in *On Wealth* as a baseline, and proceed to explore how subsequent experience and empirical investigation modified his early ideas into potentially more practicable reform programs.

71. Philip A. Kuhn, *Origins of the Modern Chinese State* (Stanford: Stanford University Press, 2002). The quotation is from page 117.

72. For example, Liu Guangjing, "Shijiu shiji chuye Zhongguo zhishifenzi."

CHAPTER 3

Farming

Within the frequently back-biting Qing bureaucratic culture, having "the smell of the vegetable garden" about him was a deprecating way to refer to an *arriviste* scholar-official of humble family origins. Bao Shichen, however, wore this as a mark of the highest pride. We have seen that during Shichen's youth, when his father took ill, the young man had supported his parental household for a time primarily though his own efforts at market gardening. This experience, coupled with a lifetime of research into the practical experience of farming in his native lower Yangzi region, led Bao to confidently believe in his own expertise—that he knew as much or more about agricultural policy than any other literatus in the Qing empire.

Bao Shichen expounded his views on agriculture in various writings throughout his adult life.[1] These collected writings, in the view of the

1. Bao's 1801 *On Wealth* (*Shuochu*) contains considerable comment on agricultural policy. In several essays supplementary to *On Wealth*, notably those on agricultural administration and local decimal-unit household regimentation (*baojia*), Bao expands these ideas considerably. In other policy papers and correspondence produced over nearly a half century, and especially an essay dismissively entitled "Notes from the Year 1820, Part Two" (*Gengchen zazhu, er*), he presents a comprehensive program of agrarian reform. The 1844 preface to the *Anwu sizhong*, and that to the subsection of that work on material welfare entitled "Four Works for the People" (*Jimin sishu*), both address agrarian issues in more general terms. Finally, we have the record of Bao's single political posting, as magistrate of Jiangxi's Xinyu county in 1839, where he was forced, rather uncomfortably, to confront many rural issues on the ground.

esteemed agricultural historian Li Bozhong, constitute one of "the two most important books" on farming practice in late eighteenth- and early nineteenth-century Jiangnan.[2] Li cites Bao authoritatively on such various matters as crop selection, crop rotation, planting and harvest schedules, use of draft animals, rice yields per acre, and per capita grain consumption.

As in his other areas of policy advocacy, Bao became progressively less utopian and more cautiously pragmatic over the course of the Jiaqing and Daoguang reigns. His ever more guarded optimism regarding the potential to fundamentally jump-start the empire's agricultural output and dramatically improve the lives of its farming population was certainly a function of Bao's own personal aging process, but it is very tempting to see it as well as reflecting a genuine deterioration of Qing rural economy and society in the half century of the great divergence.

Population and Productivity

Though Bao Shichen was thirty years younger than Hong Liangji (1746–1809), both men had been at one time or another protégés of Zhu Gui, former tutor to the eventual Jiaqing emperor and, during the first years of Jiaqing's personal rule, probably the most powerful minister in the empire. Despite this common patronage, Hong and Bao disagreed profoundly on two of the most pressing policy issues of the day. As we have seen, Hong famously urged a thorough purge of the bureaucracy in the wake of the downfall of Heshen, while Bao, like Zhu Gui himself, advised a general amnesty for most officials in the interest of administrative stability. And, more relevant to our concerns here, Bao and Hong held diametrically opposed views of the potential of the empire's agriculture.

Bao Shichen remained convinced throughout his youth and middle age that the productive capacity of the Qing agrarian economy was much greater than assumed by others, and was supremely confident that,

2. Bozhong Li, *Agricultural Development in Jiangnan, 1620–1850* (New York: St. Martin's Press, 1998), 44 and passim. The other book mentioned by Li is Jiang Gao's 1834 *Pumao nongzi.*

following his formulas, this economy might quickly be brought back to good health. "People regularly say that the population is growing daily, while new land can no longer be found, so popular immiseration is the inevitable result," Bao argued in 1801, in unstated reference to the dire demographic predictions of "China's Malthus," Hong Liangji. "But they have not made their case persuasively" (*fei dinglun ye*)—that is, they have not worked it out mathematically, the way Bao himself proceeds to do.[3] Twenty years later, Bao wrote that "there are those who say that because the population is growing daily, the productive capacity of the land cannot keep pace with food supply needs. These are merely the words of petty Confucians [*xiaoru*], who do not understand the situation today or the way the world works [*bu ta lizhi*]."[4]

Bao was right, at least, about Hong Liangji's arguments, which though they have served as the basic point of reference for such influential historical demographers of China as Ping-ti Ho, do not include much in the way of quantification.[5] Bao was very different. Indeed, he seems to have had an intense infatuation with numbers, to a degree not remotely matched by even the most sophisticated economic analysts of the preceding "high Qing" century, and he clearly presented this as evidence of his own superior expertise. He argued that "The empire's land [*tianxia zhi tu*] nourishes the empire's people [*tianxia zhi ren*]. It is self-evident that if the population grows, so does the number of producers [*shengzhe*]; this

3. Bao, *Shuochu*, in *Quanji* (1991), 188. A similar reading of Bao's views, as a valid "refutation" of those of Hong Liangji, is made by James Z. Lee and Wang Feng, in *One Quarter of Humanity: Malthusian Mythology and Chinese Realities* (Cambridge, MA: Harvard University Press, 1999), 167.

4. Bao, *Gengchen zazhu, er*, in *Quanji* (1997), 210.

5. The classic text is Ping-ti Ho, *Studies on the Population of China, 1368–1968* (Cambridge, MA: Harvard University Press, 1969). Only recently have scholars such as James Lee and Li Bozhong begun to doubt Ho's argument that the turn of the nineteenth century saw the population-to-land ratio begin to turn more adverse, and find there the beginnings of contemporary China's population "problem." As Sui-wai Cheung has recently pointed out, Hong Liangji "did not . . . provide any data to support his hypothesis" of a looming population crisis; Sui-wai Cheung, *The Price of Rice: Market Integration in Eighteenth-Century China* (Bellingham: Western Washington University Press, 2008), 75–76. For selections from Hong's 1793 population essays, translated by K. C. Liu (Liu Guangjing), see Wm. Theodore de Bary and Richard Lufrano, eds., *Sources of Chinese Tradition*, 2nd ed. (New York: Columbia University Press, 2000), 2: 174–75.

is the very basis of wealth [*fuji*]. It is true that there is no longer much virgin land [*kuangtu*] remaining, but the real problem is that human work capacities [*lizuo*] have not been been utilized efficiently or systematically [*bu ru fa*]."[6] In effect, Bao was reasserting, in the face of Hong Liangji's pessimism, a classic article of Confucian statecraft faith: the ability of human beings to triumph over the limitations of nature (*yiren shengtian*).[7]

In his youthful treatise *On Wealth*, Bao proceeds by pointing out that, by statute, one *li* (a unit of distance, roughly equivalent to one-third of a mile) is defined as 360 paces (*bu*=5 *chi*, or Chinese feet) or 180 *jiang* in official feet (1 *jiang*=5 paces).[8] A *mou* of farmland is 240 paces in area, or 77.4 feet squared (*qi jiang qi ci si cun*). Accordingly, one *li* squared (*fangli*) equals 530 *mou* of land; 10 *li* squared (*fangshili*) equals 53,000 *mou*; 100 *li* squared (*fangbaili*) equals 5,300,000 *mou*; and a thousand *li* squared (*fangqianli*) equals 530 million *mou*. Official statistics claim the breadth of the country today, from Tingzhou (Manchuria) in the east to Dunhuang (Gansu province) in the west, to be more than ten thousand *li*. Altogether then, Bao concludes, the *neidi* (the "inner land," often translated as "China proper"), or that area between the Great Wall to the north, the Jiayu Pass (Gansu) to the west, the seacoast to the east, and the Burmese borderlands to the southwest—that is, the region directly subject by the throne to land tax and corvée levies—comprises 3,600 *li* squared, or some 6,868,800,000 *mou*. Granting that 40 percent of this is made up of mountains, water, towns, and villages, that leaves altogether some 4,121,280,000 *mou* of arable farmland.

Since the empire has been free from military devastation for many years, Bao argues, the population has accordingly grown during this prosperous era (*shengshi*) to more than 700 million (*ren qiwanyuwan kou*).[9]

6. Bao, *Gengchen za zhu, er*, in *Quanji* (1997), 210.

7. Bao, "Liuzhi Jiangxi xin fubu Chen Yusheng," in *Quanji* (1997), 258–59. Bao's characteristic optimism, in line with that of earlier statecraft thinkers but increasingly challenged in his own day, not only by Hong Liangji but also by younger contemporaries such as Gong Zizhen, is also noted by Liu Guangjing, "Shijiu shiji chuye Zhongguo zhishifenzi," 995–1030.

8. Bao, *Shuochu*, 188–89.

9. Bao does not indicate his source for this figure, which historical demographers today would deem wildly high. Lee and Wang, *One Quarter of Humanity*, 27, for example, estimate the empire's population in 1800 to be roughly 350 million.

From here he calculates the likely yields from agriculture. Excluding from the total population persons who are artisans, merchants, soldiers, and other nonfarmers, leaves an average of 5 *mou* of arable land per farmer. In an average year, one *mou* of land will yield 2.5 *dan* of unhusked grain (*gu*), or 12.5 *dan* per farmer.[10] If we allow for the small percentage of arable land that is set aside for crops other than grain, we still have an annual grain yield of 12 *dan* per farmer. The average farm family consumes about 7 *dan* of grain per year. Even setting aside the chaff that is fed to chickens and pigs, then, this is only about two-thirds of what each farmer can produce.

Now, a healthy adult male is capable of cultivating 20 *mou* of land, Bao continues; the elderly and infirm can assist him, and offer him the benefit of their experience. Bao calculates that such healthy adult males comprise about 30 percent of the empire's total population. If one in six of these is employed in one of the other legitimate nonfarming occupations, and the other five (that is, one-quarter of the empire's total population) devote themselves to agriculture, their labor alone will be sufficient to reclaim and cultivate every plot of arable land in the empire, allowing all other necessary occupations still to be staffed. Beyond the food he produces himself, the farmer needs other items such as salt, iron, candles, and cooking oil, but his surplus grain production will be quite sufficient to exchange for these. Adult males in the agrarian household farm and gather fuel; adult women produce cloth and cook; the elderly are kept warm and well fed; children study diligently. If, after the present rebellion is suppressed and good officials put in place, all this can be brought into being, Bao concludes. Within seven years after the restoration of good government by a heroic ruler (*yingyi*)—the newly empowered Jiaqing emperor?—the people will be well supplied with their needs and happy with their lives, the country will become rich, and the ruler will be well respected and secure.

It is instructive to compare Bao's numbers and projections with those of historians today. Li Bozhong, as we have seen, accepts much of Bao's

10. As a unit of weight, a *dan* (usually translated "picul") was equivalent to 100 *jin* (catties), or slightly over 130 pounds. See Sui-wai Cheung, *The Price of Rice: Market Integration in Eighteenth-Century China* (Bellingham: Western Washington University Press, 2008), x.

quantitative data as reliable (though, concerned as he is with regional rather than national performance, Li does not comment on Bao's estimates for empire-wide numbers). Li comes down most emphatically on the side of Bao Shichen versus Hong Liangji on the major question of population pressure. Li concedes that over the late eighteenth and early nineteenth centuries average family farm size in Jiangnan shrank considerably. However he sees this retreat to an "optimum" population-to-land ratio as an active advantage, as the intensification of double cropping and crop rotation, and the more efficient allocation of household labor (especially the dedication of female labor more exclusively to sideline sericulture and cotton processing work), led to greater labor productivity and greater per capita output. Going perhaps still farther than Bao Shichen himself might have, Li argues that "there was a shortage, not a surplus, of labor" in the early nineteenth century, even in the empire's most densely populated region, Jiangnan.[11]

However, focusing instead on the national level, the widely respected historian Guo Songyi reaches very different conclusions. Whereas Bao calculates the empire's total arable land in the early nineteenth century at more that 4 billion *mou*, Guo takes the official figure (*Qingmou*) for 1812 of 791,525,000 *mou* and converts it to an actual figure (*shimou*) of 1,050,436,000 *mou*—that is, a total empire-wide arable of less than a quarter of Bao's cheery estimate. Guo also estimates the population in 1812 as roughly 350 million, or one-half that of Bao's odd estimate of 700 million. Guo's estimate of per *mou* annual grain yield is only somewhat less than Bao's (2.34 *dan* vs. 2.50 *dan*), but his yield per working farmer is lower. The agricultural historian Zhou Bangjun, working with population and land figures from 1812 similar to those of Guo, computes per capita farmland at 2.19 *mou,* noting a dramatic decline from the 6.13 *mou* per capita of 1381.[12] Most significantly, in Guo Songyi's view both per capita productivity and standards of living had been in decline already for decades by the time Bao Shichen wrote, in 1801, and would continue an accelerated decline over the subsequent century, primarily the result of unchecked

11. Li Bozhong, *Agricultural Development*, 147 and chap. 6, passim.

12. Zhou Bangjun, "Bao Shichen de bianji tudi liyong jixu sixiaang" (Bao Shichen's thought on techniques for utilizing marginal farmland), *Zhongguo nongshi* 21.4 (2002): 99.

population growth—a factor about which Bao professed himself unconcerned.[13]

It appears, then, that modern scholarly opinion remains divided on the salient issue of Bao's day, the impact of population pressure on per capita food production. Whether or not one finds Bao's data credible may depend on the question of scale: if his microlevel numbers reflect his own close observation, his extrapolations to empire-wide numbers appear wildly wrong. There is no indication that Bao had been to Beijing, where he might have seen official figures, before he wrote; his patron Zhu Gui had been recalled there to serve the Jiaqing emperor in 1799, and repeatedly invited Bao to join him, but apparently he did not. The revised Jiaqing-era *Da Qing huidian,* though published only in 1812, was well in preparation by the turn of the century, and both Guo Songyi and Zhou Bangjun accept its figures as reasonably accurate, but again there is no indication that Bao had been in communication with the *Huidian*'s editorial staff before he wrote his *On Wealth.* His national-level numbers, then, seem to have been largely or even entirely self-generated.

While in youth and middle age Bao assumed that the problem of population pressure could be resolved solely by more efficient use of existing resources, in later years he more frankly acknowledged the negative impact of declining per capita farmland. He thus pressed enthusiastically for expanding cultivation into marginal lands, including polder lands along riverbanks and seacoasts, greater utilization of vacant plots in cities, and above all more systematic exploitation of highlands. Bao urged local officials to divide mountainsides in their districts into seven strata (*ceng*), and, leaving the highest three strata in their natural state, work upward to progressively bring under cultivation the lower four. Bao suggested as suitable crops for this terrace land corn, cotton, medicinal herbs, and taro, and offered concrete advice on how each of these might successfully be introduced. In other words, even considering the growing population pressure, and despite evidence of the ecological deterioration observed by scholars today, Bao remained cautiously optimistic that,

13. Guo Songyi, "Ming-Qing shiqi de liangshi shengchan yu nongmin shenghuo shuiping" (Grain production and rural standards of living in the Ming-Qing era), *Zhongguo shehui kexueyuan lishi yanjiusuo xuekan* 2001.1: 373–96.

following his own expert advice, Qing agriculture would prove sustainable over the long run.[14]

Agricultural Practice

In his early essay "Agricultural administration" (*Nongzheng*), Bao marshals all he knows about actual farming practice to flesh out his vision of empire-wide sustainable agriculture. He states his credentials:

> I grew up in an area that was rustic and remote. We had only coarse food to eat. In my youth, I personally grew vegetables. In more recent years, I have traveled widely, observing how officials carry out their duties. I have gone thousands of *li* from east to west, all the time enquiring about local practices and getting a sense of what works and what does not in each locality, comparing older and newer techniques, and those in this locality with those in use in other distant places.

This long essay is, in effect, an agricultural handbook (*nongshu*), the twenty-six-year-old Bao's precocious take on a genre that had already had, at least since the expansion of commercial publishing in the late Ming, a substantial history. There are seven major sections. The first, on crop selection, runs through various grains, beans, and other staple crops, explaining for each their appearance, their various substrains, their proper growing season, their hardihood and yields, their uses as food, and specific techniques for their cultivation. The second section, on land utilization, is divided into subsections on paddy, irrigated fields, and dry fields, listing which specific crops are best suited for each; it argues that any land that can be converted to high-yielding paddy ought to be, but outlines conditions under which this may not be feasible. There follow sections

14. Zhou Bangjun, "Bao Shichen de bianji tudi liyong jixu sixiaang," 99–107. For modern scholarly studies of mid-Qing ecological decay, see Evelyn S. Rawski, "Agricultural Development in the Han River Highlands," *Ch'ing-shih wen-t'i* 3.4 (1975): 63–81, and Peter C. Perdue, *Exhausting the Earth: State and Peasant in Hunan, 1500–1850* (Cambridge, MA: Harvard University Press, 1987).

on planting, labor allocation during the growing season, sericulture, arboriculture, and animal husbandry.

Bao's penchanat for numbers is much in evidence here as well. For example, he opens his section on aquaculture with the well-known passage from the Daoist classic, the *Zhuangzi*: "Fish swim all around their habitat, an untold number of thousands of *li*." He then calculates how many times the fish flap their tailfins in order to move: an average of between eighteen and thirty-six flaps before shifting direction. Each flap, he speculates, propels the fish between two inches and one foot. In laying out a fish pond, the farmer wants to place in the middle nine islands, at irregular intervals. However, he needs to carefully calculate the placement and distance between them, so as to allow the fish to move in accordance with their natural inclination (*yuxing*), and therefore develop to the fullest and fattest possible extent.[15]

But the *Nongzheng* is not merely a how-to book, nor in fact is it addressed directly to farmers themselves. Rather, it is an impassioned tract intended, as its title suggests, for *administrators*, arguing for greater empathy with the rural population's precarious existence and for much more personal knowledge of, and involvement with, agricultural practice on the part of imperial officials. This starts with the ruler himself. Opening his essay with well-known passages from the *Analects* and *Mencius* on the imperative for government to respect the demands of the agrarian calendar, Bao then rather conventionally contrasts the "government by fundamentals" (*benzheng*) of the former kings (*xianwang*) with the careless disdain for agrarian practice of recent rulers. This loss of imperial interest has led directly to popular waste and extravagance, inefficient farming techniques, disregard of the rites, and, as seen today, the growing flight out of settled agrarian households into "vagrancy" (*yumin*). Imperial indifference to agriculture has been paralleled by that of local officials and literati, most of whom have no understanding at all of how to farm, or of how tough farm life is, preferring to devote themselves to intellectual dalliance with metaphysical issues (*xingming*). Agricultural expertise, as presented in this treatise, "can no longer be left simply to the common people themselves" (*bu yiwei xiaomin zhi zhi*).

15. Bao, *Nongzheng* (Agricultural administration), in *Quanji* (1997), 208.

It is the task of the official (and also the literatus-landlord) to instruct. He must make the effort to be intimately aware of local practices (*tufeng*), but at the same time not necessarily take them to be the most efficient use of resources. Lands should all be put to their most productive use (*yindi zhili*); potential paddy should never be left as dry fields. Indication that local practices are less than optimal are that commodity prices seem out of balance: grain is cheap but firewood expensive, for example, or livestock abundant but clothing scarce. In these situations, the scholar-official's superior depth of knowledge and comparative experience of local practices elsewhere must be called into play, to relieve popular immiseration (*minkun*) and in the process strengthen the "lifeblood of the nation" (*guomai*).

Bao then outlines a scheme by means of which the state sector at the local level can directly jump-start agricultural development. Let's presume, he says, that we have a large and densely populated county, with some 50,000 farm households. Each household pays taxes twice a year, and those payments each include an assessment of one man-day of labor. That amounts to 100,000 workdays per year. Now, three workdays are generally enough to bring under cultivation one *mou* of fallow wasteland, so this modest levy is capable of contributing over 30,000 *mou* of new farmland to the county. Alternatively, if wasteland is not a problem locally, or after it has in this way turned into arable, each assessed workday may be used (on public land?) to yield an additional 0.2 *dan* of grain, amounting to 20,000 *dan* county-wide. Bao reiterates that corvée assessments must be made with absolute respect for the annual work schedule of the private farm households. But, this being done, he has presented the local official with two very practical ways to increase the productive assets of the community as a whole.[16]

Property

Bao Shichen professed himself a devoted believer in private proprietorship. In 1844, toward the end of his life, he wrote that there are three cardinal

16. Bao, *Nongzheng*, in *Quanji* (1997), 187.

principles that policy makers must grasp in order to achieve agricultural productivity: *li* (ritual correctness), *yi* (righteousness), and *xin* (faith). As applied to agriculture, *li* referred to the proper division of wilderness space into arable fields, as in the model of the well-field system of antiquity. *Xin* referred to the division of time into the agrarian calendar—the confident belief that the seasons will follow each other in rational succession, and the knowledge of what action is appropriate to each moment in the year. And *yi*, or "what is right," is deferential respect for the system of private/household ownership of agricultural land (*minyou zhi*). At the root of the current crisis is wanton expropriation of the people's property and wealth by "thieving officials" (*taochen*), clerks, and local elites.[17]

Yet, in practice, Bao proved in numerous ways no unambivalent champion of private property rights and personal liberties. In his youthful *On Wealth*, for example, he proposed a detailed and fussy code of sumptuary laws for all classes of society; farmers were to wear garments of any solid color other than green (*qing*), which was reserved for merchants and artisans, and simple, unpatterned cotton footwear.[18] As we shall see, he also imposed strict limits on production and personal consumption of a range of regulated goods. But his most striking qualifications to the principle of private property came in relation to natural resources and famine relief policies.

In a lengthy disquisition in *On Wealth* on the salt monopoly, Bao argues that salt, along with other natural resources such as copper, lead, and timber, represents "wealth bequeathed by Heaven" (*tiandi zhi cang*) to all humanity, and should be managed by the state in the public interest. They are collective assets and belong to no private individual or household (*fei minjia siye*). However, as in his later, successfully adopted policy recommendations regarding the Liang-Huai salt gabelle in the 1820s and 30s—discussed in detail in chapter 4, below—Bao combines his argument for collective ownership of natural resources with a call for private commercial management of extraction and distribution: merchants bidding for distribution contracts for salt in feasible job lots will deliver it more efficiently than will hereditarily enfranchised official-

17. Bao, "Preface" (*xuyan*) to *Jimin sishu*, in *Quanji* (1997), 159–61.
18. Bao, *Shuochu*, 139–40.

merchants, resulting in better prices for the consumer, well-earned profits for themselves, and—by no means least important—much increased salt tax revenues for the state.[19]

In a less celebrated policy paper of 1804, Bao applies analogous reasoning to another resource, the cedar forests in the Western Hills outside Beijing. Ever since the relocation of the capital in the early Ming, he observes, trees in these sparsely inhabited highlands have been communally harvested by local people, with the wood sold in Beijing for use primarily as incense sticks. The yield was modest but sustainable, and the activity was effectively taxed by the state at a wood tax collection station in the Miyun county (Shuntian prefecture) seat. Over time, somewhat larger-scale commercial timber-farming enterprises were staked out in the area, and this too, Bao says, was equitable and appropriate. The problem came in 1799 when, at the height of the White Lotus campaigns (unclear whether this was before or after the demise of Heshen early in that year), the woodlands were seized by the state (*zhao ru guan*), and soldiers sent in to strip the forests for profit, to be applied to military uses. Bao condemns this abuse of fiscal policy, which rightly should be tailored to balance the legitimate revenue needs of the state, the livelihoods of private households, and the sustainability of the resource base.[20]

Provisioning

The second major policy area in which Bao's enthusiasm for the sanctity of private property was compromised was in provisioning, especially in the handling of dearth. In his youthful essay on the decimal-unit household regimentation system (*baojia*), written in conjunction with his *On Wealth* around 1801 but first published only in his 1844 collected works, Bao presents a utopian scheme to turn this hoary institution into nothing short of an instrument for economic redistribution.[21] In his essay,

19. *Shuochu*, 184–86.

20. Bao, "Miyun shuikou shuo," in *Quanji* (1997), 245–46.

21. Bao, "Shuo baojia shiyi," in *Quanji* (1997), 271–82. In considering the possibility of state-sponsored redistribution of private wealth at all, Bao seems to have differed from the views of his contemporary Gong Zizhen, who argued that levels of wealth and

Bao offers considerable detail on the posting of household door placards (*menpai*), even offering a handy model to be copied. The placards bear what might be seen as "class labels," identifying the household as belonging to one or another income grade, based on the amount of cultivated acreage per family member, modified by the number of draft animals owned and other factors. The basic categories are "upper household" (*shanghu*), "middling household" (*zonghu*), and "lower household" (*xiahu*), but there were also categories for the extremely wealthy—"well-off household" (*raohu*) and "rich household" (*fuhu*)—and others for the extremely poor—"poor household" (*pinhu*) and "indigent household" (*qionghu*), the latter comprising those with no land, no livelihood, and no family to support them. Better-off households will be required to keep grain in storage according to their rank: three years worth for *fuhu*, two years for *raohu*, one year for *shanghu*, and a half year for *zhonghu*. Grain beyond this amount should be sold off by the household, to keep an adequate supply on the local market.

Redistribution in normal times proceeds along ties of kinship. The local *baojia* headman is ordered to track down any wealthy relatives of indigent households, and persuade (not command) them to help out their poor relations. Those who do so will have the characters "righteous household" (*yihu*) stamped on their *menpai*, along with their class label. (Analogies to post-Mao "civilized household" [*wenming hu*] labels seem inescapable.) Those who fail to comply will be stigmatized by the label "unneighborly" (*buyou*), and if this appears several years in succession will face expulsion from the group. In times of dearth the redistribution process takes on a greater degree of compulsion, and reaches beyond kinship. In the eleventh month of a bad year, the magistrate will issue official letters (*zhizhao*) to the poorest families, authorizing them to approach their wealthier neighbors and demand loans of grain, in specified quantities, for a maximum of three months, to be repaid with only token interest.

Bao then extends this to a higher level. Once the *baojia* system has been fully implemented in a county, with calculations made of the aggregate well-being of all its households, the county itself can be classified

---

poverty are naturally generated, and not to be tampered with by government; Sun Guangde, "Gong Zizhen de jingshi sixiang," 280.

as a "wealthy county" (*raoxian*), an "upper," "middle," or "lower" county, or a "barren county" (*jixian*). The prefect, then, can impose redistribution in times of need on the magistrates involved, just as the magistrates do within their counties, and the *baojia* headmen within their tithings. Bao calls his system "encouraging assessment and extension of relief" (*quanpai yanggei*, or *paigei* for short). It amounts almost to a planned economy scheme for rural society at the local level.

In practice, however, both in an advisory and an administrative role, Bao's actions in the face of dearth were considerably less radical and idealistic. His redistributionist impulses were first tested by a looming famine in his adopted hometown of Nanjing in 1814–15.[22] Over the first six months of 1814 no appreciable rain fell in the Jiangnan region. The crops failed, and over the following winter and spring there was major dearth, both within Nanjing city and in surrounding areas. The situation was complicated by the fact that a local rebellion in southeastern Henan province the year before had spilled over and gathered additional recruits in the Yangzhou hinterland of northern Jiangsu. Refugees from both fighting and drought further besieged Nanjing.

Ever since the posting of Bailing to Nanjing as governor general of Liang-Jiang in the summer of 1811, Bao Shichen had served on his staff as an advisor on river conservancy matters. As the drought worsened during the course of 1814, Qin Changye (Yitang), a reader of the Hanlin Academy, native and resident of Nanjing, and one of the most eminent men on the scene, several times approached Bao to express his concern about the likelihood of famine and inquire about how it might be dealt with. Bao drew upon his research into past experience, determined that the closest analogy was to a famine in Changzhou prefecture in 1785 that had been successfully managed by the Changzhou prefect Jin, and drew up a twenty-point program (in five sections) that adapted Jin's policies to the current time and place. Among other things, Bao argued that effective famine relief frankly necessitated redistribution of wealth from the rich to the poor (*shuaifu yipin*). He submitted this plan to Qin, who dithered

22. Sources for this affair include Bao, "Wei Qin Yitang shidu ge hua Baimen Huangzheng" (Plans for famine relief in Baimen presented to Hanlin Reader Qin Yitang), "Shang Bai jiexiang shu" (Letter submitted to Governor General Bailing), and "Da Fang Baoyan shangshu shu" (Letter in response to Board President Fang Baoyan), all in Bao, *Jimin sishu*, *juan* 2, 222–28, 230–32, and 232–34, in *Quanji* (1997).

over it. (Bao claimed that Qin really understood almost nothing about agrarian policy and that he had to explain even the simplest things repeatedly to him.) But when Qin began to observe poor rural people (*xiangmin*) plundering the grain stores of their richer neighbors he understood that the time to act had come, and he sent Bao's plan and a cover letter to Governor General Bailing proposing a systematic famine relief operation.

On Jiaqing 16/7/24 Bailing convened a meeting at Nanjing's Zhongshan Academy to discuss such plans. In attendance were Qin Changye, Fang Baoyan (board president and, along with Qin, the most eminent man resident in the city), the provincial treasurer, the provincial salt commissioner, the Nanjing prefect, and the two magistrates of Shangyuan and Jiangning counties, which divided the city of Nanjing and its suburban areas. There were essentially three components to the plan they arrived at. First, the salt commissioner disbursed 15,000 *dan* of grain from the salt administration granary for immediate discount sale (*pingtiao*) on the local market. Second, Bailing ordered the allocation of 60,000 taels from the provincial treasury for assigned purchase of rice from the thirty-two rice mills along the river outside the city gates. Finally, a subscription drive was launched among local wealthy households to contribute charity relief (*yizhen*) for distribution via a system of tickets of eligibility. Bailing issued a proclamation to start this drive and summoned wealthy gentry and merchants for a second meeting at the academy on Jiaqing 16/8/4 to urge them to contribute. Four of the wealthiest households in the city immediately contributed a total of 100,000 taels, and another hundred households eventually donated smaller amounts up to 5,000 taels apiece. Altogether 177,000 taels were collected.

But problems and contention plagued the project from the start. First, although the rice mills were glad to sell the rice at reasonable cost to the state for relief purposes, the Jiangning magistrate Cai Junbi unilaterally decided to order them to sell at a 20 percent discount below market price, and the mill owners balked. They took their protest to the provincial treasurer, who was furious at Magistrate Cai. Eventually, a compromise was worked out whereby the mills sold the grain at a discount of 8 percent.

Second, a dispute broke out among the officials about who was to be in charge of the relief program. All agreed that the seniority and reputations of the Hanlin reader Qin and Board President Fang made them the obvious candidates to head up the subscription drive, but who was to manage the investigation of eligibility and the actual distribution of relief? At the Zhongshan Academy meeting, Prefect Qiu Shutang argued that the project should be categorized as *minjuan guanban* (nongovernmental local elites contribute the money but it is managed by the officials—that is, by the prefect and county magistrates), while others felt it would be more appropriately handled as *minjuan minban* (both funded and managed by local elites themselves). Again, brokered by Fang, a compromise was reached, whereby 27,000 taels was entrusted directly to the two county magistrates for distribution to urban residents (for some unexplained reason the Shangyuan magistrate, Shen Bangji, suddenly recused himself on grounds of incompetence, leaving the Jiangning magistrate, Cai, to handle the task by himself), and the remaining 150,000 entrusted to a mixed commission of twenty-four men—twelve "assistant magistrates" (*zuo'er*) and twelve provincial degree holders—for distribution to rural people.

Related to this was the issue of just who were eligible recipients of relief. There was some sentiment among officials that urban residents alone be ministered to, rural populations left to fend for themselves. Bao Shichen persistently argued against this position, noting that "the rural townships are the foundation of the city" (*sixiang wei cheng zhi genben*), and also that famine refugees from outside the prefecture ought to be fed directly in rural areas, while preventing them from entering the city. On both counts his position won out, and eventually at least 89,000 rural dwellers and another 9,000 refugees received aid.

Things did not go smoothly for Bao, however, despite the eventual determination that the relief program he advised was a success. Fang, for example, was reportedly unhappy about several elements of the project's management, and conveyed his discomfort to Governor General Bailing, prompting Bao to write Fang directly in spirited defense of his reasoning. Bailing himself was yet more of a problem. At several points during the subscription drive he chose to call it to a premature halt, only to revive it when corpses and near-corpses numbering in the thousands were deposited outside the city gates. Relations between Bao and his patron and employer progressively soured during the process, and by the time of Bailing's transfer out of his post (he died shortly thereafter, in 1816) they were clearly on rather bad terms.

This uncomfortable episode may well have soured Bao Shichen on even the most cautious of redistributionist solutions to provisioning crises. As Xinyu magistrate in 1839, in the face of torrential rains that had wiped out much of the grain crop, the now elderly Bao did no more than request the deferral of the county's land tax and grain tribute obligations to the future (*dihuan*), just as his predecessors had routinely done in repeated bad harvests before him.[23]

Agriculture and Commerce

Bao Shichen's writings are suffused with empathy for the agrarian population, and for farming, which, like nearly every author in the Confucian statecraft tradition, he considered the foundation of the economy. Farming is brutally difficult, Bao insists, and farmers are genuinely immiserated. In the *Nongzheng*'s central section on labor allocation (*zuoli*), Bao lays out this case:

> Farmers tending to their work, except for New Year's and other ritual observances and exercising familial obligations, spend all their time planting and weeding when the weather allows, and spinning and weaving when it rains. Their backs are sunburnt red from weeding; they wade barefoot through manure-soaked paddy while ploughing. They work very long days, well into the night. Those who work the hardest, and have their own land to til, realize from their labor no more than 14–15 copper cash per year. You can imagine how much less those who are tenants, or are not fully able-bodied, are able to realize. If on top of that they suffer exploitation or fraud on the part of county tax clerks, their annual earnings may be reduced to virtually nil. If they also suffer (climate-induced) dislocations or bad harvests, it can take many generations for them to recover, if at all.[24]

Bao's consistent emphasis on the primacy of agriculture, however, cannot be read as a corresponding deprecation of commerce. The major

23. *Xinyu xianzhi* (1849), 3:19. We will return to Bao's contentious tenure in this county below.

24. Bao, *Nongzheng*, in *Quanji* (1997), 186–87.

fear is not that farmers will desert their fields in order to adopt other trades, but that they will become unemployed vagrants (*youmin*). He frequently invoked the term *simin*—the four (legitimate) occupations—to suggest that merchants and artisans were indeed worthy and contributing participants in the multisectoral Qing economy (though, as we shall see, he thought they were relatively undertaxed). And his conception of agriculture itself was by no means one of self-sufficiency; rather, he envisioned an active participation in the commercial market and cash cropping. Lengthy sections of his agricultural manual *Nongzheng* were devoted to market-oriented sericulture, aquaculture, arboriculture, and horticulture.[25] And in *On Wealth* he radically proposed that the domestic customs be abolished altogether, so that all commodities can move about the country more easily, "for the benefit of farmers" (*junhuo biannong*).[26]

Bao, however, is unwilling to grant to cultivators complete freedom in crop selection and land allocation. He is emphatically opposed to dissipating potentially productive resources on the evils of tobacco and alcohol. These are familiar complaints from statecraft reformers over previous generations, though Bao gives them a numerical spin of his own. Tobacco, he notes, was at first only imported to China (charmingly, he refers to the place of origin as "Tan-ba-gu guo," or, literally, "Tobaccoland"), but by the sixteenth century it was cultivated domestically. Whereas several decades ago only 20–30 percent of the population used it, he writes, today it is ubiquitous throughout the empire and used by both men and women. He calculates that each user spends no less that 7 or 8 copper cash on tobacco per day; for a large household of ten members, then, this adds up to several dozen taels per year. Then there is the otherwise productive grain land that has been turned to tobacco. To say nothing of the night-soil requirements, which Bao estimates at six times the amount per unit of land required to fertilize rice paddy, and four times the amount required for dry fields planted in grain. In terms of labor costs, a comparable plot of land planted in tobacco requires fifty man-days (much of this devoted to defense against insects) versus eight to nine man-days for rice paddy, or twelve to thirteen for cotton or dry-field grains. Thus, tobacco is six times more costly in labor than rice. And this doesn't even

25. *Nongzheng*, 189–208.
26. Bao, *Shuochu*, in *Quanji* (1991), 186.

count the labor involved in postharvest processing. Moreover—and here is the typical elite complaint—farmers who use tobacco lose as much as 20 percent of their labor time sitting in the fields enjoying a smoke![27]

Bao notes that tobacco is not currently a prohibited substance, and argues (typically for him) that any attempt to ban it immediately would be unenforceable and therefore mistaken. He suggests instead a three-year program. Tobacco already planted will be allowed to be harvested and sold, but no more may be planted next year; this protects the farmers. Sale of tobacco will be allowed for two more years, until this year's crop has cleared the commercial supply channels; this protects the merchants. Consumption of tobacco will be allowed for three more years, and after that banned.[28]

Alcohol, says Bao, was consumed in antiquity only for ritual or medicinal purposes, but now, in a wealthy prefecture such as Suzhou, it is ubiquitous. This prefecture is about 170 *li* square, he notes, and then he makes some calculations; If we subtract the 40 *li* that are occupied by mountains, rivers, towns, and historical landmarks, we are left with 130 *li* square of farmland. This computes to a total of 9.1 million *mou* of fields. Agricultural practice here is highly developed, so that each *mou* yields, in a good year, 3 *dan* (piculs) of rice or 1.2 *dan* of wheat, and even in a poor year 2 *dan* of rice or 0.5 to 0.7 *dan* of wheat. In the year in which he is writing, for example, the prefecture's total yield was over 22 million *dan* of rice. It is a densely populated prefecture, and its people (4–5 million adult males and an uncounted number of women and children) consume an annual total of 14–15 million *dan* of rice. Another 700,000 *dan* go to tax payment, leaving a projected annual surplus of 5–6 million *dan*. Half of this surplus is purchased by merchants from Zhejiang, Guangdong, and Anhui for interprovincial export, but the other half goes to alcohol production.

Bao then calculates the amount of grain (rice, sorghum, wheat, or millet) needed to distill decent wine, and compares the average daily consumption of a Suzhou adult male of wine versus grain. He concludes

27. Bao's arguments against tobacco cultivation are noted as well in Carol Benedict, *Golden-Silk Smoke: A History of Tobacco in China, 1550–2010* (Berkeley: University of California Press, 2011), 45 and 75.

28. Bao, *Gengchen zazhu, er*, in *Quanji* (1997), 210. Compare also *Shuochu*, 186, which makes a similar argument.

that the average Suzhou male consumes seven or eight times the amount of rice, and roughly twice the amount of lesser grains, in the form of alcohol that he eats as food. The waste of the empire's food supply, in this one prefecture alone, is astounding. There are existing bans on private distillation of alcohol, which should be strengthened, as they were in past times. Bao does not say here, but it appears that, since he does not propose a prohibition on alcohol consumption, that production would be left as a monopoly of certain government-licensed distillers.[29]

Bao enthusiastically included coastal trade in the circulation of agricultural produce he sought to encourage. As we will see in chapter 4, he was a consultant and drew up detailed plans for the adoption of the "sea route" for commercial shipment of tribute grain northward along the coast in the Daoguang reign. Indeed, more than two decades earlier, in 1804, he had championed the shift from Grand Canal to coastal shipments, mounting detailed arguments to dismiss fears of excessive costs, delays due to the uncertainty of coastal winds and currents, and the hazards of piracy.[30] Less celebrated are his arguments in favor of opening coastal trade in commercial farm produce, such as the one he advanced for Haizhou, northern Jiangsu, in 1815.

In the fall of that year, Bao made a personal inspection tour of Huaizhou's Ganyu county. He observed that, although much of the area was mountainous and uncultivable, it was capable of commercialized production of beans, miscellaneous grain, pigs, and fish. Moreover, in several of the region's market towns there were processing plants for bean oil and bean cake. For the most part, it was a case of "having commodities but no market for them" (*youhuo wushou*). In fact, though, there was a ready market for these goods in the cities of Jiangnan, where there were also raw and processed cotton, paper goods, and other commodities which might be exchanged for them. Unfortunately, the interior waterways linking Ganyu and Jiangnan were mostly impassible, so the small quantity of goods that were traded this way were carried by overland foot porters, and the resulting high transport costs constituted a "waste of commercial capital" (*fou yu maiben*) for Ganyu producers. There was an obvious

29. Bao, *Gengchen za zhu, er*, in *Quanji* (1997), 211.

30. Bao, "Haiyun nancao yi" and "Haiyun shiyi," both in *Quanji* (1997), 11–13 and 81–85.

alternative, that being export via Ganyu's one good maritime harbor, Qingkou, but in order to enforce collection of customs on the trade at the Huai customs, in inland Huai'an, coastal trade via that port was prohibited by law. Not that some smuggling via Qingkou didn't already take place, but this was controlled by violent "evil gentry" and "thugs," costing the producers dearly while netting the government no revenues whatsoever. The solution, for Bao Shichen, was simple: legalize the coastal trade via Qingkou and set up a branch of the Huai customs at that port. After all, some coastal shipping such as that of Shandong beans to Manchuria was already legally under way. As with his favored reforms of the Liang-Huai salt administration and the northern grain tribute, Bao argued that the removal of excessive bureaucratic restraint in this instance would predicate a "progressive expansion of commercial exchange" (*liutong riguang*), from which the farmers and merchants would derive profits and the state enhanced tax revenue.[31]

Maritime Trade

Domestic coastal trade was one thing, but overseas trade was quite another. In his youthful *On Wealth*, he allows the need for some officially regulated intercultural exchange with central Asia but, as we have seen, absolutely prohibits all overseas trade (*chuyang maoyi*) and all maritime navigation to Southeast Asia and beyond (*dongnan kaiyang*), and calls for beheading of those who would dare import Western manufactures.[32] As of 1801, he has not yet identified opium imports as the major evil—indeed, he does not need that particular argument in order to buttress his fundamental antiforeignism. His animus against maritime trade here seems instead rooted in protectionism for domestic textile producers, and in his more general sumptuary concerns—foreign manufactures are simply one more extravagance that Bao's new and improved population must be denied.

31. Bao, "Qingkou shuo," in *Quanji* (1997), 246–48.
32. *Shuochu*, 141.

By 1820, Bao has begun to relax his antipathy to maritime trade *in toto*, while coming to see opium imports as the greatest evil facing the empire. Whereas tobacco and alcohol are dissipations of "primary wealth" (*benfu*)—that is, production inputs such as labor, land, and fertilizer—opium is a waste of "secondary wealth" (*mofu*), or money, he argues. He continues: Opium is produced and imported by foreign barbarians (*waiyi*), and it kills our people. Although there are strict prohibitions against it, in recent years its use has expanded tremendously, in all parts of the empire. In the city of Suzhou alone there are more than 100,000 users. Assuming each user consumes about 0.1 tael worth of opium per day, that yields a total of 10,000 taels of silver expended on opium per day, or 3 to 4 million taels per year, in this one city alone! In cities throughout the empire (Bao seems to consider opium use largely an urban phenomenon) it adds up to 100 million taels per year. The cost of this is largely borne by "poor working households" (*pinku gongzuo zhi jia*), and the profits all go to foreign barbarians.

Bao estimates that the state/nation (*guojia*) collects no more than 40 million taels each year on the salt monopoly and customs revenues combined (that is, the major sources of government revenue other than the land tax). So the amount of silver sent out to foreign barbarians is more than double that collected in taxes. Since silver, he says, is the primary medium of wholesale exchange, and domestic silver mining is insignificant, the strangulation of the domestic currency markets in recent years is completely due to this. It is a case of *xuzhong shiwai*—China is emptied out of real wealth, which is exported to enrich foreigners.

Opium use, Bao observes, has multiplied in spite of repeated bans. Because it is addictive, it is nearly impossible to get users to quit. But because it is not produced domestically (Bao notes that efforts to cultivate it in Zhejiang and Yunnan have so far failed), the effective way to curtail opium use and trade is to cut it off at its root, the maritime trade. Indeed, "the entirety of foreign imports [*yanghuo*] are things for which our country [*neidi*] has no use." Even though the revenue from maritime customs yields some 2 million taels per year, sacrificing this pittance in order to save the 100 million per year dissipated on opium is a small price to pay—it is a true example of a policy of "storing wealth among the people" (*cangfu yumin*).

Some will protest, Bao adds, that unilaterally suppressing the opium trade risks foreign war. He suggests, instead, that there is no foreign threat without domestic collaborators (*neijian*): Of the foreign barbarians, the English are by far the strongest, and yet their population does not amount to 1 percent of that of China (Zhonghua). Chinese merchants and coastal defense officials have been complicit in the foreigners' crimes, and overly fearful of their power. What the British want from the Chinese most of all is tea and rhubarb. They can have this, paying for it with foreign copper (*yangtong*). Any traitorous Chinese (*Hanjian*) or foreign merchant who defies the ban on opium will be put to death, he declares. "If the foreign trade is managed the way I have laid out, things will be made right, the price of rice will return to the stable price that it ought to be, and grain supply will be plentiful throughout the land."[33]

Over the course of the 1830s Bao came ever more sharply to link the problems of opium imports and silver outflow with the crisis in the domestic economy caused by an increasingly skewed silver-to-copper exchange rate. As we will see in chapter 6, in a series of letters to various correspondents, including the otherwise obscure Jiangnan literatus Wang Liu, he discussed Wang's proposal to introduce paper currency. In Wang's view that step would resolve the silver shortage and also, by requiring foreigners to accept Chinese paper currency in payment for their imports, would gradually disincline them to bring opium into China; Bao thought the latter notion was unrealistic, but did offer qualified support to the basic idea of paper money.[34]

It is notable that Bao's remedy did not include cutting off all foreign trade, with which by now he had become reconciled. Indeed, in the late 1820s he had actually served for a time as an advisor in the Superintendancy of Maritime Customs at Guangzhou.[35] In a series of letters written in observation of the rapid expansion of foreign trade after the Opium War, however, he anticipates the call of early twentieth-century anti-imperialist politicians and scholars by decrying the impact of foreign imports on local handicraft products. It is no longer luxury novelties like

33. Bao, *Gengchen zazhu, er*, in *Quanji* (1997), 213.

34. Bao, "Yu Zhang Yuanfu shu," "Ta Wang Liangsheng shu," and "Cai ta Wang Liangsheng shu," all in *Quanji* (1997), 214–20. See also Man-houng Lin, *China Upside Down*, and chapter 6 below.

35. Hummel, *Eminent Chinese*, 610–11.

cuckoo clocks, nor simply opium, that are the problem, but instead cheap factory-made consumer staples. Bao observes that by this time farmers throughout the lower Yangzi region have become completely dependent on the subsidiary income derived from cotton spinning and weaving to meet their tax obligations and bring their household budgets up to subsistence levels; in recent years foreign machine-made cotton cloth has flooded the Chinese market, undercutting the price of handicraft cloth by as much as two-thirds. At least in Jiangnan, he laments, cottage industry in cotton is effectively dead, and raw cotton dealers in fact rarely visit rural producers anymore to supply them. Again, though, Bao sees the available remedies as restricted to tax and currency reform, the open maritime trade now established as a fait accompli.[36]

The Role of the State

As much of the foregoing suggests, one of Bao Shichen's consistent themes throughout his writings about agriculture is the responsibility of officials to pay personal attention to the conditions of farm life and to routinely intervene to ameliorate and improve such conditions. This was understood as the essence of governance (*tizheng*) by the rulers of antiquity (*xianwang*), but in recent generations it had greatly declined. Officials of the past understood how to encourage appropriate crop selection, farm labor allocation, the techniques of irrigation, and how to stabilize consumer commodity prices, but no longer. In his own day, he writes, while rural people (*xiangli yumin*—implying an inability to make rational production decisions on their own) rarely visit a town or city and never see the face of an official, the latter devote themselves to poetry and literary pursuits, leaving any contact with the people to predatory underlings. The people are reduced to privation, and no matter how diligently they labor they see their parents and children cold and malnourished, even without the arrival of a dreaded natural disaster. "Exhausting their finances at the

36. Bao, "Ta zuzi Meng Kai shu," dated Daoguang 26/5/24, and "Zhi qian dasima Xu Taichang shu," dated Daoguang 26/6/18, both in *Quanji* (1997), 234–39.

hands of extortionate bullies, exhausting their bodies in service of their oppressors, year in and year out, how are they able to bear it?"[37]

Take, for example, the case of irrigation. Bao states confidently that there is no part of the empire that is incapable of being irrigated, so that the grain production in even the arid northwest can eventually equal that of the fertile southeast.[38] The state's responsibility for maintaining the hydraulic infrastructure is at the center of a detailed letter Bao wrote to the incoming Jiangxi governor Chen Luan in 1836.[39] In Beijing the preceding year Bao had been notified of his impending appointment to a magistracy in that province, and had eagerly sought out as many Jiangxi natives as he could find in the capital, including the staff of the long-in-the-making revision of the Jiangxi provincial gazetteer, to inform himself of conditions in his impending jurisdiction. At the point of writing, however, Bao had been forced to delay his acceptance of his magistracy to undertake a two-year mourning for his mother at home. This did not prevent him from lecturing the incoming governor on just what was wrong in Jiangxi and what should be done about it.

Bao points out that virtually all the rice produced in Jiangxi is grown in polder fields reclaimed from lakes and riverbanks. "In the past people gobbled up the lakes to make fields, but now the lakes gobble up the people as if they were fish." Ecological decay has set in, primarily because of a failure of maintenance. Small polders, usually owned by households or lineages, are encompassed within large polders. The small polder walls are maintained, albeit indifferently, but in a classic free-rider syndrome no one has tended to the large polders, which have fallen into great decay. Without systematic repair to these, repairs to the small polders are increasingly ineffective. Decades of neglect have progressively worsened the situation, but the years since 1830, he writes, have been an out-and-out disaster, with major floods wiping out most of the crop every year.

37. Bao, *Nongzheng*, in *Quanji* (1997), 163–64.

38. Bao, *Gengchen zazhu, er*, in *Quanji* (1997), 210.

39. Bao, "Liu zhi Jiangxi xin fubu Chen Yusheng," dated Daoguang 16/4/13, in *Quanji* (1997), 256–60. Bao addresses this man as "Chen Yusheng," but the *Jiangxi tongzhi* (1881), 16:24–25, identifies the Jiangxi governor in this year as the well-known activist official Chen Luan. Bao routinely addresses his correspondents by their alternate names. I have not seen confirmation that "Yusheng" was an alternate name of Chen Luan, but I believe that he is the same individual.

Local and regional officials have turned a blind eye to the problem, concentrating their efforts solely on collecting the land tax and the grain tribute. Indeed, the continuing need to meet these tax obligations even while their farm income shrunk to nothing has left these households, literally and figuratively, under water—many have responded by abandoning their holdings and becoming wandering vagrants (*liumang*). At this stage in the game, neither the financial capacities of the people themselves (*minli*) nor the public works budgets (*gongxiang*) of county and prefectural governments are capable of meeting the challenge. Bao urges the incoming governor Chen to tackle this problem systematically: commission detailed topographical maps and cadastral surveys, draw up plans for large-scale hydraulic reconstruction, apportion costs to landholders who can afford it and can expect to benefit from the increased hydraulic security, and make up the remainder out of provincial revenues. The job is surely daunting, but, characteristically, Bao is fully confident that with proper management it can be successfully done.[40]

Tax and Currency Reform

In 1801, after returning from the White Lotus front, Bao toured Jiangnan and was deeply struck by the immiseration of the people due to imposition of agrarian taxes. He was particularly "broken hearted," he recalled, by their willingness to court death (*changsi*) in resistance to these crushing impositions. This formative experience stayed with him all his life.[41] In his lengthy essay on agricultural administration, written shortly after this tour, he argued that the most urgent and fundamental thing that officials can do to alleviate popular plight is to reduce agrarian taxes:

40. For a remarkably detailed account of large-scale polder maintenance organization in the Pearl River delta in the early nineteenth century, involving provincial coordination and seed money, gentry management bureaus, landholder subscription, and merchant contributions, see David Faure, *Emperor and Ancestor: State and Lineage in South China* (Stanford: Stanford University Press, 2007), chap. 18. This is clearly the kind of arrangement Bao had in mind for Jiangxi and, given his service in Guangzhou in the late 1820s, it might even have provided the specific model for his proposals of 1836.

41. Bao, preface to *Anwu sizhong*, dated Daoguang 24/9/26, in *Quanji* (1997).

> The farmers are greatly overtaxed. The land itself is subject to a semiannual assessment. The labor service levy is added to this, with 90 percent of the farmers being conscripted and sent out of their home community. Plus there are various public and private fees imposed by local officials, mutiplying several-fold the basic tax rate. Then there are meltage and commutation fees [*haozhe*], which fall more heavily on the poor than on the gentry or wealthy, because the latter pay in bulk with fewer expenses of collection. When it comes to the (corrupt and dysfunctional) grain tribute, those with wealth and influence are even better able to escape their fair share of the burden. It is no wonder that tax resistance and rebellion has arisen.[42]

And in the main text of *On Wealth*, Bao offers a concrete scheme for effectively shifting the state's fiscal burden from agriculture to the commercial sector; his plan calls for lowering the land tax by 10 million taels (ounces of uncoined silver specie) per year.[43]

The chief impetus to Bao's more pragmatic agrarian reformism throughout his mature life was to reduce this crushing tax burden. Toward the end of his life he recalls this long battle, and notes with some irony that he has not been arguing his own case, since he owns merely a token piece of property in his native place. His income, rather, derived primarily from sale of his writings and his calligraphy, and was neither taxed nor significantly affected by monetary exchange rates. This, while those with real property and productivity (*youye zhi min*) were squeezed without mercy.[44]

Bao agreed that the "great way of producing wealth" (*shengcai zhi dadao*) is to leave as much of it as possible in private, productive hands, and that the best means to enrich the public as well as the private, as if by an invisible hand, is to allow popular wealth (*mincai*) to flourish.[45] Yet this was not merely liberal rhetoric: it must be emphasized that Bao, notwithstanding his genuine empathy for popular tax burdens, Bao never sought tax reform in order to benefit the people at the expense of the state. At the very beginning of his first major work, *On Wealth*, he identified state finances as a critical cause for attention: an underfunded

42. Bao, *Nongzheng*, in *Quanji* (1997), 163.
43. Bao, *Shuochu*, 182.
44. Bao, "Zhi qian dasima Xu Taichang shu," in *Quanji* (1997), 239.
45. Bao, *Shuochu*, 182; preface to *Jimin si shu*, in *Quanji* (1997), 159–61.

state is by necessity a predatory state, as well as a weak one. Throughout his life he continued to recognize the Qing administration as cripplingly poor, and tailored his policies to enhance the *guofu*. This was one major area in which he differed, in emphasis at least, from High Qing reformers, who tended to take the financial health of the state as a given, rather than a cause of concern. Bao's tax and currency reform proposals normally argued that they would serve both ends at once: profiting the state above and the people below (*shang li guo, xia li min*), profiting the state while conveniencing the people (*liguo bianmin*), or, in a usage anticipating that of reformers such as Feng Guifen later in the century, benefiting the people while still "enriching the state [*fuguo*]."[46]

Over the course of his career, Bao ever more strongly associated the problem of rising tax burdens with that of currency mismanagement. In 1820 he wrote that currency had been an invention of the Yellow Emperor, as a means of moderating surplus and lack, and thus cultivating the people's wealth. Today, however, skewed silver-to-copper exchange rates work precisely against this effect. In an era of ever more intensive agricultural commercialization, a process which we have seen Bao applauded in itself, farmers are subjected to a worsening price scissors: they calculate their budgets in copper coin, while the merchants with whom they deal price their merchandise in silver. Thus, although silver is only a secondary repository of wealth (*mofu*)—grain being the primary (*benfu*)—the value of the latter is directly influenced by that of the former. It is the duty of officials to work intelligently and diligently to bring the silver-to-copper exchange back as close as possible to the 1:1,000 par rate.[47]

Increasingly, Bao linked the currency imbalance specifically to the problem of growing popular tax burden. In 1839, coincident with the outbreak of the Opium War, Bao wrote his most fully formulated analysis

46. Bao, preface to the supplement (*fulu*) to *Zhongqu yishao*, in *Quanji* (1993), 8–10; "Ta Wang Liangsheng shu," in *Quanji* (1997), 214–15.

47. Bao, *Gengchen zazhu, er*, in *Quanji* (1997), 209–13; see also the 1844 preface to *Qimin sishu*, in *Quanji* (1997), 159–61. For a well-informed analysis of this problem, see Peng Zeyi, "Yapien zhanzheng hou shinianjian yingui qianjian bodong xia Zhongguo jingji yu jieji guanxi" (The Chinese economy and class relations in the post-Opium War decade under the impact of rising silver-to-copper exchange rates), in *Shijiu shiji houbanqi de Zhongguo caizheng yu jingji* (Government finance and the economy in late nineteenth-century China) (Beijing: Renmin chubanshe, 1983), 24–71.

of the currency crisis, "A Simple Remedy for the Silver Famine."[48] Farmers in many parts of the empire, Bao noted, were assessed their taxes in silver taels but actually paid them in copper cash. Though the par rate for conversion from taels to cash was 1:1,000, the market rate (observed by Bao in Nanchang that year) was 1:1,630, and tax collectors often imposed rates of 1:1,800 or higher. Thus farmers, who were paid for their goods in cash prices that did not reflect the skewed exchange rate, were increasingly squeezed by their rising tax burden. Bao's "simple remedy" was assessment of most agricultural taxes directly in copper—as had been the case prior to the late Ming.

Bao increasingly came to believe that it was desirable to demonetize silver as much as possible, and advocated the introduction of paper currency as one means of doing this. He did so most emphatically during his exchange of letters with Wang Liu in the 1830s (see chapter 6, below). A decade later, however, Bao was still emphasizing the need to introduce paper currency to resolve the still-worsening silver-to-copper exchange rate. In 1846, he estimated the average market exchange rate in the lower Yangzi at around 1:2,000, but added that clerks often demanded commutation rates of up to 1:3,000 in their collection of the land tax and the grain tribute, which frequently exceeded the value of the entire yield on their land, driving them into abandoning agriculture. Once again, he argued for the mandating of copper cash as the government's sole money of account, and the introduction of paper currency, which as he notes the Daoguang court had entertained and rejected in 1845, as one means of effecting the demonitization of silver.[49]

On the Ground

After a lifetime of advising others on how to carry out various agrarian reforms, Bao Shichen got his first and only chance actually to enact policies in practice during 1838–39, at the age of sixty-four. In the summer of

48. Bao, "Yinhuang xiaobu shuo," in *Quanji* (1997), 228–30. See also "Cai ta Wang Liangsheng shu," in *Quanji* (1997), 215–20.

49. Bao, "Zhi qian dasima Xu Taichang shu," dated Daoguan 26/6/18, in *Quanji* (1997), 237–39.

1838, he received an imperial appointment to Jiangxi as an expectant county magistrate, and in the fall, when the magistracy of Xinyu county opened up, he was assigned to proceed there to fill the post.[50] It was, to say the least, a chastening experience. Xinyu was officially categorized as a "simple" and "prosperous" jurisdiction (*jianyou*), but in 1838 it was clearly nothing of the sort. It was a county in what Bao himself described as open tax rebellion (*kangwan*). The previously assigned magistrate had actually refused to take up his appointment to Xinyu, leaving it to Bao. When Bao himself arrived in the county, he was intercepted by sympathetic local elites and advised not to enter the county seat, which was in total chaos. Accepting their hospitality, he remained for several weeks some fifteen *li* outside the city, while conducting extensive fact-finding interviews and planning his strategy.

Xinyu was plagued by active conflict between (and among) local people and various higher-level officials, including the prefect, the provincial grain tribute intendant, and the provincial treasurer, whom Bao variously presents as corrupt or well-intentioned but incapable. The county was several years in arrears on its grain tribute payments. Rural property holders were subjected to a multiplying number of transport and collection fees (*caogui*), which Bao wasn't loathe to describe as "squeeze" (*lougui*). On top of this, commutation and bimetallic exchange rates were greatly inflated: the prevailing silver-to-copper rate in Xinyu markets was bad enough, at 1:1,600, but in tax collection practice it went as high as 1:2,000. Tax and commercial litigation was hopelessly backlogged, with a group of sojourning merchants engaged in a protracted legal struggle with locals over defaulted payments (apparently related to the inflated exchange rates). A group of local elites had taken up a subscription for a fund which would help subsidize these inflated commutation and exchange rates, but at the moment there was heated local disagreement about how these monies were to be allocated. Police runners (*zaoyi*) charged with tax collection were detested and often met with violent resistance. A particular cause of local grievance was the seizing by grain

50. Sources on Bao's tenure as Xinyu magistrate include "Fu Chen Qumi shu," in *Quanji* (1997), 239–44; preface to *Zhongqu yishao*, in *Quanji* (1993), 8–10; *Nianpu*, in *Quanji* (1991), 236–37; and *Xinyu xianzhi* (1849) (reprinted Taipei: Chengwen, 1988), 3:19.

tribute functionaries of a local Confucian school to serve as a collection depot. Two local lower degree holders named Wan Guoyu and Hu Xiangyou had initiated petitions to cashier the grain tribute intendant, to which the provincial treasurer had responded by declaring them "grain tribute thugs" (*caogun*) and ordering their arrest. Provincial authorities, in Bao's view, had come to the conclusion that the entire county ought to be severely punished for its intractability.

Characteristically, Magistrate Bao sought to resolve the issues with reasoned moderation. Once he felt emboldened to enter the county seat, he convened a large meeting of taxpayers and tax collection functionaries, at which he patiently explained that the grain tribute itself was a legitimate fiscal obligation that should be met, and that there were indeed some collection fees that were burdensome but unavoidable. Working through these with all parties to determine which were justified and which not, Bao presents himself as having reached some consensus. He then engaged in a somewhat contentious correspondence with provincial authorities to have the schedule of collection fees for Xinyu pruned of excess. He also pledged to discipline any local functionaries who had egregiously "oppressed the people" (*nuemin*). When the 1839 grain crop was badly affected by summer flooding, he sought successfully to have payments of past arrears deferred again until some future more bountiful harvest.

But whatever his level of actual success in these matters, Bao Shichen clearly failed to resolve the two most compelling problems in Xinyu's fiscal mess. He deposited the elite-solicited funds with the prefectual treasury, while trying repeatedly to negotiate their fair redistribution to their original donors, but to no avail; once he had been relieved of his magistracy, the provincial governor personally seized the money and arbitrarily decided who and how much to repay. Worse still was the issue of the two "thugs," Wan and Hu. Bao tried repeatedly to coax them into his yamen on the promise that he would hear them out fairly and present their cases with sympathy to higher authority, but they were not persuaded and fled to neighboring jurisdictions. The exasperated provincial authorities responded with brutal force. Troops were sent down to the Xinyu region to apprehend them directly; both were caught and Wan, at least, died in confinement. In the process some three hundred family farms in the two culprits' home villages were burned to the ground.

Conclusion

Earlier in this book I noted a current interpretation of Bao Shichen's policy views as comparable to Western economic "liberalism," and my own reticence about embracing this position. As we have seen here, Bao adamantly supported private property rights, but by no means unqualifiedly so. He favored in most instances private (merchant) management of economic enterprises, but only on condition of close state supervision, and in what he felt to be the public interest. Indeed, one of the most consistent themes in his agrarian policy advocacy was the need for greater state activism and intervention.

Perhaps a better characterization of Bao's position would be the more neutral "utilitarian." This would encompass at least three strains. First, the determined pursuit of greater economic efficiency and productivity. Second—and here he falls closely in line with many "statecraft" scholar-officials of the "prosperous age" of the mid-eighteenth century—a persistent emphasis on ameliorating fiscal and other burdens on the farming population. Third, however, was something relatively newer: an abiding, genuine, and urgent emphasis on attending to the needs of state finance (*guoji*). As we shall see in chapter 7, late in life Bao summed up his approach to political economy as the maximization of advantage or profit (*li*), especially by combatting the siphoning off of wealth at a middle level (*zhongbao*), to the detriment of both the people and the government. He argued that this misappropriated profit should be reallocated roughly 70 percent to society and 30 percent to the state.[51]

Bao as we know was a highly influential policy advocate, but was he equally successful or effective? He was clearly very bright, extremely knowledgeable, and bold in his thinking—and contemporaries respected him for these qualities—but he also strikes me as cripplingly naïve. In concrete situations, as we have seen, notably in his advisory role in managing the Nanjing dearth of 1814 and in his handling of local fiscal matters in Xinyu county in 1838, he was pretty much a failure. He was fascinated

51. Bao, "Ta zuzi Meng Kai shu," dated Daoguang 26/5/24, in *Quanji* (1997), 234–36.

by numbers, to an extent that I have not seen matched by any other policy analyst of the mid-Qing era, but his approach to such numbers was, to say the least, cavalier. And his foundational confidence that the productivity of Chinese agriculture (both per capita and per acre) could be continually increased by attentive management was, I think it is fair to say, misplaced.

Bao Shichen's adult life and writings span the years between two major crises: the Qianlong-Jiaqing transition at the turn of the nineteenth century (the generation of reform writers such as Hong Liangji, Yan Ruyi, Tao Zhu, and—a bit later—Wei Yuan), and the great mid-century rebellions (the generation of Hu Linyi, Zeng Guofan, and—a bit later—Feng Guifen).[52] His writings over this half-century consistently display his sympathy for the rural producer, and also his deep concern with the financial well-being of the state. The latter concern was much more deeply felt among the later generation of reformers than among the earlier one, and on this score Bao was somewhat ahead of his time. So too were his constant efforts to root out exploitative middlemen between the producers and the state, a long-time concern of *jingshi*-minded officials, but a genuine obsession of those in the mid-nineteenth century. If the continuities in Bao's writings are striking, however, so too is the gradual decline from the utopian optimism of his youth, in the heady era of the "Jiaqing restoration," to the dejected perseverance of his later years. Writing in 1846, he found both the exploitation of the livelihoods of the people (*minsheng*) and the exhaustion of state finances (*guoji*) to be more severe than ever, and worsening every day.[53] In spite of his having enjoyed enormous influence and some notable practical policy successes, by the midpoint of the nineteenth century the problems seemed all too familiar, and the things that concerned him had only grown worse, rather than better.

52. Feng Tianyu draws out Bao's significance as the single figure most exemplifying this transition from the intellectual concerns of the high Qing to the muscular statecraft of the mid-nineteenth century. See Feng, "Daoguang Xianfeng nianjian jingshi shixue," 138–51.

53. Bao, *Quanji*, 234–36.

CHAPTER 4

Grain

The Qing empire in the early nineteenth century was, as we have seen, wracked by a pervasive sense of crisis, which led to a broad-based reform movement, both in and out of government. One of the major policy areas of both the crisis and the reform efforts—arguably *the* centerpiece of it all—was the highly controversial and protracted debate over the reform of the grain tribute system and the proposed move from shipment of southern tax grain north via the Grand Canal under bureaucratic auspices to shipment along the maritime coast via private commercial carriers. This debate has been reasonably well studied, both in East Asian and Western languages, but there remain gaps in our overall understanding of the issues at stake.[1]

Bao Shichen was very close to the center of the debate, although his connection to it remains relatively underappreciated, if not altogether obscured; having never served in a provincial-level official post, of course, Bao remains invisible in any scholarship based on archival or published

1. Jones and Kuhn, "Dynastic Decline"; Jane Kate Leonard, *Controlling from Afar: The Daoguang Emperor's Management of the Grand Canal Crisis, 1824–1826* (Ann Arbor: University of Michigan, Center for Chinese Studies, 1996). For background on the late imperial grain tribute system, see Harold C. Hinton, *The Grain Tribute System of China, 1845–1911* (Cambridge, MA: Harvard University, Chinese Economic and Political Studies, 1956); Hoshi Ayao, *Dai unga: Chūgoku no sōun* (The Grand Canal: grain tribute in China) (Tokyo: Kondō shuppansha, 1971); Hoshi Ayao, *The Ming Tribute Grain System*, ed. and trans. Mark Elvin (Ann Arbor: University of Michigan, Center for Chinese Studies, 1969).

court documents.[2] My goal in this chapter is to determine what Bao and other reformers felt was at stake in this crisis—that is, what needed to be defended or protected—as well as what the capabilities and limitations were of the faltering imperial state to deal with this, and what might have been the impact of changing times on the situation as a whole. In short, what I hope to present is a contribution to our overall understanding of what the reformism of this era was about, and of the significance of this historical moment in Qing and imperial history.

The Problem of Grain Tribute

Bao Shichen consistently expressed his belief that the grain tribute was the single greatest policy problem in central China, and the most difficult to remedy. The difficulty was not that the cause of the problem was not obvious: it was the corruption of local and regional government clerks, which siphoned off revenues from the people below and the state above (and also the legitimate income of transport workers in the tribute collection system). Nor was it that the existing laws were not adequate: they had simply been subject to five hundred years of accumulated abuses. Nor yet was it that the solution was not also obvious: even without adopting the sea route, which Bao himself came to favor, simply establishing more localized military collection depots and keeping the details of shipment secret from local administrative meddling would save so much in corruption and overhead that the tax rate could effectively be lowered

2. Jones and Kuhn ("Dynastic Decline") mention Bao in their general discussion of reformism in this era, but not in direct connection with the grain tribute reforms. He does not appear at all in Leonard's book *Controlling from Afar*, nor is he mentioned significantly in Ni Yuping's recent and detailed studies of the sea transport experiment of 1826; Ni Yuping, "Daoguang liunian caoliang haiyun de jige wenti" (Some problems regarding the sea transport of tribute grain in 1826), *Qingshi wenti* 2002.3: 70–75, and Ni Yuping, *Qingchao Jia Dao caizheng yu shehui* (Financial administration and society in the Qing Jiaqing and Daoguang reigns) (Beijing: Commercial Press, 2013), 244–76. Bao's role in grain tribute reform was, to my knowledge, first explored by Ōtani in "Hō Seishin no jitsugaku shisō ni tsuite" in 1969, and later in greater depth in Zhang Yan, "Bao Shichen yu jindai qianye de 'haoyun nancao' gaige" (Bao Shichen and the seaborne grain tribute shipment reform), *Jindaishi yanjiu* 2000.1: 129–53.

throughout the lower Yangzi region. The problem was that fixing the system would require such a concerted and "heroic" effort on the part of well-placed officials that it was unlikely to occur.[3]

In a 1836 letter to the Jiangxi governor Chen Yusheng, Bao analyzed the problem of grain tribute arrears in that province, a problem that had been steadily worsening over the course of the Daoguang reign.[4] Although a clerical mafia had gotten control of the collection and reporting process, they had concentrated their deceptions on reporting as paid taxes that in fact had not, rather than, fortunately, the reverse. The shortfalls they reported fell into two categories: *minqian* (tax dues actually not paid by the taxpayer) and *guanqian* (taxes paid by the taxpayer to local authorities but not forwarded upward to higher authority). In 1835, in a gesture of imperial benevolence (but also, certainly, one of recognition of genuine incapacity to pay) the throne had forgiven all *minqian* incurred in Jiangxi before the year 1830. At the same time, however, a stepped-up coercive campaign got under way to collect the popular arrears incurred *since* that year, an amount the provincial tax investigation bureau (*qingcha ju*) placed at about 700,000 taels. The result had been that the clerical mafia extending from the provincial bureau on down had grossly abused the collection process, ruthlessly "oppressing the helpless and unconnected while fattening up themselves" (*lei gugua er fei shuyi*).

Bao also pointed out to the governor that the grain tribute burden fell very differently in different parts of Jiangxi. For one thing, not all counties in Jiangxi were assessed the same amount of tribute dues, and some were not assessed any at all. Whereas this was supposed to reflect their relative grain surplus, it more accurately reflected simply historical accident and the difficulty of collection. Another factor was the differing means employed to collect the grain. In some localities, taxpayers collected their own tribute grain and brought it to the central collection point themselves (*minzheng mindui*); in others, taxpayers collected it but turned it over to administrative functionaries for shipment (*minzheng guandui*);

3. *Quanji* (1993), 8. For a detailed analysis of dysfunctions in the grain tribute during the Daoguang reign, and the resulting loss of government revenue, see Xia Nai, "Taiping tianguo qian hou Changjiang gesheng zhi tianfu wenti" (The land tax problem in the Yangzi provinces before and after the Taiping rebellion), *Qinghua xuebao* 10.2 (April 1935): 409–74.

4. Bao, "Liu zhi Jiangxi xin fubu Chen Yusheng," in *Quanji* (1997), 259–60.

while in still others, grain was both collected and shipped by bureaucratic authorities (*guanzheng guandui*). The first alternative had the benefit of keeping administrative manipulation to the minimum, but the second, and still more the third, brought with them the levying of surtaxes and fees (*duifei*, *caogui*, and so on) on the taxpayer to cover the supposed costs of government shipment. Needless to say, those taxpayers whose property lay farther upriver from the collection center paid relatively higher surtaxes, out of all proportion to the product of their land. Bao urged Governor Chen to conduct a detailed survey of provincial realities in order to apportion the burden of tribute payment more equitably and more in line with taxpayers' ability to pay, in order to put the clerical racketeers out of business and improve both popular and official morale.

Early Reform Proposals: 1801

Bao's first known proposal for grain tribute reform came in 1801, when he was just twenty-six years old, in the context of his comprehensive treatise on administrative restructuring, *On Wealth*. In keeping with the spirit of that work, Bao's analysis of the problem was far-reaching and his proposed solutions frankly idealistic. Although the specific problems inherent in grain shipment north via the Grand Canal had not yet become obvious (as they would but two years later), Bao condemned the grain tribute system in and of itself, both for imposing an undue tax burden on the people and for spawning another unnecessary and bloated bureaucracy. His solution was effectively to abolish it altogether.[5]

The group served by the grain tribute was primarily the bannerman population of Beijing and its environs, who were very largely unemployed. Yet everyone knew that the coastal salt marshes of Zhili province were potentially arable, and Bao proposed that they be reclaimed as military colonies (*tuntian*), in which these bannermen might be resettled as part-time farmers and part-time soldiers. Seed, farm tools, and farming instructors could be brought in from the south to get these new settlers

5. *Shuochu*, 186–87.

started. The boatmen on the Grand Canal were mostly southerners themselves, and so they might easily be resettled on reclaimed *tuntian* estates along the central coast; they presumably knew how to farm paddy land already, and would certainly prefer securing their subsistence via agriculture, on land to which they held title (Bao proposed for both groups that *tuntian* land be reallocated in each generation according to the model of the ancient well-field system), instead of via the backbreaking labor of hauling canal barges.

Relying on military personnel, housed in *tuntian* colonies, as grain tribute boatmen was the way the system had initially been designed to operate, and in fact had done so under the Ming. This system had been inherited by the Qing. However, by the Jiaqing reign the percentage of soldiers among Grand Canal boatmen had been dramatically reduced: their *tuntian* lands had been mostly privatized by the expanding land market, and their work on the boats largely taken over by contracted civilian laborers (*shuishou*).[6] What Bao Shichen was suggesting, then, was a reversion to the *tuntian* model of agricultural production, but with the actual grain transport activities eliminated from the equation.

Bao acknowledged that given the greater per capita productivity of agriculture in the south versus the north a certain amount of geographic redistribution of grain would still be required, but he argued that this should be accomplished by means of the commercial market. The market was clearly more efficient for this purpose than the official bureaucratic means then in use. It is worth noting, however, that Bao's proposal was not simply a call for greater marketization; the outcome of his reforms, if enacted, would in fact be to make a greater percentage of the population largely self-sufficient in foodstuffs and hence *less* market-dependent. He clearly preferred market over state redistribution when called for, but, in the context of his 1801 tract more generally, it is clear that he was offering a brief in favor, not of merchant interests, but of burdened agrarian taxpayers.

6. Hinton, *Grain Tribute System*, 11; Hoshi, *The Ming Tribute Grain System*, 86; Jones and Kuhn, "Dynastic Decline," 121.

Early Reform Proposals: 1820

Over the course of the Jiaqing reign, in a wide range of policy areas, Bao moved away from the idealistic proposals of his youth, tending to concentrate on more pragmatic piecemeal reforms. With regard to the grain tribute, however, he still sought to find a means to its abolition, and continued to recommend a more energetic use of *tuntian* as a means to reduce corruption and actual tax burdens. In two of a series of essays on political-economic issues that he compiled a month after the accession of the Daoguang emperor, under the title *Gengchen zazhu* (Miscellaneous writings from the year 1820), and eventually published five years later, Bao revisited the grain tribute problem.[7]

The first of these two essays focuses on the corruption and inefficiency inherent in the many layers of bureaucracy that have been imposed over the years on the grain tribute, and proposes a streamlined chain of command to alleviate these problems. One of the most significant early Qing innovations in the tribute process had been the introduction of the "official collection and official transfer" system (*guanshou guandai*), which took the responsibility for direct collection of tribute dues from the taxpayer out of the hands of militarized grain tribute personnel and placed it in the hands of local officials in the regular field administration.[8] While the intent of this move had been to reduce the opportunity for racketeering on the part of a corporate tribute mafia, it had in fact opened up the tribute to profiteering by unscrupulous officials and county clerks, in the process exacerbating chances for dishonorable local taxpayers (*jianmin*) to evade their assessments and shift the burden onto their honest neighbors (*liangmin*). Bao suggests cutting county administrations out of the system altogether, and returning to direct collection by grain tribute soldiers. In many areas these men remain on the scene anyway, organized into depots (*weisuo*) and residing in military agricultural colonies (*tuntian*); Bao would systematically augment their numbers and reclaim

7. *Gengchen zazhu*, essays 3 and 4, in *Quanji* (1993), 65–68. On the early publication history of these materials, see Bao, preface to *Zhongqu yishao fulu*, in *Quanji* (1993), 8–10.

8. Hoshi, *The Ming Tribute Grain System*, 86, 91–93.

additional *tuntian* land. He had of course argued for a similar augmentation in his *On Wealth* of twenty years earlier, but by now he had pragmatically reconciled himself to the continued need for the grain tribute system itself, and presented *tuntian* as a means to alleviate its problems rather than obviate it altogether.

The second of Bao's two 1820 essays on grain tribute is remarkable in part for its display of his growing obsession with quantification, to a degree rarely equaled by political-economic writers of his day or earlier. He points out that between 3 and 4 million *dan* of grain are sent northward to the Tianjin depot each year, carried aboard more than five thousand boats. All of this passes through numerous canal locks en route, requires hauling by laborers along the canal banks, and necessitates constant repair of both boats and channels. These added costs amount to no less than 10 million taels per year, and result in a price of southern rice on the Beijing market nearly triple what it commands in the production area.

Returning to a theme of his youthful *On Wealth*, Bao hints that the ideal way to eliminate these problems would be to undertake a massive overhaul of the agrarian ecology and hydraulic infrastructure in north China, not only reducing the problem of silting the Grand Canal with Yellow River sand—which had become a critical issue in recent years (see below)—but optimally making paddy rice cultivation possible on a much greater scale in the hinterland of the capital itself. However, in a relatively rare concession to political feasibility, Bao admits that this is unlikely; though such well-informed and highly placed ministers as Zhu Gui have studied this in the past, it is clear that the huge project expenses could not be borne by the government alone (*guanli*) and passing them on to private farmers (*minli*), who would see the up-front costs but not envision the long-term benefits, would incite great popular resistance.

But there is a better solution. Bao notes that the total amount of tribute rice assessment each year is around 4 million *dan*, which is the equivalent of the product of 2 million *mou* of good farmland in the southeast during an average year.[9] If we assume that there are actually 4 million

9. One *mou* was the equivalent of approximately 0.15 acre. One *dan* was a volume measurement, sometimes translated "bushel," and equaling just under 104 liters; one *dan* of rice would have weighed approximately 185 pounds. See Sui-wai Cheung, *The Price of Rice: Market Integration in Eighteenth-Century China* (Bellingham: Western Washington University, 2008), x and 7.

mou of such farmland in this region, and the yield of this land is divided equally between landlord and tenant, then the annual tribute assessment is exactly equivalent of the total rents collected.

Bao then calculates the area of one hundred *li* squared to equal approximately 5,300,000 *mou.* He identifies an area in north China to the west of the Imperial Estates, comprising parts of Henan, Shandong, and Shanxi provinces, that is crisscrossed by small waterways, portions of which are horse pasture and portions simply marshland. This is suitable for reclamation as *tuntian.* We should invite in experienced farmers from the south who are currently without leaseholds, and provide them with state grants of start-up capital in order to fashion a proper irrigation network and a grid of paddy fields, and provide them with farm tools and draft animals. The project can begin with an experimental tract of ten *li* squared and, once the benefits of this reclamation are clear to all, progressively expand over the course of ten years to one hundred *li* square. Allowing 300,000 *mou* for residences, granaries, and other nonfarming purposes, this will leave some 5 million *mou* of newly created rice land. The cultivators on this *tuntian* land will be tenants of the state (*guandian*). Their annual rent payments, in kind, will equal 5 million *dan* of rice, or a million *dan* greater than the total amount of grain tribute collected from the south. As the new land is gradually brought on line, tribute assessments on southern land can be reduced accordingly, eventually eliminated altogether, and the extra million *dan* of grain generated can be applied to official salaries, troop rations, and so on. The start-up costs for this massive reclamation project, Bao estimates, will be no greater than one year's grain tribute revenues, a negligible investment in a project that will provide stable state revenues for "a hundred generations" (*baishi*), while at the same time relieving "the tribulations of the southeast" (*dongnan zhi kun*).

As in his youthful *On Wealth*—and indeed as throughout his life—Bao thus identified with agrarian interests of his native lower Yangzi region. But he was more than simply a spokesman for the Jiangnan gentry, as he is sometimes claimed to be. His career had been forged in the suppression of the White Lotus in central and northwest China, which left him deeply sensitive to two other factors: first, the legitimate grievances of poor farmers exploited to their limits by local officials and petty state functionaries and, second, to the legitimate fiscal needs of the state itself—an impoverished state is perforce a predatory state, and hence an endangered one. In his 1820 essays Bao invokes the familiar mantra of eighteenth-century statecraft, arguing that his tax-cutting measures will "store wealth among the people" (*cang fu yu min*) rather than in state treasuries, and in this way enhance their inherent productive capacity (*yuanqi*). He clearly means it. But he is also quite genuine in arguing that his proposed reforms will safeguard not only state revenues (*guoji*), but more basically the stability of the government itself (*zhengti*). The system as it stands risks inciting popular wrath (*zhongshu*) and spawning uprisings similar to the White Lotus, this time in the southeast (*dongnan zhi huan*). Bao sounds here his characteristically frank pursuit of advantage or profit (*li*), but insists that this is profit accruing to the state as well as the people (*gongsi zhi liyi*). It is worth noting as well that his proposed reforms here—a dramatic expansion of military colonies and a massive program of government-financed land reclamation—are essentially state- rather than market-driven. In other words, these are not the writings of a single-minded small-government advocate.

Although Bao's proposals on the phasing out of the grain tribute were of course never enacted, it is clear that they were read by the growing number of persons both in and out of government who felt that the system was fundamentally broken. These included Lin Zexu, who reportedly endorsed them. Wei Yuan and He Changling thought Bao's recommendations on expanded use of *tuntian* plausible enough to include the third of his 1820 essays in their influential 1826 compilation *Huangchao jingshi wenbian* (Writings on statecraft from the present dynasty), but they omitted his fourth essay, presumably because they thought it too radical.[10] The Jiangsu governor, Tao Zhu, rejected both Bao's ideas on expanded military colonies and his call for elimination of the grain tribute as impractical.[11] It would be Tao, however, who eventually turned to Bao Shichen as a major architect of his own very dramatic grain tribute reforms.

10. Essay 3 was republished under the title "Rooting out Dysfunctions in the Grain Tribute System" ("Ti caobi") in *Huangchao jingshi wenbian* (Selected writings on statecraft from the ruling dynasty), ed. He Changling and Wei Yuan (1826), 46:23–24.

11. Duan Zhao, *Tao Zhu yu Jia-Dao jingshi sixiang yanjiu*, 196–97.

The Sea Route Alternative

In 1803 a dike ruptured at Hengjialou in Henan province, spilling water and silt into the Grand Canal. Northbound grain tribute boats on the canal were halted at Zhangqiu (Shandong) by the silt buildup, and many failed to reach their destination. The alarmed Jiaqing emperor opened the "pathways of words" (*yanlu*), calling upon all of his provincial-level officials to submit suggestions on how to fundamentally rehabilitate the canal and the tribute system.[12] Bao Shichen, who at age twenty-eight, having already written on the subject in his *On Wealth*, had conducted an inspection tour of Shanghai and its environs the preceding year, and considered himself highly expert on grain tribute matters, submitted a "private letter" (*sishu*) from Suzhou to the Jiangsu governor, calling for a complete abandonment of the Grand Canal as an artery for grain shipments and a move instead to shipment by sea (*haiyun*). This idea, though bold, was not wholly original. Northern grain shipments by sea had been utilized intermittently in both the Yuan and Ming eras. Several early Qing officials, most notably the grain tribute commissioner Cai Shiying in 1664, had considered this possibility, and so had several of the provincial respondents to Jiaqing's 1803 call for advice.[13] All of this past experience and current advice, however, had in common the fact that transport by sea was to be conducted by military or other bureaucratic personnel. Bao's proposal was wholly unique in its provision that coastal grain tribute shipment be handled entirely by private commercial contractors.

Bao's "Proposal in Favor of the Sea Route for Southern Grain Tribute" ("Haiyun nancao yi") begins by listing the most common objections to utilizing coastal shipping: (1) pirates would steal the cargoes, (2) because of the uncertainties of maritime shipping there would be frequent losses and delays, and (3) the cost of constructing new boats for this purpose would be prohibitive. Bao, characteristically, dismisses these arguments

12. Bao, preface to *Anwu sizhong*, in *Quanji* (1997); Hu Pu'an, *Nianpu*, 217; Jones and Kuhn, "Dynastic Decline," 122.

13. *Huangchao jingshi wenbian*, 47:26–32; Wei Yuan, "Haiyun ji," in *Huangchao jingshi wenbian*, 48:70–71; Zhang Yan, "Bao Shichen," 130–31.

as the "unfounded ramblings of scholars with book-learning only" (*shusheng yutan*), and sets out to refute them on the basis of his own on-site investigations.[14]

First, the pirates. The eastern seas are divided into the Nanyang and the Beiyang, south and north of Shanghai, respectively. These have different depths and pose different obstacles, requiring different sorts of vessels, observes Bao. The deep Nanyang demands deep-draft "island-hopping ships" (*daochuan*), whereas the sandbank-strewn Beiyang calls for shallower-draft "sand ships" (*shachuan*). Pirates inhabit the Nanyang, but their deep-draft vessels are not built to threaten traffic in the Beiyang.

Second, the threat of loss at sea or delay. Bao counts some 3,500 to 3,600 *shachuan* home-ported in Shanghai, each capable of carrying between 1,500 and 3,000 *dan* of cargo. They are all owned by wealthy commoners (*fumin*), with normally forty to fifty boats owned by a single master (*chuanzhu*), and all belonging to a single guild headed by a guild manager (*dongshi*). Since Kangxi's lifting of the sea ban in 1684, these boats have plied routes north from Shanghai to Manchuria and other northern regions, with their southbound cargo comprised primarily of bean-cake fertilizer (to the extent of more than 10 million *dan* per year) and their smaller northbound cargo made up of tea and other lower Yangzi specialty products. The trade has proceeded prosperously for years without significant loss; the guild manager has told Bao that losses affect no more than one in a hundred or a thousand ships—far less, Bao adds, than the percentage of loss in the Grand Canal shipments.

Clearly, then, the ships already exist and there would be no need for the government to construct new ones itself. Moreover, since the really lucrative portion of the existing trade is the southbound carriage of bean-cake fertilizer, the private ship owners are always looking for northbound cargoes and would be happy to carry tribute grain at reasonable freights. Brokers (*yaren*) at Shanghai routinely arrange such cargoes; dockhands in Tianjin are well practiced in receiving and offloading them. Bao's historical research reveals to him that as early as the Tang the venerated finance minister Liu Yan successfully contracted private commercial vessels (*minchuan*) to transport some northbound tribute rice.

14. Bao, "Haiyun nancao yi," in *Quanji* (1993), 11–13.

Today, asserts Bao, with the manifest greater development of private commerce, using private contractors for maritime shipments will be much easier yet. It just makes sense.

But there were additional factors that Bao had failed to take into account. According to Bao's own testimony, the deathblow to his proposals in this period was administered by the great Hanxue scholar and incumbent Zhejiang governor Ruan Yuan (1764–1849), who would not be persuaded. In 1803 Ruan dismissed the sea route altogether, out of concern that its adoption would put tens of thousands of canal boatmen out of work and that these unemployed and unaccountable (*shiyewulai*) men would be a far greater risk than the losses incurred in canal shipment. When these shipments showed signs of failure again the following year, Ruan modified his position to accept the necessity of *some* supplemental coastal shipments, but only aboard Qing naval vessels (*bingchuan*). There would be no layoffs required.[15]

Bao Shichen spent the next two decades on the staff of various lower Yangzi and north China provincial officials, researching and offering technical advice on matters of hydraulic reconstruction on the Yellow and Huai Rivers and the Grand Canal. During the severe Jiangbei dearth of 1814–17, he was assigned to help work out relief programs for the afflicted. But the issue of the grain tribute was never far from his mind, and he continued to discuss this with whoever would listen to him. While in Beijing to sit (unsuccessfully) for the *jinshi* examination, he secured an interview with the venerable Grand Secretary Dai Quheng, regarded as a leading expert on river control. Bao insisted that hydraulic issues could not be separated from that of the grain tribute, and discussed in detail with Dai his plans for paddy land reclamation and retooling of idle bannermen as agricultural colonists to offset the popular burden on lower Yangzi farmers of the grain tribute. He mentioned that he had other solutions in mind as well, on which he declined to elaborate—utilizing the sea route seems to have been one of these. Nothing substantial came of this conversation.[16]

15. Ruan Yuan, "Haiyun kao," parts 1–3, in *Huangchao jingshi wenbian*, 48:1–10; Bao, *Quanji* (1993), 11; Zhang Yan, "Bao Shichen," 137–41.

16. Hu Pu'an, *Nianpu*, 222–23; Liu Guangzhi, "Bao Shichen yu Wei Yuan," 1000–1001.

In 1809 and 1810, as silting on the Grand Canal continued to worsen, the Jiaqing emperor once again opened the *yanlu* for discussion of grain tribute problems. By this time employing the sea route had become at least a viable option, and the agenda for the debate was set at working out of some possible combination of canal and coastal shipments. No one, however, endorsed Bao Shichen's proposal to use commercial contractors; nor was any real policy innovation decided upon.[17] Jiaqing effectively left resolution of the problem to his successor.

The Daoguang Crisis

During the first years of the Daoguang reign, the situation noticeably worsened, with successful grain shipments reduced and social unrest in the capital area threatened. In the tenth month of Daoguang 4 (1824), the critical Gaojia yan dike ruptured, silting up the canal at Qingjiang (present-day Huai'an) in northern Jiangsu, so that the great majority of the tribute-bearing boats were either beached or obstructed from their northward passage. The emperor ordered a conference among high officials, headed by the grain tribute commissioner, Wei Yuanyu, to come up with a speedy resolution to the crisis, but their deliberations were inconclusive and none had the temerity to suggest moving to the sea route. Reportedly Daoguang himself, normally something of an indecisive ruler, had come to the conclusion that adopting the sea route was unavoidable, at least as a temporary expedient, but was wary of the use of commercial vessels for this purpose. The decisive argument came in the form of a memorial from the Board of Revenue president, Yinghe (1771–1839, *jinshi* 1793), a Manchu whose career had been made by his father's principled opposition to Heshen and by his own successful suppression of the Eight Trigrams rebellion of 1813, but who would be alternately in and out of imperial favor under both Jiaqing and Daoguang.[18]

17. Zhang Yan, "Bao Shichen," 137.

18. Wei Yuan, "Haiyun ji" (Record of sea route grain tribute shipments), *Huangchao jingshi wenbian*, 48:72–75; Zhang Yan, "Bao Shichen," 141. On Yinghe, see his biography in Hummel, *Eminent Chinese*, 931–33.

It is hard to assess the degree to which Bao Shichen's influence lay behind Yinghe's memorial, but it was likely considerable. Bao himself claimed that the memorial was mostly based on his own earlier ideas.[19] The historian Zhang Yan writes that Yinghe's text was based on consultations with the newly arrived Jiangsu governor Tao Zhu, the Jiangsu provincial treasurer He Changling, and the reformist writer Wei Yuan, but that all three men had themselves been influenced by Bao; he also notes that Bao and Yinghe had known each other for several years, from a time when both had been living at Yangzhou. In subsequent years, Bao was employed by and in regular correspondence with Tao Zhu, and interacted frequently with He and Wei, but I have found no solid evidence that Bao had personally met any of them prior to 1825. He Changling and Wei Yuan included Bao's 1803 call for implementing the sea route, "Haiyun nancao yi," in their *Statecraft Compendium* of 1826, but, interestingly, none of his subsequent writings on the subject. Even more oddly, Bao is not mentioned in either of Wei's own summaries of the affair which *are* included in the *Compendium*—was this an indication of personal rivalry? Still, it seems fair to assume that Bao's 1803 text had circulated widely for decades prior to the *Statecraft Compendium*'s publication, that it had attracted growing appeal, and that Yinghe had been aware of its general contents prior to submitting his memorial.

Citing the Song Neo-Confucian culture hero Cheng Hao, Yinghe began by arguing that the current crisis called for bold solutions: the way of governance (*zhidao*) dictates that major benefits (*dayi*) can be attained only if we are to willing to undertake major changes (*dabian*). After offering advice on what to do with the few boats and cargoes that have made it through the impasse and those that are currently beached, Yinghe offers his major changes. Boats that have not yet made it to the point of obstruction on the Grand Canal should back up and their cargoes be transferred to different vessels for maritime shipment. In the following year, they should *temporarily* abandon canal shipment altogether. A portion of the tribute should be commuted and the monies used to undertake major repairs on the canal and the river systems. That portion still collected in kind—one and a half million *dan*—should be shipped by the sea route via Shanghai, using hired commercial vessels for this purpose.

19. Bao, preface to *Zhongqu yishuo*, in *Quanji* (1993), 3–7.

Any resulting shortfalls in grain in the capital region can be made up by purchases on the local market, which is sufficiently developed for such purpose. The Daoguang emperor endorsed Yinghe's memorial with a simple order for compliance (*xunshi*).[20] This set in motion a new series of bureaucratic transfers, on-site investigations, and court discussions, all preparatory to implementing reform.[21]

Meanwhile, in the eleventh month of Daoguang 4, Bao Shichen himself was invited by the Jiangsu provincial treasurer, surnamed Cheng, to accompany him on an inspection tour of the affected Grand Canal and Yangzi delta area; Cheng was convinced that a shift to the sea route was desirable, but was either unwilling or unable to convince his superiors to make the shift. The following month an old acquaintance visited Bao at Yangzhou, and they discussed the crisis. This was Qi Yanhuai, whom Bao describes as his *tongnian* (that is fellow graduate, presumably of the provincial degree), who had previously served as magistrate of Jingui county (today's Wuxi), and currently served as a board secretary in Beijing. Following his discussions with Bao, Qi submitted a report up the chain of command recommending shift to the sea route. This report seems to have reached the court, and received imperial approval, but little was done in practical terms.[22] In the second month of the following year (1825), an edict ordered investigation of the availability at Shanghai of potential tribute carrying boats; despite the arrival in the delta area of an army of clerks tasked with the investigation, and the issuance of a second edict in the fourth month, little effectively was done to implement the new system.

20. Yinghe, "Chou caoyun biantong quanju shu" (Memorial advocating thorough changes in grain tribute transport), in *Huangchao jingshi wenbian*, 48:37–44.

21. For a summary of edicts and memorials in 1825, in the wake of Yinghe's proposals, see Ni Yuping, *Jia Dao caizheng*, 249–56. For a detailed series of maps on the affected areas of the Grand Canal, see Leonard, *Controlling from Afar*.

22. Qi Yanhuai, "Haiyun nancao yi" (Discussion of the sea route for grain tribute shipments), in *Huangchao jingshi wenbian*, 48:33–34. See also Bao Shichen, "Shang Ying xiangguo shu" (Letter to Grand Secretary Yinghe), in *Quanji* (1993), 101–3; *Nianpu* 231; Zhang Yan, "Bao Shichen," 145. On the basis of Qi's report, the early twentieth-century historian Meng Sen credited him, not Bao, with having been the originator of the sea route plan. Zhang Yan refutes this (p. 145), noting that Qi's report simply replicates Bao Shichen's identically titled 1803 essay.

In the fifth month, a friend visited Bao and showed him a copy of Yinghe's memorial, and on the 18th of that month Bao wrote to Yinghe congratulating him on his perceptive reading of the situation; he noted the irony that despite the fact that so many so close to the scene had recommended the sea route for years, in the end it was only Yinghe, writing from so many miles distant from the area, who had been able to come up with an effective solution and gain imperial approval.[23] Even so, he noted, there had been foot-dragging and endless bickering on the part of those in charge (*dangshi*). Whereas most scholarship on the sea route debates identifies organized resistance on the part of an entrenched Grand Canal bureaucracy and workforce as the chief roadblock to a shift to maritime transport, Bao himself identifies to Yinghe another source: clerks and lower officials in the Maritime Customs (Haiguan) at Shanghai. These vermin, he says, have been pocketing 20–30 percent of all customs duties on southbound shipments of bean-cake fertilizer from Manchuria, and they fear that utilization of these boats for grain tribute shipments on their return voyage will expose the racket. Bao goes on to sketch his proposed system of regulation for the sea route fleets, the details of which he has been working on assiduously at the time.

In the sixth month of Daoguang 5 (1825), Bao produced a set of ten highly detailed proposals for implementation of maritime transport of the grain tribute ("Haiyun shiyi"), presenting them to newly installed Jiangsu governor Tao Zhu in anticipation of that year's shipments.[24] Since winds at this time of year are inconstant, he says, if we expect grain to arrive at the northern ports by early in the ninth month, we should send it north as soon as possible.

The core of Bao's proposals is a detailed organizational analysis of maritime commerce at Shanghai. There are, he reports, eleven fleets/guilds (*bang*) of boats at the port, each named after the native place of their propritors (*dahu*), the three largest of which are the Chongming, Tongzhou, and Haimen bang. These fleets average between thirty and fifty boats apiece. Within each fleet there is also a headman (*lingshou*), who negotiates the interests of the boatmen with the proprietor. There are also

23. Bao, "Shang Ying xiangguo shu," in *Quanji* (1993), 101–3.

24. Bao Shichen, "Haiyun shiyi," in *Quanji* (1993), 81–85. See also Duan Zhao, *Tao Zhu*, chap. 6.

smaller independent boatmen who compete for small shipments not claimed by the larger bang. Usually, they will attach themselves to a single large bang and its proprietor to serve as their guarantor.

Details of paying customs duties, arranging pier services, and hiring on casual boatmen are entrusted by the bang proprietors to one of eight "cargo management firms" (*baodai hang*). Bao expresses his opinion, however, that since tribute grain is a nondutiable good, we can cut these middlemen out of the process in our tribute shipments for this year, and deal with the fleet proprietors directly.

Bao goes on to give more detail: There is a guildhall (*huiguan*) at Shanghai to which all boat proprietors and independent boatmen belong. Nominally, the heads of all bang meet together regularly to discuss conditions and deliberate policy for the trade, but in recent years, they have less often met as a body. Policy is now effectively made by personal negotiations among the three leading bang proprietors, acting on the advice of the guilds professional manager (*dongshi*), whose authority has correspondingly also grown over time. The flow of authority in the entire trade is thus channeled through the guild. For example, each boat has its own distinctive floral painting, and these markings are registered with the guild and reported to the local administration. When a boat first arrives at Shanghai, it must register with the guild manager who has it inspected for seaworthiness and its owner investigated for financial solvency.

This existing centralized structure of authority, Bao suggests, will serve well in arranging grain tribute shipments. The guild manager can attest to the reliability of each boat employed for this purpose. The boat headmen will be issued letters of commission by him, which they will surrender for inspection when the boat and its cargo reach Tianjin. The Shanghai guild manager and the boat headmen together can confer with officials to establish a per unit schedule of payment for tribute grain to be carried. Since there is also an existing private trade of southern trade north, it can be assumed that northbound ships will want to continue to carry some private rice along with their contracted government grain, and the proportion of each will be determined by the managers of the trade. The cargo to be carried on each boat's return trip south, notably but not exclusively bean-cake fertilizer from Manchuria, may be determined together by the guild manager and the relevant cargo management firm.

Bao goes on to address other details of maritime shipment, including financial responsibility for losses of government grain at sea (some combination of individual boatowner and collective guild liability), supplementary pickups of tribute grain at ports enroute in counties that have their own modest tribute assessment, and so on.

Bao concedes that there will be practical problems to be worked out, and that it will take a few cycles of grain shipment before the system can operate with complete smoothness. The important thing is for the government not to swamp the boats with regulations and with invasions of regulatory clerks, and to maintain their goodwill, by convincing them that grain tribute shipment is as profitable a business for them as private commerce. One thing to be alert to is the historical tendency for the larger bang to grow at the expense of the smaller ones, those with five boats or fewer, and to push them out of the trade. Government will want to nurture the smaller bang as well as the larger ones, and to demonstrate that there is profit to be made from grain tribute shipment for them as well.

Bao notes that the court's first two efforts to implement the sea route for 1825, in the second and the fourth month of that year, both came to nothing for the same reason: they involved sending in an army of lower officials and clerks that spooked and effectively paralyzed the maritime trade infrastructure. His program will feature a much reduced hand of the state, and greater reliance on established patterns of authority within the merchant community itself. It would be a mistake, however, to see Bao's program as laissez-faire liberalism. For example, he mandated that southbound cargoes on grain boats be regulated by licensing on an annual basis, and argued for the promulgation of regulations for this trade on the model of those already governing the Taiwan rice trade. He demanded that the Shanghai guild maintain detailed records of payments to each boat under its jurisdiction, and that these ledgers be submitted for regular inspection by local officials. And he stipulated that stops by tribute-bearing boats at coastal ports en route to the north be in accord with a schedule promulgated in advance by officials, "to avoid confusion and corruption." In other words, Bao still recognizes the responsibility of the state, in concert with the private leadership of the trade, to maintain an orderly market.

Moreover, he remains centrally concerned with the security of state revenues. The shift to the sea route itself is of course a means to protect, not abandon, the grain tribute system. And in Bao's proposed regulations he points out that tribute-bearing boats will likely continue to carry a much greater percentage of their cargoes in the form of private freights. He agrees that this is appropriate, but also sets down procedures for this cargo to be inspected for collection of customs duties at Shanghai and Tianjin.

In his first publication of his "Ten Proposals" more than two decades later, in 1848, Bao proudly adds a note that incoming governor Tao Zhu accepted virtually all of them and used them as a blueprint for his reforms. The reforms, he adds, were totally successful, with the recipient areas receiving all the southern grain due to them, at the same time that great profits accrued to the shipping merchants and boatmen.[25]

As Bao Shichen had predicted, shipment of tribute grain via the sea route itself went quite smoothly.[26] And yet, the grain tribute system remained a critical and worsening problem over the second quarter of the nineteenth century, for a variety of reasons extraneous to those Bao had addressed. First was social unrest on the part of petty officials and canal boatmen increasingly deprived of their income by the shift to coastal shipment. Incidents of collective resistance by these men became ever more serious over time, merging with grievances over other issues, and climaxing in an internationally reported attack by tribute boatmen on three English missionaries at Qingpu, Songjiang, in 1848.[27] Second, despite the understanding in the 1820s that shipment by sea would be only a temporary expedient while the Grand Canal and its surrounding hydraulic infrastructure was systematically repaired, the canal continued to deteriorate. In 1853, rendered the *coup de grâce* by its severance by Taiping armies, the millennium-old canal was abandoned once and for all as a means of tribute grain transport.[28]

The third set of problems involved that portion of tribute dues which, in accordance with Yinghe's plan, was commuted to cash payment. Over

25. Bao, *Quanji* (1993), 85.

26. Ni Yuping, however, argues that historians have been perhaps oversold on the success of the experiment by the effusive reports of Wei Yuan, He Changling, Tao Zhu, and others of the program's sponsors; the overhead costs of the 1826 shipment, for example, may have been considerably higher than recognized by anyone involved.

27. Hoshi, *Dai unga*, 233–36.

28. Hinton, *Grain Tribute System*, 28; Jones and Kuhn, "Dynastic Decline," 122.

the course of the Daoguang reign the silver-to-copper monetary exchange rate had grown ever farther from the prescribed par of one tael silver=one thousand copper cash, and manipulation of this spread on the part of tribute collectors had resulted in an increasingly crushing burden on agrarian taxpayers—especially the poor, who were less able than their wealthy neighbors to negotiate a favorable rate for their payments. By the 1850s, popular anger at the burden of grain tribute collections contributed to the success of Taiping recruitment among the poor of the lower Yangzi valley. Despite the unpopularity of commutation, however, the administration's inability to carry out tribute shipments *either* by canal or by sea under the chaos of the Taiping campaigns gave it no choice but to commute to cash the entirety of tribute grain levies beginning in 1857–58.[29]

Historicizing Grain Tribute Reform

Writing in 1826, just a year after the first seaborne shipment, Wei Yuan made an effusive claim for the revolutionary nature of what had just occurred. For him, "nothing like it has ever been seen in the past" (*qiangu weiyou yu shi*). Shipment by sea instead of inland waterways, using private merchants instead of bureaucrats (*yihai daihe, yishang daiguan*), was a complete success on every level: it had benefited both state and society, merchant and official, canal and tribute shipments (*guobian minbian shangbian guanbian hebian caobian*). For Wei, use of the sea route was less an expedient adopted in time of crisis than a long-sought opening to a whole new world, a liberation that had not been possible in the past, but only in the world of today (*jinri*). It could only be achieved when human capacity had developed to be sufficient for its adoption (*zhishun*). Chinese rulers had long wished to utilize the sea, but had created imaginary impediments against doing so; Wei Yuan quotes Laozi: "The Way is direct and straightforward, and yet people insist on taking byways instead" (*Dadao shen yi, er min hao jing*). This shift, however, represented a milestone

29. Xia Nai, "Taiping tianguo qian hou Changjiang gesheng zhi tianfu wenti," 419–25; William T. Rowe, "Hu Lin-i's Reform of the Grain Tribute System in Hupeh, 1855–58," *Ch'ing-shih wen-t'i* 4.10 (December 1983): 33–86.

in human progress, a moment in cosmic time when such barriers could be overcome (*cheng tianshi renshi*).[30]

By contrast to Wei's remarkable paean to human progress, Bao Shichen is relatively modest in what he claims for the significance of the sea route. Much as he pleads for its feasibility, he never describes its adoption as historically liberating—the fact is, he notes, it is already in heavy use by the private sector. Part of this difference may be a function of the two men's age. Bao was fifty-one in 1825, while Wei was twenty years younger, and the Bao of twenty years earlier was clearly more idealistic than he was in his later years. Part may stem from the difference in the two men's educational background. As we have seen, Wei Yuan, like Gong Zizhen, came out of a subset of statecraft thought that derived from study of such new text classics as the Gongyang commentary which heavily emphasized temporal relativism and a classically ordained need for continuous progressive reform, whereas Bao was a largely self-taught technocrat who simply wanted to fix things.[31] In this sense, Wei seems more of a "modern" man than does Bao.

The mature Bao Shichen, while often bold in his policy innovations, was arguably the most centrist and representative reformer of his era. He was, as several scholars have described him, an "accomodationist,"[32] who sought neither fundamental political change, nor economic restructuring, nor changes in the land or property regime. Unlike Hong Liangji, he was optimistic about the empire's evident demographic growth, and the expansionist capacity of agrarian productivity to meet food supply needs. He believed that agriculture was the basis of the economy, and that it should be both promoted and improved by government intervention (no laissez-faire here). At the same time he was fully comfortable, indeed

30. Wei Yuan, "Haiyun quan'an xu" (Preface to a complete account of the sea route shipment), in *Huangchao jingshi wenbian*, 48:70–71.

31. Duan Zhao, *Tao Zhu yu Jia-Dao jingshi sixiang yanjiu*, 122. As we saw in chapter 1, both Wei and Bao were influenced by the Changzhou school, epitomized by Li Zhaoluo and Liu Fenglu. Both Li and Liu had reformist bents, but Liu was a proselytizer of the Gongyang commentary, which posited cosmological grounds for change, whereas Li was more empirical, favoring study of history and geography. Wei Yuan was an avowed disciple of Liu Fenglu and the Gongyang school, while Bao, though exposed to Liu's ideas, was much closer to Li Zhaoluo and his empiricist teachings.

32. Hu Qizhuang, *Zhongguo jingji sixiang shi*, 585; Lin, *China Upside Down*.

enthusiastic, about most forms of commercialization and monetization: "The roots (agricultural produce) and the branches (commodities and currency) are equally forms of wealth" (*benmo xifu*). And he consistently sought to *use* the market and private commercial entrepreneurship for state and societal purposes; he was not, in other words, a knee-jerk antistatist. But in order to use merchants effectively, he insisted, policy must be solicitous about their need for profits. In this, as Liu Guangjing pointed out, he anticipated the much more thoroughgoing government reliance on merchants in the later nineteenth century.[33]

While not seeking basic systemic change, Bao was deeply aware of pervasive dysfunctions in the existing political and economic system, and devoted his public career to rooting them out. His approach was formed during his service in the White Lotus wars, a debacle he saw as clearly attributable to exploitation of the local population, and excessive grasping on the part of a revenue-starved state. That experience had taught him that the basic concerns of policy must be twofold: popular well-being (*minsheng*) and state finances (*guoji*). At the present time, both are under threat: the *minsheng* are being expropriated (*zuixiao*) while the *guoji* are becoming daily more insolvent (*rixu*). As I will discuss more fully in chapter 7, Bao's candid goal is to pursue "profit" (*yanli*) for both—again, he is no antistatist—by removing dysfunctions of "engorgement at the middle level" (*zhongbao*) on the part of traitorous people (*jianmin*), who impose unnecessary costs or unfairly pass along financial burdens to their neighbors. (*Zhongbao* would, of course, become a standard bogeyman for reformers of the next generation, such as Hu Linyi.)

While vocal and influential in a wide range of policy areas, it was the grain tribute that Bao consistently saw as the major plague affecting his region of chief concern, the lower Yangzi. He noted, for example, that evident differences in prosperity between even neighboring counties could be attributed to differences in the manner of their tribute assessment, and also that collection of a tax in grain unduly burdened agricultural areas that had, in the interests of efficient production, shifted to cultivation of nongrain commercial crops.

Bao's sympathies, as we have seen, were primarily—though not exclusively—agrarian. His personal interests no doubt lay with the agrarian

33. Liu, "Bao Shichen yu Wei Yuan."

elite, but the cause he championed was that of all farmers, not simply of the so-called landlord class alone. As early as 1808 he took notice of the buildup of broad-based popular grievances (*zhongshu*) against grain tribute exactions, and increasingly warned of the likelihood of large-scale "rebellion in the southeast" (*dongnan zhi hui*), an implicit counterpart to the White Lotus uprisings in the northwest. And he was clear-sighted enough to point out that local "great households" (*dahu*), through proxy remittances and other means, routinely passed along the most excessive burdens of the grain tribute to their poorer neighbors (*xiaomin*).[34] The "accomodationist" Bao was by no means a friend of popular insurrection—in the northwest he had contributed significantly to its violent suppression—but he could understand, and even perhaps empathize with, its motivations.

34. Ōtani, "Hō Seishin no jitsugaku shisō ni tsuite," 178.

CHAPTER 5

Salt

The subject of this chapter, Bao Shichen's role in the nineteenth-century reform of the Qing salt monopoly, invites us to foray a bit "beyond binary histories"—specifically those of Western progress versus Asian stagnation, or Western challenge and Asian response—and focus momentarily instead on the common features among polities at either end of the great Eurasian land mass in the early modern period. As the historian of France James Collins puts it, "Between the fifteenth and the eighteenth centuries, Western European political units shared with political units elsewhere in Eurasia both underlying structural factors—population trends, bullion influx, an increasingly integrated world economy—and challenges, above all the rising costs of military activity." At one level of generality, the responses of these polities, east and west, also shared certain features, among them "greater territorial integration, . . . stepped-up efforts to establish cultural hegemony in given territorial units, [and] higher levels of taxation."[1]

There seem to have been at least two distinctive forms of this administrative reaction to the conditions of early modernity. A common response

1. James B. Collins, "State Building in Early-Modern Europe: The Case of France," in *Beyond Binary Histories: Re-imagining Eurasia to c. 1830*, ed. Victor Lieberman (Ann Arbor: University of Michigan Press, 1997), 159. See also the similar analysis in John F. Richards, "Early Modern India and World History," *Journal of World History* 8.2 (1997): 197–209.

in Western Europe was the rise of what has been called the "fiscal-military state," described by Michael Kwass as "an awesome beast that could tax and borrow on an unprecedented scale to field mighty armies on the continent or deploy blue-water navies around the world."[2] Historians of the Qing have occasionally sought to find a comparable fiscal-military state there as well, but not, to my mind, fully convincingly. What did seem to characterize much of Eurasia outside of Western Europe was the rise of a new form of early modern, land-based, multinational empire, exemplified by Muscovy, the Ottomans, the Moghuls, and the Qing. The last of these, as envisioned by Evelyn Rawski and others, shared more with other Eurasian empires than it did with the Ming or other predecessor empires on the Chinese subcontinent: a capacity to administer (more or less directly) territory of vast scale and populations of great diversity, enabled in part by new administrative technologies such as the Eight Banners (*baqi*), the Grand Council (*junjichu*), and the palace memorial system (*zouzhe*), and financial mechanisms like the Imperial Household Department (*neiwufu*).[3] Both of these new political forms demanded enhanced fiscal extractive capabilities, and, especially in France and in the Qing, these prominently included taxes not on persons or on real property but rather on consumer goods.

Kwass demonstrates how the "consumer revolution" of the eighteenth century—a product of empire and globalization but, significantly, *not* of industrialization—was met with dramatic extractive interventions on the part of the French state. Chief among the commodities affected were New World tobacco, on which the state declared a monopoly in 1674, which it contracted out to a private company, the so-called General Farm, and South Asian calico, on which out of protectionist concerns it declared an import prohibition in 1686, later replaced by a steep tariff, enforced by the same "Farm." Together, these state initiatives spawned "a spectacular

2. Michael Kwass, *Contraband: Louis Mandrin and the Making of a Global Underground* (Cambridge, MA: Harvard University Press, 2014), 41–42. The classic articulation of the "fiscal-military state" thesis is John Brewer, *The Sinews of Power: War, Money, and the English State, 1688–1783* (Cambridge, MA: Harvard University Press, 1988).

3. Evelyn S. Rawski, "The Qing Formation and the Early Modern Period," in *The Qing Formation in World-Historical Time*, ed. Lynn A. Struve (Cambridge, MA: Harvard University Asia Center, 2004), 207–41.

growth of illicit markets," a shadow economy that Kwass terms "the dark side of globalization."[4]

In the Qing empire, neither tobacco nor cotton cloth were subject to similar state monopolization or protectionism. Imports of South Asian cotton cloth by the British East India Company and other Western traders were fully legal, and modestly taxed, but—Bao Shichen's own concerns notwithstanding (see chapter 7)—in the view of most did not present a serious challenge to the thriving domestic handicraft cloth industry.[5] New World tobacco was introduced as part of the Columbian exchange in the late sixteenth century, but a process of import substitution markedly more successful than that in Europe made tobacco largely a domestic product by the mid-Qing. Numerous literati reformers—not least, as we saw in chapter 3, Bao Shichen—railed about the waste of land and money that tobacco represented, and called for its prohibition, but to no great effect.[6]

The closest Qing counterpart to imports of New World tobacco and South Asian calico in France was arguably South Asian opium. Elsewhere in this volume we see how Bao Shichen inveighed against the drug's import, for fiscal as well as other reasons, and sought sometimes quixotic means to delimit its importation. Because of its multiple debilitating effects, however, opium was something of a special case, and need not concern us in the present context.

The most exact parallel between early modern France and Qing was in fact salt—in both polities almost completely a domestic product, understood not as a luxury good but as a necessity of life, and production and distribution of which was a declared government monopoly. Salt in France had been taxed as early as the fourteenth century, but the first salt "gabelle" was established in 1547; characterized by Kwass as "the most loathed tax in French history," it was the stimulus to persistent popular resistance in the seventeenth century and beyond. Significantly, the salt

4. Kwass, *Contraband*, 9.

5. Peng Zeyi, "Qingdai qianqi shougongye de fazhan" (The development of handicrafts in the early Qing), *Zhongguo shi yanjiu* 1981.1: 43–60.

6. Declarations of a tobacco monopoly by Chinese governments, both in Taiwan and on the mainland, came only in the mid-twentieth century. See Carol Benedict, *Golden-Silk Smoke: A History of Tobacco in China, 1550–2010* (Berkeley: University of California Press, 2011).

gabelle was abolished as one of the first acts of the revolutionary regime in March of 1790, but for much of the preceding century Enlightenment intellectuals had spiritedly attacked the institution. They did so on a number of grounds, but one of the most far-reaching, and ultimately persuasive, was the argument for "free trade" or "economic liberalism."[7]

It is very tempting to see the increasingly strident literati attacks on the Qing salt administration as reflecting the same liberal attitudes, and some scholars have done just that.[8] As this chapter suggests, however, I believe the matter to be somewhat more complex. Above all, even the most perceptive and radical critics of the salt monopoly in the early nineteenth-century Qing empire understood that empire to be under threat both internally and externally, and under such conditions they could not afford to be straightforward antistatist liberals.

Calls for Reform

Along with the grain tribute administration and the Yellow River Conservancy Superintendency, the salt administration comprised one of the three great functionally specialized bureaucracies (*sandazheng*) of the Qing empire. Salt production and distribution had been declared an imperial monopoly in the second century BCE by Emperor Han Wudi; the state salt administration had been restored and reconfigured in the Tang and Song by the economic planners Liu Yan and Wang Anshi, and given its basic late-imperial form under the early Ming. By the middle of the eighteenth century, when it was operating at what most considered peak effectiveness, it provided state revenues at close to 9 million ounces of silver per year. By Yeh-chien Wang's well-informed estimates, this comprised 11.8 percent of all state revenues, ranking behind only grain taxes as a fiscal source.[9] The salt administration was a hybrid state-merchant enterprise, and modern students have differed on its role in China's economic and political development: Ping-ti Ho described it as an outstanding

7. Kwass, *Contraband*, esp. 287–88.

8. Man-houng Lin, "Two Social Theories Revealed" and *China Upside Down*.

9. Yeh-chien Wang, *Land Taxation in Imperial China, 1750–1911* (Cambridge, MA: Harvard University Press, 1973), 72. Wang's figures are for the year 1753.

early example of "commercial capitalism," whereas probably the system's greatest scholar, Saeki Tomi, saw it instead as the epitome of Qing imperial "absolutism" (Japanese: *zettai kunshu*)—analogous to the early modern European model of a throne-merchant alliance in opposition to the feudal landed classes.[10]

Even throughout the "prosperous age" of the eighteenth century, salt smuggling had been active, and a locus of popular resistance, at times violent. In 1718, for example, a racketeer named Big Pockmarked Yu (Yu Damazi) "openly set up shops" (*gongran kaidian*) in towns of Shandong to trade in contraband salt, intimidating the local population (who nevertheless eagerly patronized his wares) and administrators alike. In 1736 a salt superintendent reported that the price of salt in Yangzi delta cities, which had recently spiked due to flood-induced disruptions in the transport network, had now stabilized due largely to the opportunistic influx of the smuggled product; welcome as this price relief was, he felt it his duty to combat the smugglers.[11]

But, along with the other two specialized bureaucracies, the salt administration was broadly recognized, inside and outside of government, to have become critically distressed by the early nineteenth century. There was a manifest decline in sales of official salt and a corresponding loss—in this age of mounting internal and external threat—of desperately needed state revenues. Observers agreed that the reason was the loss of the market to private, smuggled salt—the Qing's own "shadow economy." Government salt had effectively priced itself out of the market due to corruption and inefficiency in the salt administration, a legacy in part of the Heshen years but also due to more basic structural failings in the system's

10. Ping-ti Ho, "The Salt Merchants of Yang-chou: A Study of Commercial Capitalism in Eighteenth-Century China," *Harvard Journal of Asiatic Studies* 17 (1954): 130–68; Saeki Tomi, "Chūgoku kinsei ni okeru zettai kunshu no keizai sei" (Absolutism in modern China), in *Chūgoku shi kenkyū* (Studies in Chinese history) (Kyoto: Tōyōshi kenkyūkai, 1971), 2.61–74.

11. Chinese People's University Institute of Qing History and Archives Department, comps., *Kang-Yong-Qian shiqi chengxiang renmin fankang douzheng ziliao* (Resistance struggles of urban and rural people in the mid-Qing) (Beijing: Zhonghua shuju, 1979), 2.555–58. For the contribution of salt smuggling, suppression, and armed resistance to twentieth-century revolutionary movements, see Ralph A. Thaxton, Jr., *Salt of the Earth: The Political Origins of Peasant Protest and Communist Revolution in China* (Berkeley: University of California Press, 1997).

design. As Susan Mann Jones and Philip Kuhn have argued, by comparison with the grain tribute administration, the salt administration was politically easier to fix: the thousands of persons who would suffer financially from reform were private smugglers, not—as with grain tribute boatmen—government employees, and there was also an influential state agency, the Imperial Household Department that stood to profit substantially from the salt administration's improved performance. Plus, salt smuggling was demonstrably linked to sectarian and other social disorders that continued to threaten the regime in the wake of the White Lotus and Miao rebellions. Thus the normally indecisive Daoguang emperor had far less reluctance to sign off on basic overhaul of salt versus grain tribute matters.[12]

Amid a chorus of reform proposals, many of which were published by Wei Yuan and He Changling in their 1826 *Huangchao jingshi wenbian* (Collected writings on statecraft from the present dynasty),[13] the Liang-Jiang governor general Tao Zhu in 1832–33 undertook a fundamental reform of operations in the Liang-Huai salt district (map 2), of which he was collaterally commissioner. "Liang-Huai" was the most lucrative of the several geographic districts into which the imperial salt administration was divided. It was tasked with distributing the rich product of the salt fields in the Yangzhou hinterlands throughout two subdistricts: "Huainan," encompassing portions of northern Jiangsu and most of Jiangxi, Hubei, and Hunan, and "Huaibei," covering most of Anhui and Henan. Distribution of Liang-Huai salt from the production to the consumption areas was the job of some two hundred official-merchants, each of whom held one or several hereditary licenses known as *gang*. Each *gang* specified the amount of salt the holder might purchase at the saltyard, the consumption areas in which he held the exclusive right to sell it, and also the route and entrepôt via which his salt was to be transported. At each designated entrepôt (*kou'an*) through which the salt passed—Nanchang and Hankou being the largest of these—the salt would be taxed and repackaged into smaller lots, adding additional "superfluous expenses" (*foufei*) and raising the ultimate price to the consumer. Each

12. Jones and Kuhn, "Dynastic Decline," 125–26, 140.
13. *Huangchao jingshi wenbian*, *juan* 49–50.

MAP 2. Map of the Liang-Huai salt districts.

gang licensed its holder to distribute a very large amount of salt—as many as 12,000 *yin*, each *yin* weighing something under a thousand pounds.[14]

In order to resolve the problem of the noncompetitive price of government versus smuggled salt, Tao Zhu first considered the strategy of limiting all salt taxes to a single imposition levied at the original point of merchant purchase at the saltyard; he eventually rejected this approach

14. According to the *Matthews' Chinese-English Dictionary* (Cambridge, MA: Harvard University Press, 1954), a *yin* of salt weighed 6.75 piculs (*dan*), and each *dan* was the equivalent of 133.3 pounds. By this standard, a *yin* would weigh approximately 890.78 pounds.

as unworkable due to the dispersed nature of the salt production areas themselves. He focused instead on reducing as much as possible the "superfluous expenses" accrued in transit. Tao's remedy for this was a dramatic abolition of the centuries-old *gang* system. This involved: (1) throwing open the occupation of marketing government salt beyond the hereditarily enfranchised few to any enterprising merchant who could obtain a certificate of authorization (*huzhao*) from his home county magistrate (the merchant's home county being the presumed, though apparently not necessarily sole, target market for his salt); (2) allowing these licensed though nonofficial merchants to purchase "tickets" (*piao*) to receive far smaller job lots of salt (as few as ten *yin* vs. the average of 12,000 *yin* under the old system); and (3) relaxing many of the restrictions on transport routes, to allow more flexible and cost-efficient shipping. According to one of the reform's students, Thomas Metzger, Tao's 1832–33 reforms "quickly and fully" revived both the sales of, and tax revenues from, Liang-Huai salt.

Bao Shichen and Liang-Huai Salt Reform

What was Bao Shichen's involvement in this reformist project? Classic accounts of the reform connect him to it only indirectly, if at all—as with studies of the grain tribute reform, studies based on official court correspondence can miss his presence completely. In both his pioneering 1955 article on Tao's reforms, and his 1956 monograph on the Qing salt administration, Saeki Tomi left Bao out of the story altogether, as does a recent detailed study of the reforms by Ni Yuping. Metzger in 1962, citing the entry on Tao Zhu in *Eminent Chinese of the Ch'ing Period* (1943), acknowledged Bao's general contribution to Tao's understanding of the problems in the Liang-Huai administration, but identified no specific influence on reform policies.[15] More recently, however, Tao's biographer,

15. Saeki Tomi, "Shindai Dōkō cho ni okeru Kainan ensei no kaikaku" (The reform of the Huainan salt administration during the Qing Daoguang reign), in *Chūgoku shi kenkyū*, 2.621–66; Saeki Tomi, *Shindai ensei no kenkyū* (A study of the Qing salt administration) (Kyoto: Tōyōshi kenkyūkai, 1956); Ni Yuping, *Jia Dao caizheng*, 276–311; Metzger, "T'ao Chu's Reform of the Huaipei Salt Monopoly (1831–1833)," *Papers on China* 16 (1962): 1–39. For follow-up reforms affecting the Huainan portion of the

Duan Zhao, has been able to trace point by point how his protagonist was closely adhering to Bao's advice.[16] My own reading of Bao's essays and correspondence supports this view of his direct involvement in the reform efforts.

Throughout his life, the dysfunctions of the salt administration, as well as its near unique potential for rescuing the empire from its then multifaceted crisis, was one of Bao Shichen's central concerns. In his 1801 treatise *On Wealth*, salt revenues were the cash cow upon which he financed a totally revamped system of government finance. With the disastrous White Lotus rebellion still under way (Bao himself had only recently returned from several years at the front), he sought remedies for the twin evils that he believed had driven the rebellion: official venality and a crushing popular tax burden. As we saw in chapter 2, he laid out plans simultaneously (1) to raise official and subofficial salaries from the anachronistically low levels that had, in his view, left such functionaries no choice but to exploit the people, (2) to raise operational budgets (*gongfei*) throughout the administration to needed levels, and at the same time (3) to undertake a major empire-wide reduction in the land tax and grain tribute levies. Bao acknowledged that his reforms would be tremendously costly, and so proposed corresponding cost savings and new revenues from other sources. Among the latter was a historically prescient tax on commercial capital. Chief among the former was a thorough purge of salt administration functionaries (*yanchai*), for a projected annual savings of 4,600,000 taels.[17]

Elsewhere in *On Wealth* Bao undertakes an analysis of the crisis in the Liang-Huai administration and offers a set of proposed solutions, both of which closely anticipate the debates surrounding Tao Zhu's reforms of more than three decades later.[18] He notes that the average price of government salt to the consumer at present is approximately twenty copper cash per catty (*jin*), whereas that of smuggled salt is no more

---

Liang-Huai district, see William T. Rowe, *Hankow: Commerce and Society in a Chinese City, 1796–1889* (Stanford: Stanford University Press, 1984).

16. Duan Zhao, *Tao Zhu yu Jia-Dao jingshi sixiang yanjiu*, 178–84.

17. Bao, *Shuochu*, 182.

18. Bao, *Shuochu*, 184–85. Bao notes that his evidence is drawn from the Liang-Huai district, but that he understands similar conditions to pertain in other salt districts throughout the empire.

than three to four cash. Clearly, the profit margins for salt officials and government-franchised merchants must be "unspeakably exploitative" (*yuanku ke sheng yan*) on the people. Moreover the inflated cost of government salt has empowered a class of racketeers (*yantu*), he claims, strong and daring tough guys who scoff at death, so quick and deft in their movements that officials are helpless to intercept them; they do great harm to both the state and local society, and yet no one can stop them.

Bao proposes three steps, simple but dramatic, to rectify the situation. First, government salt should be taxed just one time, at the point of sale from the saltyard to the distributer. This, of course, is a proposal that Tao Zhu eventually dismissed as unworkable, and Bao must have considered the same objections, for in *On Wealth* he goes into considerable detail about how this strategy could be successfully implemented. Second, in anticipation of reforms that Tao did in fact adopt, he argues for total abolition of the district structure of the salt trade, and elimination of the bloated bureaucracy of salt officials at all levels, as well as police and soldiers assigned to enforce that structure. Salt should be allowed to be bought and sold and to circulate freely within the empire, just like other commodities such as grain and cooking oil. This would at one stroke eliminate the incentive to smugglers, reduce official harassment of private merchants, and eliminate the criminalization of common people who are currently forced to buy the more affordable smuggled salt. Third, Bao would eliminate the monopoly of the few government-franchised salt merchants and throw the trade open to the countless more smaller scale merchants who wish to enter the trade. If we legalize this, he argues, many of the individuals who presently operate as "traitorous" smugglers (*jianmin*) would transform themselves overnight into "good merchants" (*liangshang*) pursuing a lawful occupation.

Two of Bao's arguments on salt reform in *On Wealth* are especially interesting. The first of these is revealing because it displays Bao's seemingly precocious—and not wholly credible—affinity for quantification, as well as his optimism regarding the ease of restoring the empire's financial well-being, if only policy experts such as himself were heeded. He notes that the total Qing population was estimated by the throne in 1793 as some 700 million. Assuming that the population has declined 30 percent due to the recent warfare, he calculates, we are left with more than 500 million people.[19] If each person consumes roughly 0.1 *shi* of salt per year, empire-wide total consumption is more than 50 million *shi.* If the government taxes this salt at 25 percent in kind, it will take in some 12.5 million *shi.* And if each *shi* of salt is valued at 0.8 taels of silver, this works out to a total salt tax revenue of 10 million taels per year—that is, more than 8 times the revenue actually collected from salt today. What a remarkable payday, he implies, if those in authority only follow my advice!

Bao's second revealing argument is his consideration of a reform he understands to have recently been enacted in the Shanxi salt district. As in Bao's own proposals, the Shanxi reform declared salt a commodity like any other, free to circulate in private hands according to the dictates of the market. Salt taxes in Shanxi were eliminated altogether, and to compensate for lost government revenue a corresponding surtax was added to the land tax. Bao concedes that this is a seductively attractive solution: by reducing the cost of salt to the consumer by at least half without forfeiting government revenue, the reform would seem to benefit the people (*limin*) and state finances (*guoji*) simultaneously. But he rejects the model for two reasons. Folding the salt tax into the land tax (*ke tan dingdi*), having already folded the head tax into that on land (*dingyin gui tian*), would leave agrarian landowners bearing nearly the entire fiscal burden of the population, and potentially drive persons of substance and competence out of agriculture, precisely opposite to state aims.

Bao's second objection to the Shanxi model is yet more revealing of his priorities. The practical result of privatization of the salt trade in this northern district has been to encourage the import of "green salt" from Mongolia (Menggu *qingyan*) to serve the Shanxi market. He writes:

> Now, the financial resources of the interior [*neidi shengcai*] are fixed, while the salt production of Mongolia is limitless. The salt flows in while the wealth flows out [*yanru caichu*] at the rate of several million [taels?] per year. This puts China [Zhongguo] on a treacherous course: the progressive

19. As discussed in chapter 3, above, these figures for the Qing population would be judged by historical demographers today to be too high. Lee and Wang, *One Quarter of Humanity*, 27, put the empire's population in 1800 at roughly 350 million. A 30 percent population decline due to the White Lotus and other rebellions likewise seems greatly exaggerated.

> weakening and impoverishment of the interior [*pinruo neifu*] along with the strengthening and enrichment of the outer pale [*qiangfu waifan*].

Bao thus counsels the immediate prohibition of the import of Mongolian salt. What is striking in this 1801 passage is Bao's frank (anti-"liberal") protectionism, and his prescient protonationalism (the choice of "China" rather than "Qing" as the entity to be enriched and strengthened). His logic here would be echoed and expanded upon in his later analysis of the economic evils of opium imports and his strident rhetoric of resistance to British encroachment in the prelude to the Opium War.

Bao Revisits the Problem

Although we know that many important scholars and policy makers of the day had occasion to read Bao Shichen's *On Wealth* in manuscript over the early nineteenth century, we cannot be certain that it was read by Tao Zhu and that it therefore directly influenced his Liang-Huai reforms. This is not the case for an essay Bao wrote in 1820, his most comprehensive general statement of his program for salt administration overhaul. The essay was part of a series of five that Bao composed in that year, entitled "Random Notes from the Gengchen Year" ("Gengchen zazhu"), reflecting his thoughts on various problems of political economy.[20] Taking a different tack than he did with *On Wealth*, Bao opted to publish this essay, in 1825, in a collection entitled *Zhongqu yishao*.[21] If Tao Zhu did not read Bao's essay in this form, which he very likely did, he would certainly have seen it in the version republished the very next year by Wei Yuan and He Changling, in their comprehensive anthology *Collected Writings on Statecraft from the Present Dynasty* (*Huangchao jingshi wenbian*).[22]

20. Bao, "Gengchen zazhu, wu," in *Quanji* (1993), 68–71.

21. Bao discusses this publication in his preface to a supplement to *Zhongqu yishao*, available today in *Quanji* (1993), 8–10.

22. *Huangchao jingshi wenbian* 49:11–14. Bao's essay is here very little altered from the 1820 original, but it is assigned a new title "Huaiyan sance" (Three policy recommendations regarding Huai salt).

Bao's 1820 essay is an ambitious piece of political-economic analysis. He begins by observing that government figures from the early Kangxi reign put the consumer population of the six provinces comprising the Liang-Huai salt district at just over 2 million (presumably the unit is households). In the subsequent century and a half there has been steady population growth, he tells his readers, so that it can be safely assumed that the current population is over 3.5 million (households). Many analysts of the salt administration attribute its current smuggling problem primarily to the failure of official salt quotas to meet this growing consumer demand, Bao notes, but this, he counters, is greatly oversimplified. In fact, there is a large variety of types of smuggling going on simultaneously (he describes eleven of these), in most of which the official-merchants, not private smugglers, are the principal culprits. The size of each *yin* shipment authorized to be carried by official merchants is set by statute at 340 catties, but in fact this amount is expanded in practice to more than 500 catties. This, he comments, constitutes smuggling. So too is the distribution and sale by official merchants of additional salt, not registered under the *yin* system at all. Then there is the import of salt from other salt districts into consumer areas legally served only by the Liang-Huai administration: Shanxi salt into northwest Hubei, Sichuan salt into western Hubei, Guangdong and Fujian salt into southern Jiangxi, Zhejiang salt into Jiangsu, and so on. Supposedly empty boats returning southward on the Grand Canal from grain tribute shipments to the capital routinely carry salt from the Tianjin district for sale in Liang-Huai, Bao points out. Finally, he cites the percentage demanded as "merit salt" (*gongyan*), and resold for private profit, by government inspectors at the various stations along salt distribution routes.

Bao then proceeds to a detailed and seemingly well-informed analysis of the structure of smuggling organizations, and their geographic distribution. He applies this model to an inquiry into why so many formerly honest boatmen have been drawn into the illicit trade. In the past, he says, boats hired on for the official trade were authorized to carry between 1,000 and 3,000 *yin*, depending on their size, and made two to three runs bearing this cargo per year. The profits were good enough that there was no incentive to engage in smuggling. Today, however, runs have been legally restricted to two per year, and cargoes to between 300 and 800 *yin*. Moreover while the per *yin* wages for sailors have remained constant, the payoffs demanded by pier headmen have risen fourfold in recent years. Combined with other forms of official squeeze, this has reduced profit margins for boatmen so much that they have no choice but to engage in smuggling, either directly themselves, or in collusion with full-time smugglers. Ringleaders known as "tiger heads" (*laohu tou*) orchestrate the entire racket. With their authorized tax revenues steadily diminishing, Liang-Huai officials themselves have no choice but to impose ever more onerous illegal fees. Thus, Bao argues, overall the salt business in Liang-Huai is doing very well indeed; it is only the official monopoly that is stagnating.

Bao then proceeds to discuss and dismiss more piecemeal solutions previously proposed for the problem, before going on to propose his own fundamental restructuring of salt distribution in Liang-Huai. Bao's proposed reforms of 1820 look very much like those that Tao Zhu had actually implemented a dozen years later. Bao claims that he wants salt distribution to conform in general to systems currently used for iron and saltpeter; it will be, in effect, a regulated commodity but not a government monopoly. Bao would eliminate at a stroke the entire specialized bureaucracy of salt supervisors (*daxiao guanyan guanyi*), and no longer mandate specialized sites for merchant sales (*buli shangyuan*) nor segregated distribution routes (*bufen zhenyu*). Ordinary merchants (*shangfan*) will instead proceed to their own county magistrate (*bendi zhouxian*) and receive a certificate (*yinzhao*) authorizing them to buy a job lot of salt for sale in that county, paying the magistrate a processing fee (*zhizhu zhi fei*). At the saltyard, the merchant will purchase his entitlement of salt, and pay up front the government tax (*zhengke*). Bao acknowledges that this tax cannot be made entirely uniform, based on distance to the consumer area and other factors, but it will be assessed according to a standardized schedule. There will be no other fees, for repackaging, inspection, and so on, imposed en route.

The resulting benefits will be multifold, Bao says. The cost of salt to the consumer will be reduced by as much as 50 percent. As official salt thereby better competes with smuggled salt, government tax revenues will be restored. Bao notes that as a side benefit all fees collected beyond the base tax, that is, the processing fee imposed by local magistrates, will be allocated to county operating budgets—*gongfei*—rather than simply lining the pockets of mid-level bureaucrats, as is the case now. Finally, there should be little unemployment (*shiye*) resulting from this reform, since even those merchants currently engaged in salt smuggling will be welcome and encouraged to enter the profitable legal trade.

In contrast to Bao's proposed reforms of the grain tribute administration, where he argued for removing the local field administration from participation and for actually increasing the specialized workforce involved, his reform of salt distribution entailed eliminating the specialized bureaucracy but involving regular local officials more heavily in the process. This is yet one more reason why Bao's reformist agenda cannot be categorized simply as "privatization" or "economic liberalism."

If Bao's 1820 essay provided, as I suggest, the basic blueprint for reform of the Liang-Huai salt administration, he would become yet more directly involved in the process a decade later. In 1830 the Board of Revenue submitted a memorial to the throne proposing a shift of Liang-Huai to a "private commercial shipment and sale" system (*minyun minxiao*), and the Daoguang emperor responded by ordering the memorialists, Board President Wang Ding and Vice President Baoxing, to proceed to Nanjing to confer on the details of this with the Liang-Jiang governor general, Tao Zhu. In preparation, Tao sent a "trusted deputy" (*qinxin renyuan*)—quite possibly Wei Yuan—to the salt production areas to investigate the situation. Bao Shichen tells us that this deputy had previously read his own writings on salt reform and, despite some hesitation about certain provisions, had come to accept the basic policy ideas he advanced. After consultations, Bao in the winter of 1830–31 prepared a yet more detailed set of twenty-five detailed provisions for reform, presumably for the attention of Governor General Tao.[23]

These new provisions offered a yet more thoroughgoing "deregulation" (*jiesan yanjin*) than did Bao's 1820 proposals: significantly, he now announced as his model the trade in grain, rather than the more closely controlled substances iron and saltpeter. A prospective salt merchant (*maiko*) will proceed first to the office of the salt dispatcher (*yunsi*) and pay all his tax duties up front. In return he will be given a "ticket" (*piao*),[24]

23. Bao, "Daiyi gai Huaiyan tiaolue" (General stipulations submitted for the reform of the Liang-Huai Salt Administration), in *Quanji* (1993), 163–69. See also Metzger, "T'ao Chu's Reform," 5.

24. This is the earliest time I have seen Bao use this term, the "*piao* system" being the phrase subsequently adopted to describe Tao Zhu's salt reform package as a whole.

which will then allow him to go to the saltyard and purchase the amount of salt authorized by his ticket. Salt will be sold to merchants in much smaller units (by the catty, *jin*), so as to allow those of relatively modest levels of capitalization to enter the trade. Prescribed routes will be completely abolished and markets completely opened. Currently engaged as he is in the debate over shifting grain tribute shipments from the dilapidated Grand Canal to the sea route, Bao specifies that salt distribution as well can and should where appropriate employ coastal shipment (*haiyun*). The administrative distinction between Huainan and Huaibei will be eliminated, and the huge bureaucracies ensconced in the two subdistricts' central transshipment points, Hankou and Nanchang, dismantled. The type and size of boats utilized in salt shipment will be deregulated, allowing merchants to make use of any kind of vessel that best suits their needs. Significantly as well, Bao eliminates the existing prohibition on designated "salt boats" simultaneously carrying cargoes other than salt; cargoes may be mixed, determined by market demand alone.

Lest this sound like a complete commitment to laissez-faire political economy on Bao's part, however, we need to pay attention to others of his twenty-five provisions. For example, he understands (and applauds) the fact that a large number of casual laborers, male and female, who have been involved in the cumbersome existing system, will be laid off by the reforms, and he acknowledges the administration's responsibility for them: retraining them for other work where possible, and where this fails pensioning them off or providing hostels for their maintenance. Similarly, he knows that some of the excessive profits of the franchised merchants under the old system have been devoted to philanthropic projects (charitable granaries, orphanages, poorhouses, lifeboat societies) and public works (especially hydraulic maintenance) contributions. The government must take over these responsibilities. Based on the substantial percentage of his text he devotes to the details of how this should be accomplished, it seems evident that Bao was not simply another privatizer paying lip service to such needs.

Bao recognizes that one of the byproducts of opening the market for salt distribution will be a new incidence of competition (*zhongmai*) among

---

I do not know if the use of this term originated with Bao, with Tao, or with someone else.

merchants. Tellingly, he does not see competition as a benefit, a stimulus to greater market efficiency, but rather as a dysfunction, albeit a manageable one. There will be competition between the established merchants and the new entries into the field. There will also, more significantly, be natural competition among all merchants to dispose of their cargoes at points closer to the production areas, thus reducing their transport costs. It is revealing that Bao does not seek legally to prohibit sales in markets other than that designated in the merchant's commission; instead, he hopes to manage it by controlling incentives. Each merchant's *piao*, certifying that he has paid all taxes on his shipment up front, exempts his cargo from additional payments at duty stations en route—but only those on the way to his specified consumer market. If he chooses to sell in another market, he will be liable for further tax payments, thus presumably making his salt uncompetitive with that of the merchant whose market that is.

In other words, Bao's approach embodies a halfway house between a completely open market and a tightly regulated one. This is seen as well in his discussion of another dysfunction he anticipates in the operation of the new system: merchant hoarding (*jiya*) or delayed sale of shipments, inducing shortage in order to push prices upward. Like countless officials before him seeking to manage the grain trade, Bao condemns such activity but refrains from criminalizing it altogether, understanding it to be normal market behavior on the part of profit-seeking merchants. It is only when such behavior reaches an egregious level so that it restrains the trade structurally (*bachi*) that government intervention in the form of confiscation and criminal penalties are called for.

Bao Shichen's last recorded involvement in the Liang-Huai reforms came in the immediate aftermath of the reforms' implementation, in 1834.[25] Citing exchanges of correspondence between the Liang-Huai superintendent, Tao Zhu, and his superior, the board vice president Baoxing—correspondence to which Bao Shichen has clearly been privy—he writes a fussily detailed (too detailed to detain us here) letter to Tao regarding cleaning up remaining dysfunctions in the system, offering ways to better manage prices, costs, and tax duties at each stage of the distribution hierarchy. Prices at each stage should be in logical relationship to each other, which Bao takes to be evidence that *bachi*—market

25. Bao, "Shang Tao Gongbao shu," in *Quanji* (1993), 174–79.

bottlenecking—is being held in check. Bao is, in other words, in no way abandoning salt distribution altogether to market forces. His stated goal, rather, is to use the influence of the state to ensure a fair apportionment of the costs and therefore keep all parties to the production and distribution of salt profitably in business, while still keeping down the cost to consumers, and guaranteeing vital tax revenues.

Salt and Empire

Bao Shichen's involvement in the reform of the Liang-Huai salt administration, which as we have seen was deeper than many earlier scholars suggested, helps us approach some of the larger questions regarding reformism in the early nineteenth century Qing empire more generally. Like most other reformers, Bao understood that the empire was in crisis, but what did he see as the symptoms, and causes, of the crisis? How did he think the crisis might be resolved? How fundamentally did the empire need to be transformed in this process? How optimistic was he that the empire, indeed, *could* be saved? And what social or political interests were his reforms intended to protect?

The foundation of Bao's thinking on salt matters was that salt was a public resource, granted by Heaven to serve the good of all (*Tiandi zhi cang*). It should profit ("profit" being, for Bao, a morally valid pursuit) all interests and parties to the trade. These interests included the food needs of consumers (*minshi*). When Bao talks about "profiting the people" (*limin*), how restrictive is his notion of "people"? We have seen in his discussion of the Shanxi reform experiment that he is especially solicitous of the interests of taxpaying agrarian landholders. Bao has no shortage of modern critics who are eager to identify him with the "feudal landlord class," and in a sense this view is not unjustified. But he is also a man who has seen firsthand the devastations of the White Lotus rebellion, and though rebellion itself is anathema to him, he was of the party that, along with the Jiaqing emperor, saw the White Lotus as a natural response to official exploitation (*guanbi minfan*). Thus when Bao argues that in salt reform he has the interests of "ordinary people" (*qimin*) at heart, there is no reason to disbelieve him.

The core of Bao's salt reform proposals is his belief that private commerce is the most efficient way to distribute this collective public resource, and to equitably apportion the costs of doing so. The inherent dysfunction of the existing gabelle is that it pits the interests of merchants against those of consumers, in a situation in which the enfranchised merchants have the oppressive upper hand. Bao argues that this competition of interests is entirely unnecessary. A properly calibrated system will serve the needs of consumers at the same time that it protects the profits of merchants and upholds their morale (*an shangxin*).

The same is true for the interests of the state. Like other of the fiscal systems in this moment of crisis, the salt administration exhibits "a dysfunctional government competing for profit with the people" (*yumin zhengli zhi bizheng*).[26] Again, this need not be the case. Having grown up during the heyday of the Heshen predations, and facing today the critical impoverishment of government treasuries, Bao is much more alert than his mid-Qing statecraft predecessors to the needs of state finance (*guoji*). Indeed, it might be argued that this is his first priority. However, he constantly repeats the mantra that his proposed reforms of the salt administration, among others, will simultaneously profit both state and society, and that the interests of the people are precisely the interests of the state. There is no reason to doubt his genuineness in this belief.

A final object of Bao's concern is the health of the economy, which he relates to the ease of commodity circulation (*tongshang*) and the removal of restraints of trade (*bachi*). The salt gabelle as a whole, the target of his reforms, was in fact nothing more than a massive instance of this restraint. Like many of the more promarket of his early and mid-Qing predecessors, Bao identified a flourishing commercial economy as essential to "the Great Way of producing wealth" (*shengcai zhi dadao*).[27]

Even so, however, Bao cannot be too readily equated with early modern Western liberal economic thought. An appreciation of relatively unfettered domestic commodity circulation (*liutong*) certainly existed in Qing political economy, especially regarding grain, but it does not seem

26. Bao, *Shuochu*, 182.
27. Bao, *Shuochu*, 182.

to have been ideologized the way "free trade" was in the West.[28] In any case, it is noteworthy that Bao Shichen never, to my knowledge, deployed this discourse in his reform proposals for the salt monopoly. Nor did anything approaching laissez-faire—indeed, the state, far from being conceived as the source of the problem, is central to his concerns. First, its financial interests are front and center. Indeed, Bao describes the current unsatisfactory situation as one in which the state is the big loser: consumers get their salt (albeit paying too much for it) and merchants make profits (albeit by smuggling), but the state's fair share of the proceeds is forfeited. Second, despite freeing up entry to the trade, access to markets, and transport route structures, Bao's reform proposals still contain a plethora of detailed, even fussy, regulation. For him the state still maintains its paternalist role as guardian and adjudicator of the interests of all parties, including its own. The remarkable thing about Bao, like many of his early nineteenth-century reformist colleagues (though arguably more than most), is that he steadfastly maintained his optimism that, given careful thought and empirical observation, solutions might still be found that would benefit all interests simultaneously. The *ancien régime* could be saved.

28. For thoughtful reflections on this, see Helen Dunstan, *State or Merchant? Political Economy and Political Process in 1740s China* (Cambridge, MA: Harvard University Asia Center, 2006).

CHAPTER 6

Money

Throughout the 1830s an otherwise obscure Jiangnan literatus named Wang Liu energetically circulated a series of draft proposals to issue paper currency, eventually publishing his detailed ideas on the subject in an 1837 book, *Qianbi chuyan* (Modest proposals on coin and currency).[1] Despite what most contemporaries took to be the disastrous history of such experiments in the empire's past, Wang's proposals elicited considerable debate among a wide circle of politically active scholars, among whom Bao Shichen was likely the most expert and influential.

Though firmly a believer that agriculture was the foundation of the economy, Bao understood agriculture to be necessarily commercialized: as early as 1801, in essays appended to *On Wealth*, he explored in detail the contributions to the agrarian economy of commercial cropping, sericulture, arboriculture, and animal husbandry.[2] Money was for Bao the "branch" (*mo*) of a healthy economy, secondary to but also a necessary partner of the "root" (*ben*), grain production.[3] He was also throughout his life deeply sensitive to the relative utility and value of competitive monetary mediums. This chapter seeks, through close reading of Wang's and Bao's writings on this subject, to explore Daoguang-era thinking on such questions as the operation of the economy, the possibility of shaping that

1. Wang Liu, *Qianbi chuyan* (Modest proposals on coin and currency) (1837), in *Xuxiu Siku quanshu* (Shanghai: Guji chubanshe, 1995), 838.599–65.
2. Bao, *Nongzheng*, in *Quanji* (1997), 189–208.
3. Bao, *Gengchen zazhu, er*, in *Quanji* (1997), 212.

economy through government policy, the role of maritime trade and relations with European trade partners, and the nature of the Qing polity.[4]

Silver, Opium, and the Daoguang Depression

The Qing empire inherited from its predecessor a bimetallic currency system, based on uncoined silver specie, the unit of account for which was the "tael" (*liang*), and statutory coin (*zhiqian*) made of copper alloy, the unit of the latter being the "cash" (*wen*). Whereas a string of one thousand copper cash (*chuan*) carried a par value of one silver tael, the disastrous experiences of the late Ming had convinced the Qing that efforts to maintain a 1,000:1 exchange rate, or any other rate, by administrative mandate were counterproductive. Instead, it settled for the goal of maintaining "stability" in the money market, over both time and space. In this effort it enjoyed only mixed success. In the late seventeenth century, copper-to-silver exchange rates of well over 1,000:1 were not at all unusual, but from the beginning of the eighteenth century, copper coin became increasingly "expensive," and rates of 700:1 or 800:1 were the norm. This changed again in the late 1780s, after which rates of over 1,000:1 became common, and indeed escalated rapidly over the nineteenth century.[5] In

4. Wang Liu's proposals and the ensuing debates have also been dealt with in detail in Man-houng Lin, *China Upside Down*, an impressively researched and boldly argued book, with which I find much to agree but also, as we shall see, much to differ. This chapter benefits from several personal communications with Dr. Lin on these issues.

5. The relevant literature on this subject is large, starting with Peng Xinwei's classic work, *Zhongguo huobi shi* (Chinese monetary history) (1954; reprinted Shanghai: Renmin chubanshe, 1965). See also Chen Zhaonan, *Yongzheng Qianlong nianjian de yinqian bijia biandong* (Changing relative prices of silver and copper in the Yongzheng and Qianlong reigns) (Taipei: Zhongguo xueshu ju, 1966); Kuroda Akinobu, "Kenryū no senki" (The inflation of copper cash in the Qianlong period), *Tōyōshi kenkyū* 45.4 (March 1987): 58–89; Kuroda Akinobu, "Shindai ginzen nikasei no kozo to sono hokai" (The structure and collapse of silver-copper bimetallism in the Qing), *Shakai keizai shigaku* 57.2 (1992): 93–125; Endymion P. Wilkinson, *Studies in Chinese Price History* (New York: Garland Press, 1980); Hans Ulrich Vogel, "Chinese Central Monetary Policy, 1644–1800," *Late Imperial China* 8.2 (1987): 1–52; and Richard von Glahn, *Fountain*

the province of Shanxi, for example, exchange rates went from 730:1 in 1758 to as high as 1,800:1 by 1846.[6] Bao Shichen, in his brief tenure as magistrate of Xinyu county, Jiangxi, in 1839, reported typical exchange rates of 1,600:1, but noted that in tax collection clerks often demanded payment at rates as high as 2,000:1.[7]

This last trend in copper-to-silver exchange rates was a function of the shift in the Qing empire's balance of payments in its foreign trade, which most historians attribute to the empire's inability to offset via commodity exports the mushrooming imports of foreign opium. From the sixteenth through the eighteenth century, China had been the world's greatest recipient of silver inflows, and as late as the first decade of the nineteenth century it still experienced an estimated net inflow of some 28 million silver dollars. Over the period 1828–36, however, this had been dramatically reversed, and the empire suffered an estimated net *outflow* of some 36 million dollars. This disruption of the currency system and growing scarcity of silver, further aggravated by hoarding of silver by domestic investors, was one of the major causes of the so-called Daoguang depression. The state suffered declining tax revenues, and rising real costs of maintenance led to progressive infrastructural decay. A crisis of credit caused the collapse of many native banks. Increased costs and deflated prices led to declining production by manufacturers, decreased hiring, and rising unemployment. Prices paid to rural producers also fell, and farmers experienced the familiar "price scissors" between income and needed expenditures. The real tax burden grew rapidly for smallholders who paid in the depreciated copper coin. There was thus a significant widening of the income gap between rich and poor, giving rise to a wave of civil unrest.[8]

---

of Fortune: Money and Monetary Policy in China, 1000–1700 (Berkeley: University of California Press, 1996). For my own take on this question, see Rowe, "Provincial Monetary Practice in Eighteenth-Century China," in *Chinese Handicraft Regulations of the Eighteenth Century*, ed. Christine Möll-Murata, Song Jianze, and Hans Ulrich Vogel (Munich: Iudicium, 2005), 347–71.

6. Vogel, "Chinese Central Monetary Policy," 27.

7. Hu Pu'an, *Nianpu*, 237.

8. The most sustained analysis of this is Peng Zeyi, "Yapien zhanzheng hou shinianjian yingui qianjian bodong xia Zhongguo jingji yu jieji guanxi" (The Chinese economy and class relations in the post–Opium War decade under the impact of rising silver-to-copper exchange rates), in *Shijiu shiji houbanqi de Zhongguo caizheng he jingji* (Government finance and the economy in late nineteenth-century China) (Beijing:

Some more recent scholars express skepticism that opium imports were a major cause of the silver shortage, or indeed that silver was the problem at all. He Liping, for example, doubts that the outflow of silver, which he calculates at no more than 3.6 percent to 6.7 percent of the empire's total silver supply, was unlikely to have had that great an impact on copper-to-silver exchange rates.[9] Kent G. Deng acknowledges the reversal of the Qing's balance of trade in silver around 1800, and accepts the role of opium imports in this process, but cautions that the empire's silver imports were never as high as others claim, that it was bronze coin rather than silver that played the major role in financing the Ming-Qing economic boom, and consequently that the "silver famine" of the early nineteenth century was less disastrous than usually believed.[10] Lin Manhoung, who argues emphatically that silver outflows *were* disastrous, nevertheless points out that after 1850 opium imports were even greater than they had been in the Daoguang reign, and yet the Qing once again enjoyed net silver inflows; she assigns blame for the silver outflow instead on declining overseas demand for Chinese exports and to the short-term collapse of global silver production due to the Mexican revolution.[11] Alejandra Irigoin discounts the role of political unrest in Spanish America, and argues that net silver outflow from the Qing began only in the late 1820s; prior to that time exports of silver specie by British merchants in exchange for opium were more than compensated for by imports of silver coin carried by American merchants.[12]

Richard von Glahn, like Lin Man-houng, downplays the role of opium, but differs emphatically from her in assigning the cause. Argu-

Renmin chubanshe, 1983), 24–71. See also Ramon H. Myers, *The Chinese Economy: Past and Present* (Belmont, CA: Wadsworth, 1987), 72–74; Jones and Kuhn, "Dynastic Decline," 128–31; Hamashita Takeshi, *Chūgoku kindai keizaishi kenkyū* (Studies in modern Chinese economic history) (Tokyo: University of Tokyo Press, 1989), 57–58.

9. He Liping, "Yapien maoyi yu baiyin wailiu guanxi zhi cai jiantao" (Reexamining the relationship of the opium trade and silver outflows), *Shehui kexue zhanxian* 2007.1.

10. Kent G. Deng, "Miracle or Mirage? Foreign Silver, China's Economy, and Globalization from the Sixteenth to the Nineteenth Centuries," *Pacific Economic Review* 13.3 (2008): 320–58.

11. Lin, *China Upside Down*, chap. 2.

12. Alejandra Irigoin, "The End of a Silver Era: The Consequences of the Breakdown of the Spanish Peso Standard in China and the United States, 1780s–1850s," *Journal of World History* 20.2 (2009): 207–43.

ing that the significant outflow of silver from the Qing empire began only in 1834, and that by then Mexican silver production had effectively recovered from the hiatus of the 1810–25 political unrest, von Glahn, like Irigoin, sees the role of the United States as critical. During the early nineteenth century, the United States had been by far the largest recipient of Mexican silver, a large portion of which it had reexported in payment for its imports from China. But in 1834, the United States lowered the price it paid for silver because it wanted gold instead, and American merchants shifted their means of payment for Chinese imports to bills of exchange (just as the British East India Company had already done around 1810). Without this continual stream of silver imports, the Qing rather suddenly became a net exporter of specie.[13]

Whatever historians today may see as the underlying factors in the "Daoguang depression," however, there is no question that contemporary Qing analysts, with their more restricted spatial and temporal perspective, nearly universally saw the "silver famine" (*yinhuang*) as the proximate cause and opium imports as the underlying culprit.[14] Bao Shichen himself was one of the most important voices—possibly *the* most influential voice—in popularizing this view. In 1820 he calculated the Qing empire's annual drain of silver in exchange for opium at some 100 million taels, and argued that the increasingly skewed copper-to-silver exchange rate was largely due to this.[15] And, as we saw in chapter 3, in 1839 he produced one of the most trenchant analyses of the impact of the silver shortage, demonstrating quantitively how skewed exchange rates adversely affected the rural taxpayer, leading to immiseration and—as he had just personally experienced in Xinyu—collective resistence.[16] Both Bao and Wang Liu would propose the introduction of paper currency as

13. Richard von Glahn, "Foreign Silver Coins in the Market Culture of Nineteenth-Century China," *International Journal of Asian Studies* 4.1 (2007): 61–62.

14. In his famous memorial of June 1838 that precipitated the empire-wide debate on the opium question, Huang Juezu estimated that opium imports at Guangzhou caused an annual silver outflow of 17–18 million taels in the years 1823–34, rising to more than 20 million taels in 1831–34, and over 30 million taels in 1834–37; *Chouban yiwu shimo* (Complete record of foreign affairs management), Daoguang reign (Beijing: Palace Museum, 1929), 2:5.

15. Bao Shichen, *Gengchen zazhu, er*, in *Quanji* (1997), 212.

16. Bao Shichen, "Yinhuang xiaobu shuo" (A modest proposal to alleviate the silver famine), in *Quanji* (1997), 228–30.

at least a partial solution to both the silver famine and the opium problem.

Paper Money in Chinese History

Paper money had a long history in imperial China. According to Richard von Glahn, China had always conceived of currency as "fiat money," with coins bearing stated values as a prerogative of the throne, in contrast to the metalist view of currency that prevailed in Europe, the value of the instrument determined by that of its metallic content. This difference, in von Glahn's view, allowed the world's first successful introduction of paper money in the Southern Song, several centuries prior to anything comparable in Europe. This currency was fully convertible into bronze coin, and had a fixed expiration date. After several decades of successful circulation, however, the Song court succumbed to the temptation to overissue its scrip, leading to its devaluation and eventual withdrawal. This pattern was repeated in later efforts to introduce paper currency to supplement or replace outright copper coins under the Jin and the Yuan.[17]

The Ming founder in 1375 issued paper currency known as *baochao*, and throughout the early fifteenth century his successors did as well. Each time, after initial acceptance, the paper fell out of currency; in von Glahn's view, the chief reason was the court's unwillingness to allow convertiblity of scrip into monetary metal. No less influential a scholar-official than Qiu Jun, in his repeatedly reprinted text on proper governance, the *Daxue yanyi bu* (Expanded explication of the Great Learning) of 1487, argued that paper notes should be a vital part of the empire's monetary system, provided they were convertible and closely regulated by the state.[18] In the Ming's final decades, faced by the collapsing value of copper coin versus silver and by acute fiscal distress, such notable reformist literati as Xu Guangqi, Chen Zilong, Qian Qianyi, and Lu Shiyi proposed paper money as a remedy, but the more conservative view, recollecting earlier

17. Von Glahn, *Fountain of Fortune*, 56–61, 71–74.
18. Von Glahn, *Fountain of Fortune*, 80–82.

disasters, prevailed and it was not introduced.[19] The conquering Qing, however, in 1651 issued small quantities of *chaochuan* (paper notes denominated in strings of copper cash) to help finance its consolidation of control in coastal Jiangnan, prudently withdrawing them once the mission was accomplished a decade later.[20] During the "prosperous age" of the mid-Qing, little further discussion of this issue took place.

This changed dramatically in the perceived silver famine of the early nineteenth century, when the question of paper currency again became a focus of literati debate. The most notorious instance came with Cai Zhiding, a Zhejiang native, *jinshi*, and Hanlin compiler who memorialized in 1814 that paper money should be introduced in large amounts. Cai was severely chastised by the throne for his irresponsible ignorance of similar failed experiments in the past, and his career pretty much came to an end. If such an idea was to be advanced again any time soon, the advocate would have to be far more circumspect, and do his homework very well. Wang Liu certainly learned this lesson.[21]

Wang Liu and His Proposals

Wang Liu (1786–1843) was a Wuxian (Jiangsu) native who held only a *shengyuan* degree, never held office, and enjoyed a modest reputation as a scholar of ancient scripts.[22] He worked on his book for nearly thirty years, following the keen interest in monetary issues of several senior members of his lineage. Wang's father had scoffed at the naïveté exhibited in Cai Zhiding's proposal of 1814, and wanted to make very sure that any similar proposal emanating from his own family would not share the same limitations, nor its author meet the same fate. In 1828, in Beijing, Wang Liu showed his preliminary draft for the *Qianbi chuyan* to a number of highly regarded experts, and their positive response gave him the

19. Wang Liu, "Xian zheng ming yan" (Excerpts from notable scholars of the past), in *Qianbi chuyan*, 19–37; von Glahn, *Fountain of Fortune*, 197–206.

20. Peng Xinwei, *Zhongguo huobi shi*, 807; Lin, *China Upside Down*, 40.

21. Wang Liu, "Mulu" and "Qianchao yi," part 1, both in *Qianbi chuyan*; Peng Xinwei, *Zhongguo huobi shi*, 808; *Zhongguo renming da zidian*, 1526.

22. *Zhongguo renming da zidian*, 156.

courage to have blocks carved for publication. His lineage leaders, however, still disapproved the work, and ordered him to have the blocks destroyed. After another decade of research and revision, and circulation of the text to other authorities, including most notably Bao Shichen, Wang finally published his work in 1837. The final work includes his correspondence on the draft with Bao and several others, seemingly as a means of defending himself in advance for offering such bold proposals.[23] Indeed, Wang's has every appearance of a careful and comprehensive work. He reviews in considerable detail each past experiment with paper currency, analyzing the factors in its success or failure. And he appends what is basically a sourcebook of past authorities' writings on the issue, including seven texts from the Song, two from the Yuan, eight from the Ming, and four from the Qing.[24]

Based on his knowledge of the history of paper currency in the empire, Wang argues that it has, in various times, been found useful in a wide range of sectors: salt administration, military logistics, river maintenance, and land reclamation among them. The early Ming example was among the more successful experiments, in Wang's view, and was only given up because of the court's growing and unfortunate infatuation with silver as the principal monetary medium. The early Qing experiment was likewise a success, and, he insists, would not have been tried at all had the court not recognized the successful uses of paper in the past. Where past experiments had failed, as Wang concedes most had, it was either because of insufficient understanding or, most especially, because they had not been undertaken as part of a more comprehensive monetary policy incorporating multiple media of exchange serving differing monetary needs. It is this comprehensive policy that Wang offers in his treatise.[25]

Though, as we'll see, Wang is hardly antistatist, he opens his treatise with a biting critique of the current regime's acquisitive monetary practices, which prioritize the interests of the ruler (*junzu*) over those of the people (*minzu*). This gets things precisely backward, he says, since the ruler's well-being is completely predicated upon that of the people. The imperial

23. Wang, "Mulu" and "Youpeng zengda," in *Qianbi chuyan*; Lin, *China Upside Down*, 148.

24. Wang, *Qianbi chuyan*, 19–37.

25. Wang, "Qianchao yi," parts 1–3, in *Qianbi chuyan*.

administration dutifully claims that it is keeping taxes low and encouraging economic productivity, especially in agriculture, but since it fails to manage the monetary system with due restraint it cannot succeed in either of these efforts. Wang then identifies five signs of the current empire's failed monetary system: (1) profit-minded artisans are melting down copper cash for nonmonetary uses, (2) speculators are manipulating copper-to-silver exchange rates for private profit, (3) "criminal elements" (*jianmin*) mint and circulate counterfeit cash with low copper content, (4) privately printed paper banknotes are circulated among a restrictive class of wealthy merchants, and (5) foreign currencies—notably the Spanish imperial Carlos III and IV coins—have been introduced and circulate freely within the empire's domestic economy.

Put most simply, Wang's plan to solve these problems involves the introduction by the government of two new currencies. The first is paper notes, to serve as the empire's largest denomination currency, which will coexist at the outset with both silver and copper cash. The second is a copper fiat money, "large cash" (*daqian*) with stated values independent of their copper content, to serve as a currency of intermediate value between the new paper notes and the existing small copper coins.

Wang goes to great lengths and makes extravagant claims to argue for the advantages of government-issued paper currency. He begins by recalling ten arguments in favor of paper money advanced by the late Ming minister of finance Ni Yuanlu (1593–1644), then adds a full twenty-two more of his own.[26] Though Wang himself does not do this, I would contend that all of these many arguments may be summarized under three sets of claims: those based on convenience of use, those based on elasticity of the money supply, and those based on patriotic or proto-nationalist appeals. Let us set aside the last group for the moment, and look first at the other two.

The arguments for convenience are the least original or controversial. Following Ni Yuanlu, Wang emphasizes that paper money would be lighter in weight than coin or silver, thus easier to store, to carry, and to conceal from thieves. It would more easily circulate across regions and

26. Wang, "Qianchao yi," part 1, in *Qianbi chuyan.* On Ni Yuanlu's involvement in the late-Ming paper currency campaign, see von Glahn, *Fountain of Fortune,* 205–6.

into remote areas, thus facilitating commodity exchange (*liutong*) throughout the empire. Paper money will be standardized across the empire, thus eliminating the nuisance of money changing when traveling or shipping goods interregionally. Haggling over prices, and other bottlenecks to circulation of goods (*baiwu*) will be reduced. Concerns about fineness of the metal would be eliminated, and it would not have to be weighed to assess its value, saving both effort and the opportunity for pilferage by assayers. The fact that Wang's paper money bears a stated, standardized value will preclude yamen clerks from imposing extortionate exchange rates. Likewise, with tax assessments and collections both denominated in paper money, the abominated "meltage fees" (*huohao*) demanded of taxpayers can be abolished. Furthermore, Wang argues, nearly all the current manifest dysfunctions in the *san da zheng*—the three specialized bureaucracies of the Yellow River administration, the grain tribute administration, and the salt administration—will be easily resolved once a single standardized currency is put in place.

On the advantages of elasticity, Wang may seem unduly sanguine. He writes: "When any other substance is used as currency, it is always in limited supply. But with paper money, there is no limit on how much one can produce. Produce a million, then another million. Produce ten million, then another ten million. It is an inexhaustible supply of wealth [*buhe zhi caiyuan*]." This stands especially in contrast to silver, of which the world (*tianxia*) has a finite supply, and upon the vicissitudes of imports the empire has become dependent. With paper currency, the problem of dealing with food shortages will be greatly eased; relief can be extended without imposing subscriptions upon the local wealthy (*fuhu*). Simply print as much money as the crisis demands! More generally, once paper money has made government finances comfortably secure (*guoji dayu*) there will be no further need for regulations soliciting contributions in return for brevet official ranks, civil service degrees, or other honors (*juanli*). Finally, an inexhaustible supply of money in the state's hands can be used to finance spending on hydraulic and other public works, and on land reclamation (*kaiken*), all of which will have the effect of developing the economy and creating employment (*mousheng*).

Wang Liu's actual plan comes into much sharper focus, and reveals its own distinctiveness, when one turns to his ideas of the relationship of the new paper currency to the two principal existing forms of money under the Qing, copper coin and silver bullion. Wang specifies that his newly issued paper money will both coexist with copper coins, and be fully redeemable in them. Like many before him, however, he wants copper removed from most nonmonetary uses in society. Most, that is, not all: he specifies a few uses—musical instruments, locks, buttons—where it must necessarily remain in use as a matter of popular convenience. Shops producing or selling general copperware will be shut down, but those dealing in these specified utensils may continue in operation. Wang is a bit ambiguous about enforcement of this; he repeatedly uses the phrase or "strictly banning" (*yanjin*) copper utensils, but he elsewhere insists that nonmonetary use of copper not be criminalized, which would simply provide yet one more excuse for yamen clerks to threaten and extort the population. The key for Wang is the new government "copper bureaus" (*tongju*) that he proposes setting up in major markets. Once his paper notes have been introduced into the economy (and he insists that this be done first), bureaus can be established to purchase existing copperware in exchange for paper, at highly favorable prices that will hardly be refused. The copper received can then be used to mint both additional cash and the new copper fiat money—*daqian*—that Wang proposes introducing. In other words, his new paper currency will provide the instrument to effect what others have been seeking to accomplish for years: discourage private melting down of coin for nonmonetary uses, and transform existing nonmonetary copper into additional supplies of cash, thus stabilizing the skewed copper-to-silver exchange rate.[27]

Wang's paper notes will be redeemable in silver, as they are in copper cash, but his policy toward silver is nearly the opposite of that toward copper. He has no desire to remove silver from nonmonetary use in society, but, like many before him, he wants it driven out as currency. The institution by which this will be effected is not a newly created governmental "bureau," as with copper, but instead the existing native banks or money shops (*qianzhuang*) that are ubiquitous throughout commercial centers in the empire.[28] Wang will prohibit these banks from dealing in the private banknotes (*huipiao* or *qianpiao*) that are their current stock

27. Wang, "Qianchao yi," parts 1 and 2, in *Qianbi chuyan.*

28. On *qianzhuang*, see Susan Mann Jones, "Finance in Ningpo: The 'Ch'ien Chuang,' 1750–1880," in *Economic Organization in Chinese Society*, ed. W. E. Willmott (Stanford: Stanford University Press, 1972), 37–77.

in trade, and have them deal instead in his new government-issue scrip. They will stand ready to buy silver for paper, at a favorable rate 1 percent above the prevailing market price. (The government will subsidize this favorable rate, and also a modest profit on the transaction for the banks themselves.) This will be a declining premium, however. After a year or two, once the government notes have taken hold in the economy, it will be reduced to 0.5 percent, and after a further two years there will be no premium at all for the exchange. In Wang's view, by that time the obvious superior convenience of paper will "naturally" drive the remaining monetary silver off the market (*zizhi* or *zifei*). There is therefore no need to actively criminalize its use as money. If, however, after five to ten years monetary silver is still found in circulation, it will be confiscated; the bearer will be compensated at only 50 percent of the silver's market value, but will not be subjected to criminal penalty.[29]

Wang Liu may have been optimistic in his expectations for what paper money might allow in the Qing economy, but he also presented himself as extremely practical-minded. His treatise is filled with minute details regarding the production and means of introduction of his new currencies, and with safeguards he proposes against their failure or misuse.[30] Why should paper money be accepted by the public today, Wang asks, when it failed so many times in the past? The answer betrays the strong streak of historical relativism that informs his entire work: on the one hand, he says, we have learned systematically from the experience of past mistakes and, on the other, times today are much different from what they were in the past (notably, we live now in a newly cosmopolitan, multinational world—a point to which I will return below). In addition to being issued in exchange for copperware at government bureaus, the new notes will be issued as official salaries and military pay, but initially with a premium to help underwrite the recipient's difficulty in passing them into further circulation. It shall be made clear, in advance of the issue itself, that these notes are fully acceptable by the government in payment of land tax and all other official levies and duties (it was precisely the unwillingness to accept its own notes in tax payment that doomed the paper money experiments of many earlier ruling houses).

29. Wang, "Qianchao tiaomu" (Regulations for paper money), in *Qianbi chuyan.*

30. The following paragraphs are based on Wang, "Qianchao yi," parts 6–8, and "Qianchao tiaomu," in *Qianbi chuyan.*

Wang's notes are to be printed in seven denominations: "large notes" (*dachao*) equivalent to 1,000 and 500 strings of copper cash (*chuan*), "middling notes" (*zhongchao*) of 100 and 50 *chuan*, and "small notes" (*xiaochao*) of 10, 3, and 1 *chuan*. His new fiat copper currency (*daqian*) will be minted in smaller denominations of 100 and 10 cash (*wen*). Critics will say, why such large denominations, when we have not had currency denominated so large in the past? Wang counters that the ready acceptance of foreign coin and privately issued banknotes in our current domestic economy indicates that a manifest need for such large-denomination monetary instruments now exists. Indeed, one reason he finds for the failure of paper currency issues in the past was that too many denominations, and especially notes of too small denomination, were issued at once.

Wang's proposed notes will be printed centrally by the imperial administration in Beijing, but then distributed to the various provincial treasurers' offices, where they will be imprinted with the treasurer's seal. Redistributed downward to counties, they will receive the magistrate's seal as well, and then the seal of the native bank or copper bureau that puts them into the private economy. Individual holders of this currency are free to affix their own seal to it as well. All of this will only make counterfeiting more difficult. So too will the practice of using only the finest paper, and making the original notes highly embellished. (They will also be stored in special government-issued boxes [*han*]—fancier ones for the wealthy, humbler ones for ordinary subjects). Here again Wang stresses the advantages that people enjoy today versus the past, in the superior printing and paper-making technologies now at their disposal. Notes accepted in payment of taxes in a given province must be those bearing the seal of that provincial treasurer's office, but government offices will be set up to exchange at par notes of other provinces for those in use locally.

The most intriguing of Wang's sets of regulations concern the volume of notes to be issued. When the notes are first printed, it should be done in sufficient quantity to serve the economy's anticipated need, *but no more*. After two or three years, reassess the need and issue additional notes as required. In other words, the quantity in circulation is to be a function of market demand. Officials must continually monitor the number of notes in circulation, and regularly withdraw older, worn, defaced, or superfluous notes as a means to prevent their debasement; Wang estimates the cost to the government of retiring older notes will be an easily affordable 3 percent per year. Yet Wang makes no mention of government bullion reserves, or any other government assets, as limiting factors—the notes are not to be "backed" by anything other than faith in the Qing imperium. They are a true fiduciary money. Wang insists that the population today is manifestly more ready to accept a fiduciary money than were those in past eras—they have shown this, for example, with private banknotes. We can help assure popular confidence, he says, by announcing the details of the new monetary system well in advance of actual issue, by proclaiming and demonstrating that the rules will not be changed midstream, and by being patient in awaiting full popular acceptance.

Bao Shichen's Commentary on Wang's Proposals

Before returning to the significant implications of Wang Liu's monetary ideas for early nineteenth-century Chinese political thought, it will be useful to consider the response to his proposals of the man whose approval Wang apparently most wanted to solicit, and who clearly took him more seriously than did many others: Bao Shichen. Arguably the most respected expert in the empire in a wide range of areas of public policy, from military strategy to agronomy to hydraulic management, Bao as we have seen had been throughout the Daoguang reign a chief mover in two of the major reform campaigns of the era: the shift from use of the Grand Canal to coastal shipping in delivery to the north of the grain tribute, and breaking up the monopoly of the quasi-enfeoffed *gang* merchants in the Huainan salt administration. Since both of these efforts involved essentially the shift from bureaucratic to private entrepreneurial management in a major sector of the economy, Bao has been seen by Lin Man-houng and others as something of a precocious economic "liberal."[31] In my own view, as we shall see, this is a misplaced analogy.

31. Lin, "A Time in Which the Grandsons Beat the *Grandfathers*." In her later *China Upside Down*, Lin is more cautious about using the label "liberal" to describe Bao's ideas, which she nevertheless describes as emphasizing "individual initiative," "private enterprise," and "free trade" (259). For a review article on Lin's book, emphasizing the caution necessary when applying the word "liberal" to Qing economic policies,

Bao Shichen had a deep interest in monetary management, the successful prosecution of which he held to be both essential to the lives of the entire population and an index of the overall effectiveness of the ruler.[32] He did not give the current regime high marks, and, as we have seen, wrote in detail about the devastating consequences for the rural producers of the skewed copper-to-silver exchange rate. In 1832, a mutual friend named Zhang Yuanfu gave Bao an early version of Wang's writings on the issuance of paper currency, and Bao pronounced himself delighted, saying he himself had been pondering this issue for nearly thirty years.[33] Two years later Wang was emboldened to correspond directly with the great man, and Bao said similar approving things to Wang himself.[34] And in 1837, once Wang's revised treatise had actually been published he sent a copy to Bao. Bao wrote at length to thank the author, saying that his ideas were welcomely refreshing, "not slavishly stuck in the rut of previous generations" (*bu jushou guren gezhe*) of thinking on this issue.[35]

Lin Man-houng has argued that Bao Shichen "harshly criticized" Wang's proposal to introduce paper currency, "on the grounds that they would extract money from the people and that the notes would never be accepted," and that Wang was "trying to seize the people's wealth for the state."[36] I believe this conclusion is much too strong. In Bao's replies to Wang, he acknowledged that he himself had been considering proposing introduction of paper currency as a solution to the current monetary crisis for some years, although he had not yet fully formulated his ideas nor put them in print.[37] Wang gratefully reprinted Bao's letters to him and to Zhang Yuanfu in his revised treatise, drawing from them the conclusion that Bao was in fact in general agreement with his basic proposal to introduce paper currency, even though they did have differences on the details of how to do this. I believe he was correct in this reading. Most

see Mio Kishimoto, "New Studies on Statecraft in Mid- and Late-Qing China," *International Journal of Asian Studies* 6.1 (2009): 87–102.

32. See, for example, Bao's preface to his 1844 "Qimin si shu" (Four works for the people), in *Quanji* (1997), 159–61.

33. Bao, "Yu Zhang Yuanfu shu," in *Quanji* (1997), 214.

34. Bao, "Da Wang Liangsheng shu," in *Quanji* (1997), 214–15.

35. Bao, "Cai da Wang Liangsheng shu," in *Quanji* (1997), 215–20.

36. Lin, "Two Social Theories Revealed," 8, and *China Upside Down*, 148.

37. Bao, "Cai da Wang Liangsheng shu"; see also Liu Guangjing, "Bao Shichen yu Wei Yuan," 1004.

crucially, as deeply populist as Bao Shichen genuinely was, I see no justification for arguing that he saw Wang's paper currency proposals as an attempt "to seize the people's wealth for the state." On the contrary, the attempt to bolster the power and solvency of the Qing state, at that moment threatened by foreign aggression as well as by domestic economic crisis, was an agenda both men shared.

Bao's most severe criticism of Wang's proposals concerns the latter's misplaced faith in the infinite elasticity of paper money. He cites Wang's own statement that scrip is "an inexhaustible source of wealth" and notes that kind of thinking is precisely what doomed so many attempts to introduce it in the past. In Bao's view, the first issue of paper currency should be fixed at the value of one half year's land tax revenues, and further printings should be equivalent to a year's total tax take and no more. Since it is above all silver that Wang wants paper to displace in the economy, Bao concedes that the initial modest offering of paper he favors will likely have the effect of acutally *increasing* the market value of silver, but once paper notes become generally accepted, which will take some time, the desired devaluation of silver vis-à-vis copper can be accomplished.[38]

Another distinctive difference between Bao's and Wang's optimal currency regime is that Wang wants to eliminate silver altogether as a monetary medium, while Bao does not. Bao points out that the problem is not silver per se, but more simply that it has become overly expensive relative to copper, and that it has assumed the role as money of account (*qisuan*) in too many economic arenas. He agrees with Wang that immediately banning the use of silver as currency and replacing it with paper would not work, but disagrees with Wang's premise that a successfully floated paper currency will "naturally" drive silver out of monetary use; silver will find its place in the money market no matter what tack the government takes to prevent it. What we should aim for, Bao says, is a money market with three separate mediums—silver, copper, and paper—each serving their discrete sector of the economy. Of course, we want copper to displace silver as much as possible in tax collection, where assessments in silver and payments commuted to copper at extortionate rates are killing the farmers, and to that end we want to mint more copper coin and introduce them into the economy through such means as

38. Bao, "Cai da Wang Liangsheng shu."

military pay. But the danger is that there will never be enough copper coin to meet the need, and that will only further skew the copper-to-silver exchange rate. This is precisely where the introduction of paper currency, denominated in copper cash and hence augmenting the cash supply, can help stabilize exchange rates.

Bao's third major point of disagreement regards the copper fiat money (*daqian*) favored by Wang. Bao simply sees no utility in this. Paper currency may well in time have the hoped-for effect of restoring the value of minted copper cash, but simultaneously introducing a copper currency not pegged to the value of its metalic content will likely defeat that purpose. Bao revisits the historical record on *daqian* since the Tang, noting that some issues were more successful than others. But, sounding even more historically relativist than Wang, he argues that just because something may have worked once or twice in the past there is no reason to believe that it will have the same effect in these very different times.[39]

Bao's several other questions to Wang relate more to the finer details of his program—Bao has long shown himself to be an unusually detail-oriented scholar. He offers advice on how to procure the proper paper, and on the niceties of the printing process. He has his own ideas on the optimal denominations to use for notes. He agrees wholeheartedly with Wang that the new issue of paper notes must be fully acceptable in payment of taxes. He adds further, usefully it would seem, that if purchases of gentry degrees (*juansheng*) were made possible *only* for payment in paper currency (rather than eliminated, as Wang proposed), that currency would quickly find favor among the wealthy and upwardly ambitious—precisely the sector of the population that is currently creating problems by hoarding silver. He also offers detailed suggestions on how to preclude counterfeiting and other possible future abuses.

Other Voices

Wang Liu and Bao Shichen were among the most notable participants in the debates of the Daoguang reign over fiduciary money and its relationship to the silver shortage, economic depression, and—eventually—the

39. Bao, "Cai da Wang Liangsheng shu."

foreign trade, but they were hardly alone. As with much of the political discourse of this era, the grounds of debate were set in large part by the massive and widely read *Compendium of Statecraft Writings from the Reigning Dynasty* (*Huangchao jingshi wenbian*), edited by Wei Yuan and published under the authority of He Changling in 1826. The *Statecraft Compendium* includes some fifty-three essays on monetary policy, only two of which (by my estimation) look favorably on paper or copper fiat money, and these both date from the early Qing.[40] By contrast, no fewer than seven of the fifty-three essays are by the guiding authority for most Qing policy critics, Gu Yanwu, whose views on paper currency were strongly negative. As both Richard von Glahn and John Delury have pointed out, although Gu was no great fan of the progress of the monetized economy, he was hardly the knee-jerk antisilverist he is sometimes portrayed as being. He recognized the popular need for currency (like others he attributed the Kangxi-era "depression" of his own day to a shortage of money in the economy) and advocated more mining of silver to relieve the shortage. But he saw that silver was primarily an import, and that the coastal and southern regions of the empire ran on a silver standard while other regions did not; for this reason he saw as prejudicial to the interior the policy of demanding land taxes everywhere in silver, and advocated instead separate regionalized fiscal regimes. On paper money he was unequivocal, however. No matter how starved for currency the empire was, paper money in his view would never gain popular acceptance, and paper issued by the state and unbacked by specie (as had been advocated, for example, by Ni Yuanlu in the late Ming) was no more than naked expropriation of the people's wealth by the state.[41]

Like so many of his contemporaries, Bao Shichen was a great admirer of Gu Yanwu, and in many areas his thinking was deeply influenced by

40. One of the two is Qiu Jiasui's "Tongchao yi" (On copper certificates), in *Huangchao jingshi wenbian*, 53:53–56. Qiu was a native of Shanghang (Fujian), a Kangxi-era *juren*, and a career county magistrate; see *Zhongguo renming da zidian*, 165. Qiu's enthusiastic essay on paper money was reprinted by Wang Liu himself, in the "Xian zhengming yan" (Comments of former worthies) section of *Qianbi chuyan*, 19–37.

41. Gu Yanwu's essays on currency, all but one extracted from his *Rizhi lu* (Record of daily-acquired learning), appear in *Huangchao jingshi wenbian*, 52:1–9, 53:36–40, and 53:49–50. See also von Glahn, *Fountain of Fortune*, 220–22, and Delury, "Despotism Above and Below," 226–33.

him.[42] But, as we have seen, on monetary thought they diverged, and I have not found in Bao's writings a direct commentary on Gu's dictates on currency. Wang Liu, however, was another matter. In part, most likely, to defend himself against charges of ignorance of past authorities, he devoted several pages of his treatise to an apologia for not thinking just as Gu did.

Wang reads Gu as arguing that both silver and paper should be eliminated as currency, with copper cash exclusively serving that function; in today's much more commercially developed world, however, that would be totally unwieldy. Wang argues that Gu's two chief arguments against paper are, first, that "its circulation would be obstructed and it would be withdrawn" (*yongzhi feian*), and, second, that "it would become defaced or deteriorated, and circulate at debased value" (*hunlan daohuan*). Both of these complaints, Wang says, describe late Ming conditions but are no longer legitimate concerns today. The "obstruction" of paper currency in the Ming was the product of three Ming imperial decisions: (1) that of Ming Taizu to accept silver but not paper in tax payments, (2) that of Xuanzong (r. 1426–35) to disallow paper money in upward remissions from prefectures to the central government, and (3) that of Yongzong (r. 1436–47 and 1457–64) to commute land tax payments from grain to silver. The net effect of these three decisions was to establish silver as the sole accepted medium for payments to and within the government, making it inevitable that paper currency would lapse out of circulation. Gu's second complaint reflected the poor manufacturing methods for paper currency of his day, methods that have been greatly improved since then. In short, Wang says it is easy to understand and agree with Gu's antipathy to silver—its monetary use would cease in Wang's ideal world as well—but if Gu were living in today's world, Wang predicts, his opposition to paper currency would disappear.[43]

Perhaps so, but Gu Yanwu's major champion in the Daoguang era and editor of the *Statecraft Compendium*, Wei Yuan, reached no such accomodation. Writing in 1842, Wei condemned paper money advocates such as Ni Yuanlu, Cai Zhiding, and Wang Liu (explicitly) as advocating

42. See, for example, Bao Shichen, "Du Tinglin yishu" (On reading Gu Yanwu's works), in *Quanji* (1993).

43. Wang, "Qianchao yi," part 10.

"the way of the robber." In answer to the list of "ten conveniences" of paper money drawn up by Ni and cited by Wang, Wei proposed his own list of "ten inconveniences" (*shi bubian*). As bad as the current silver famine was for ordinary people, paper money was worse, and could only be introduced by state coercion. Using language resonant of Gu Yanwu, Wei claimed that with paper currency "the benefits all accrue to those above [*shang*], while the suffering necessarily falls on those below [*xia*]."[44]

However, as the silver famine manifestly worsened over the course of the Daoguang era, other significant voices were heard in favor of the fiduciary money alternative. During his tenure as Huguang governor general in 1838, Lin Zexu, a friend of both Wei Yuan and Bao Shichen and soon to be the hero or goat (according to your perspective) of the first Opium War, responded to a call for input from the emperor in response to a memorial from the commander of the Chengdu garrison Baixing that foreign banknotes be banned. Lin instead defended their importance to the Qing domestic economy. In the face of badly skewed copper-to-silver exchange rates, he argued, the obvious answer was to both mine and import more silver; but in the interim the circulation of foreign paper monetary instruments among Qing subjects helped alleviate, rather than aggravate, the silver shortage.[45] In 1842, the censor Lei Yixian (later, as Yangzhou prefect in 1853, the inventor of the *likin* domestic transit tax) argued in favor of minting a fiat money *daqian* along the lines proposed by Wang Liu, and the Board of Revenue secretary Xu Mei issued his own call for a Qing paper currency in 1846.[46] As the silver famine worsened, and with it popular unrest, Wang's influence was clearly growing.

44. Wei Yuan, "Junchu" (Military logistics), in *Shengwu ji* (1881), 14:60–65. I thank Lin Man-houng for providing me this reference.

45. Wang Hongbin, "Lin Zexu guanyu yingui qianjian de renzhi yu yinhuo" (Lin Zexu's understanding and suspicions regarding the high cost of silver), *Shixue yuekan* 2006.9: 35–41.

46. Hamashita, *Chūgoku kindai keizaishi kenkyū*, 57–58. Lin Man-houng, "Two Social Theories," 4, identifies Xu Mei as a critic of Wang Liu, but Hamashita reads him as essentially in support of Wang on the paper currency issue.

State and Nation

One of the great insights of Lin Man-houng's study of the paper money debates of the Daoguang reign is her recognition that something far more than economic policy was under discussion. Wang Liu's treatise presents itself as a straightforward remedy to the imbalance between silver and copper values, but the work has another agenda, not exactly hidden, but revealing itself only slowly and gradually to the close reader of the text. Lin sees this agenda as Wang's advocacy of the enhanced power of the imperial state, and I would not disagree. But I see something else as well, and something shared in general terms by Wang's more celebrated correspondent, Bao Shichen: an incipient Chinese nationalism.

We may begin with the issue of opium. As we have seen, Wang and Bao shared (mistakenly or not) the assumption that the rapid rise in Qing opium imports over the Jiaqing and Daoguang reigns was the principal cause of the silver famine. Among the benefits Wang enumerated (item 12) in support of the introduction of paper currency was that border conflicts along the Inner Asian frontier were typically the result of raids in quest of silver; if paper currency were substituted for silver in the markets of these areas the raids would be discouraged. Wang's unstated assumption is that whereas silver was valuable anywhere, paper currency would be useful within the confines of the Qing empire alone. Elsewhere (item 4) he applied the same logic to the maritime trade: Foreign ships smuggle opium into China, causing the outflow of millions of taels of silver. If we adopt paper money, then the profits to foreigners will dry up and the opium imports "will naturally cease" (*zizhi*).[47] In the detailed regulations Wang offers for his new currency system, he stipulates that Chinese merchants engaged in foreign trade are allowed to offer only goods, not offer silver—in other words, he presents a crude attempt to legislate a positive balance of trade. For their part, foreign merchants arriving in China to purchase goods for export with silver will be obliged first to exchange that silver for paper currency at a government-approved

47. Wang, "Qianchao yi," part 1, in *Qianbi chuyan.*

qianzhuang, and only then use the paper currency to purchase the goods they want.[48]

This was a hopelessly idealistic scheme, as the inveterate realist Bao Shichen immediately pointed out. Bao had twenty years earlier proposed his own plan to eradicate the opium problem: a simple prohibition phased in over a three-year period, first on imports, then on domestic circulation, then finally on consumption.[49] In response to Wang's proposals, he argued that the assumption that foreigners, even if they could be coerced into accepting only paper currency in trade, would not be dissuaded thereby from importing whatever they wished; such foreign "bandits" (*taozei*) were already long accustomed to utilizing various kinds of banknotes (*huipiao*, *qianpiao*) in their commercial dealings, and they would readily accommodate to accepting Chinese currency, if it were worth anything, despite the prohibition. Besides, as Bao said consistently, disallowing the monetary use of silver was an unrealistic aspect of Wang's proposals anyway.[50]

What is most significant here, I believe, is not Wang Liu's rather unworkable scheme for curtailing opium imports, but instead what it reveals about his true motivation in pushing for the introduction of paper currency, which is far more than a simple effort to relieve the skewed copper-to-silver exchange rate. He insists that an accepted and conveniently usable government-issued paper money will "naturally obviate" (*zifei*) the use of foreign coins or other currencies on the Chinese domestic market—they will disappear without need of formal prohibition. Furthermore, *privately* issued banknotes and other commercial paper, which, whatever their convenience, currently are restricted to the use of a few privileged merchants and run the constant risk of default by the issuing bank, will likewise be driven off the market by the more democratic and secure paper currency issued by the state. What Wang is advocating, radically, is the adoption of a true *national currency*, one that will be valid throughout the entirety of China's territory and for all citizens/subjects, but not beyond its borders, and whose value will be determined by the state. All competitive currencies—those issued by provinces or

48. Wang, "Qianchao tiaomu," no. 20, in *Qianbi chuyan*.
49. Bao, *Gengchen zazhu, er*, in *Quanji* (1997), 213.
50. Bao, "Cai ta Wang Liangsheng shu," in *Quanji* (1997).

other subordinate administrative jurisdictions, by foreign governments, by domestic or foreign banks, or by previous dynasties—will be defunct.

Lin Man-houng recognizes what Wang is doing here, and assumes that the Qing was at the time well behind the historical curve in not possessing its own monetary sovereignty.[51] But, in fact, Wang was not playing catch-up at all. National currencies with exclusive authority as legal tender within sovereign borders were effectively unknown in Europe at the time Wang and Bao wrote, although a few European writers such as Jean Bodin (1530–96) had advocated the idea much earlier. By the early nineteenth century, countries worldwide typically saw both a plethora of local currencies in circulation and the widespread use of foreign currencies within their borders, just as did the Qing empire. Indeed, even in the United States, the Mexican dollar was the primary coin in domestic circulation up to the 1850s. As Eric Helleiner writes, "Only in the nineteenth century did territorially uniform and exclusive national currencies begin to emerge for the first time in world history. . . . Territorial currencies were created at quite different speeds in different countries, and it was a gradual process in most countries, spread out over a number of decades. By 1914, some Western European countries, the United States, and Japan had largely completed the process. A number of other countries in Europe [and elsewhere] would not create a fully fledged territorial currency until the interwar years or later." The principal reasons policy makers introduced such currencies in the West were similar to those advanced by Wang: the desire to unify the domestic market, to differentiate it definitively from foreign markets, and to bolster national identity. It was the solidification of the concept of the nation-state, in many cases along with new industrialized printing and coinage technologies, that facilitated this transition.[52]

Wang Liu describes the circulation of foreign currencies in the domestic economy as the "erosion" (*haoshi*) of the country by foreigners—a precocious reference, it would seem, to economic imperialism. He argues that the country enjoys economic rights (*liquan*) over all of its resources (*wanwu*), and the authority to redistribute them for popular use and to

51. Lin, *China Upside Down*, 149 and passim.

52. Eric Helleiner, *The Making of National Money: Territorial Currencies in Historical Perspective* (Ithaca: Cornell University Press, 2003), 31. See also von Glahn, "Foreign Silver Coins," 51. The circulation of foreign coins in the United States economy was legally ended in 1857; Irigoin, "End of a Silver Era," 237.

tax them for national purposes. The key word deployed here by Wang is *liquan*. Though the term had a history dating back at least to the Zhou-dynasty *Zuozhuan*, referring to the exercize of controlling power over economic resources, in my reading it was not in common use in Wang Liu's day, and enjoyed no specialized usage in reference to international relations. Intriguingly, though, the two characters that comprise *liquan*, when inversely combined as *quanli*, would become the neologism for the Western concept of "rights," and the related term *zhuquan*—like *liquan* a term of classical pedigree, in reference to the autonomous power of the ruler—would become standard modern Chinese for "national sovereignty."[53]

Even into the early nineteenth century, of course, Qing officials and literati operated under a quite different concept of sovereignty and national borders than did Western nation-states—one need not subscribe to such Fairbankian notions as a hegemonic "tribute system" to accept this simple truth.[54] *Quanli* as a Chinese-language equivalent for the Western notion of "rights" and *zhuquan* for "sovereignty" were both apparently only introduced into Qing political discourse in W. A. P. Martin's 1864 translation of Henry Wheaton's *Elements of International Law*. At least several decades earlier, however, officials and literati concerned with opium and other problems occasioned by the Western presence, including Lin Zexu, had been actively seeking a new vocabulary to meet their needs.[55] I would see *liquan* as Wang Liu's attempt to provide such. He underscores this by immediately adding that the vigorous protection of our *liquan* is necessary in order to ensure "respect for our national integrity" (*zun guojia zhi titong*)—as close, I would suggest, to a formulation for "national sovereignty" as was possible in a language lacking a precise equivalent for that foreign concept.[56]

53. *Dai Kan-Wa jiten*, 2.244; *Hanyu da cidian*, 1.706 and 2.640.

54. For recent attempts to penetrate the "tribute system" conceit, see Iwai Shigeki, "Chōkō to Goshi'chōkō taisei' ron no kokoromu" (Tribute and markets: a preliminary critique of the "tribute system" notion), http://www.hmm.bun.kyoto-u.ac.jp/asorder/meetings11–02.html; and Gang Zhao, *The Qing Opening to the Ocean: Chinese Maritime Policies, 1684–1757* (Honolulu: University of Hawai'i Press, 2013), chap. 5.

55. See, for example, Lydia H. Liu, *The Clash of Empires: The Invention of China in Modern World Making* (Cambridge, MA: Harvard University Press, 2004), chap. 4; Peter Zarrow, "Anti-Despotism and 'Rights Talk': The Intellectual Origins of Modern Human Rights Thinking in the Late Qing," *Modern China* 34.2 (April 2008): 185–86.

56. Wang, "Qianchao yi," part 1, in *Qianbi chuyan*.

Significantly as well, Wang uses not only *guojia* (the nation) with regularity, but also—in preference to "Qing empire" ("Daqing" or other terms then in existence)—habitually refers to his homeland as "Zhongguo," in a usage which can only be translated as "China." Foreign opium has been smuggled into "Zhongguo." Foreign currency, in the form of coins and banknotes, has gained acceptance within "Zhongguo." The currency Wang is proposing will be a true "Chinese money" (Zhongguo *zhi chao*), and its beneficiaries will be "the Chinese people" (Zhongguo *zhi ren*), as opposed to foreigners (*waiyang zhi ren*). As Gang Zhao has shown, it was precisely at this early nineteenth-century moment, threatened with a powerful potential enemy on the maritime coast and separatist struggles on the northwest frontier, that patriotic Chinese literati such as Wei Yuan and others began to apply the ancient usage "Zhongguo" (orginally a purely Han Chinese "central kingdom") to what they now saw as their proper homeland: the entire, newly forged multinational Qing imperium.[57] Wang Liu was clearly within this vein of protonationalist thought.

What do the differing solutions proposed by Wang Liu and Bao Shichen suggest about their perceptions of China's crisis in the early nineteenth century, and the necessary reforms? I do not see their differences, as does Lin Man-houng, as that between a statist approach to managing the economy (Wang) and a free-market "liberal" one (Bao). Bitingly critical as both men were of the policies of the existing regime, both recognized the urgency of the empire's need for a strong state. As early as the beginning of the century, Bao had been arguing that the pursuit of state wealth (*guofu*) and a sound fiscal base were critical to the imperiled Qing's survival, and he was no less adamant about this now, in this new era of foreign war. Both men linked this fiscal security, and good governance in general, with effective control over the monetary system. Wang Liu says, in a passage reproduced by Lin Man-houng, "If we want to guarantee the sufficiency of the ruler's finances [*juncai*], there is no better way than to grasp control of the monetary system [*tan qianbi zhi quan*]. If the ruler is unable to exert sovereign control over his currency, he cannot

57. Gang Zhao, "Reinventing China: Imperial Qing Ideology and the Rise of Modern Chinese National Identity in the Early Twentieth Century," *Modern China* 32.1 (January 2006): 18.

reduce the people's taxes in grain and cash, and thus facilitate their diligent pursuit of agriculture."[58] Bao said very nearly the same thing—he specifically applauded Wang's paper money proposal for the way it would enrich the state (*fuguo*) as well as benefit the people (*bianmin*)—minus the concept of sovereignty introduced by Wang. In general, the protonationalist elements I detect in Wang's treatise are less explicit, though far from totally absent, in Bao Shichen.

On the issue of foreign trade, both men want to end imports of opium. Wang is content for the remainder of the maritime trade to continue, provided his terms of trade—the use of paper—are accepted. One of the hallmarks of the contemporary age, he says, is that "Chinese and foreigners are as a single family, and merchants trade freely between them" (*Zhongwai yijia, shanggu liutong*).[59] In his youth, Bao Shichen had been unequivocally opposed to any maritime commerce at all, indeed proposing a death sentence for any Qing subject who engaged in it or purchased foreign goods; already by 1820, however, he was willing to countenance maritime trade in most commodities other than opium.[60]

Both men, as I have argued, accept the issuance of paper money as the state's prerogative, and both think it a useful means of dealing with the contemporary silver shortage. In this they are joined by others, but probably opposed by the majority of political thinkers of their day. Bao is much more cautious than Wang about the volume of paper currency that should be introduced, but though he, like Wang, wants paper fully redeemable in copper, he never stipulates that it be fully backed by any monetary metal; both men seem quite comfortable with the idea of a true fiduciary money.

In other ways, Wang Liu seems to come directly out of the more progressive economic thought of the eighteenth-century "prosperous age," a set of ideas that I have elsewhere identified with European physiocracy.[61]

58. Wang Liu, *Huozhongyuan chugao* (Preliminary drafts from the Huozhong Garden) (1835), reproduced photographically in Lin, *China Upside Down*, 150.

59. Wang, "Qianchao tiaomu," item 1, in *Qianbi chuyan*, 14–18.

60. Bao, *Shuochu*, 141; Bao, *Gengchen zazhu, er*, in *Quanji* (1997), 212.

61. See Rowe, *Saving the World*, esp. chap. 6. Other similarities between Qing political economy and French physiocracy are pointed out in Margherita Zanasi, "Frugality and Luxury: Morality, Market, and Consumption in Late Imperial China," *Frontiers of History in China* 10.3 (September 2015): 457–85.

That is, his monetary proposals are repeatedly defended on the grounds that they will help maximize the volume and velocity of domestic commercial circulation (*liutong*). Moreover, he rejects as counterproductive most forms of commandist intervention in private trade, such as imposition of fixed prices (*dingjia*)—even for the abominated opium.[62] Wang's assumptions that a superior monetary medium will "automatically" drive out (*zifei*) an inferior one, and that if a trade is rendered unprofitable it will "automatically" cease (*zizhi*), while both likely overoptimistic in their particulars, likewise fit securely into high Qing economic logic. What is new to his early nineteenth-century reformist thought, I would suggest, is primarily the emphasis on asserting sovereignty over the national economy; issuing a national currency backed exclusively by the authority of the state is his means of implementing this.

Despite the interest generated by Wang Liu's and others' proposals to introduce paper money in the 1830s, no such action was taken during the remainder of the Daoguang reign. When, under Daoguang's successor Xianfeng, a desperate court finally did opt in 1853 to float a paper currency in order to finance its anti-Taiping wars, it was calamatously unsuccessful in doing so; food and other commodity prices hyperinflated, provoking widespread unrest, especially among the salaried labor force in Beijing and other northern cities.[63] A viable paper currency was introduced into the Qing only at century's end, directly modeled on the very sort of foreign banknotes that Wang Liu had sought to drive out of the *patria*.[64] As in the Guomindang's currency reform of 1935, China was still struggling, with decidedly mixed success, to create a uniform and exclusive national currency.[65]

62. Wang Liu, "Youpeng zengta," in *Qianbi chuyan*, 43–44.

63. Peng Zeyi, "1853–1868 nian de Zhongguo tonghuo pengzhang" (China's currency inflation of 1853–1868), *Zhongguo kexue yanjiuyuan Jingji yanjiusuo jikan* 1 (1979); Hamashita, *Chūgoku kindai keizaishi kenkyū*, 59–60; Peng Xinwei, *Zhongguo huobi shi*, 808–10.

64. See Niv Horesh, "Printed in London, Disbursed on the Bund: The Hongkong Bank and its Early Note Issue in Shanghai, 1865–1911," *Late Imperial China* 27.1 (June 2006): 109–40.

65. Arthur N. Young, *China's Nation-Building Effort, 1927–1937: The Financial and Economic Record* (Stanford: Hoover Institution Press, 1971), chap. 9.

CHAPTER 7

Speaking of Profit

In the summer of 1846, Bao Shichen was seventy years old. He engaged in a correspondence with one Meng Kai, in regard to several remaining problems in the now-reformed grain tribute administration. Writing to Bao, Meng was emboldened to sum up concisely the old man's career, in the process observing that the one constant in Bao's policy proposals was his inclination to "speak of profit" (*yanli*). Since Meng's letter does not survive, we cannot be certain that he intended this in a positive sense—no less an authority than Gu Yanwu, after all, had written disparagingly of "officials who speak of profit"—but we do know that Bao Shichen was happy to take it as such. It indeed may be said that "speaking of profit" is my habitual vice, he replied, and it is the clear focus of more than half of my scholarship.

For example, how to reduce transport fees attached to the grain tribute is really "speaking of profit." So too is how to root out the practice of bribes, how to establish military colonies, and how to maximize the potential of local ecologies. Likewise the opening of mines and the printing of paper currency. Other matters, such as raising the public funding of local administrations so that officials won't be forced to gouge (*zuixiao*) the local population, and dispensing famine relief so as to prevent massive numbers of people from leaving the land, may not appear at first glance to be "speaking of profit," but if you think them through that is exactly what they are.[1]

1. Bao, "Ta zuzi Meng Kai shu" (Reply to Meng Kai), dated Daoguang 26/5/24, in *Quanji* (1997), 234–36. Meng is identified by Bao only as a "lineage head" (*zuzi*).

Matthews' Chinese-English Dictionary, reflecting usage from the early twentieth century, defines *li* as "profit, gain, advantage; interest on money." The Han-dynasty dictionary *Shuowen* offers the primary definition as *xian*=sharp, as in the blade of a knife; other classical and early imperial usages vary widely, including as *yu*=to plan or scheme.[2] But by far the most famous classical use of the character appears in the *Analects* 4:16: "The superior man understands righteousness; the inferior man understands profit" (*junzi yuyu yi, xiaoren yuyu li*). Wing-tsit Chan notes that, "This is the fundamental difference for Confucianism in general as well as for Confucius himself."[3] Bao Shichen's slightly defensive tone in his response to Meng Kai attests that, even for him, it was this pejorative usage that dominated the discourse of his day.

And yet there was a counterinterpretation, even in the classical era. Mozi, whom Bao almost certainly read and admired in his youth, argued that "any word or action that is beneficial to [*li*] Heaven, spiritual beings, and the people is to be undertaken. Any word or action that is harmful to Heaven, spiritual beings, and the people is to be rejected."[4] By late imperial times, Bao would have been familiar with, and indeed routinely employed, compounds in which the *li* component was unambiguously positive, such as *shuili*=the benefits to be gained by capable water management. As Hu Qizhuang points out, Bao's emphatically positive reading of "profit" or "benefit," striking as it may be, was not totally original, since there had been a venerable tradition of using it in this way since at least the Song, notwithstanding the heavy emphasis in neo-Confucianism on its paired alternative "righteousness" (*yi*).[5] Almost certainly the usage that Bao thought about most actively was that of Gu Yanwu, whose geographical treatise *Junguo libi shu* (Advantages and disadvantages of various localities in the empire) Bao encountered as a young man and

2. Morohashi Tetsuji, *Dai Kan-Wa jiten* (Great Chinese-Japanese dictionary) (Tokyo: Taishūkan shoten, 1955–60), 2.1325.

3. Wing-tsit Chan, *A Sourcebook in Chinese Philosophy* (Princeton: Princeton University Press, 1963), 28.

4. Chan, *Sourcebook*, 226. Chan, suggestively but perhaps ultimately unhelpfully, labels this sentiment "utilitarianism."

5. Hu Qizhuang, *Zhongguo jingji sixiang shi*, 586.

treasured as a model for his own personal scholarship.[6] For Bao, then, the logical opposite of *li* tended to be, not *yi*, but rather *bi*, disadvantage or dysfunction.

Although Bao is unabashedly positive about "profit" in most instances, he is known to use the term in the more conventional negative sense as well. He does so with revealing selectivity. Most often he associates *li* as self-interest with bureaucrats and officials—whose personal and corporate interests he clearly understands as separate and distinct from those of the state, the empire, or the *patria*. In the grain tribute, river conservancy, and salt administrations especially, bureaucratic managers habitually neglect what is best for both the state and the people in order to pursue their own narrow self-interest (*sishi zhi li*).[7] Even scrambling for examination success is an unseemly quest for personal interest. What is lost today, he laments, is a good old-fashioned Confucian sense of shame or self-respect (*chi*).[8] Bao points out that merchants necessarily act in pursuit of profit. There is nothing really immoral about this, but neither is it especially morally commendable. Bao's respect for the profit motive, in other words, is real but also guarded. What *is* definitely inappropriate is the application of personal profit-seeking, of mercantile logic, to the fulfillment of political office, and this is what characterizes bureaucratic behavior today, he says. It is not genuine *li* that is being pursued, but rather a perversion of legitimate benefit.[9]

This condemnation of middle managers is what facilitates Bao Shichen's ability to combine populism and patriotism. As Thomas Metzger long ago pointed out, a common trope in late imperial political argument is that the proposed policy will serve two—sometimes apparently conflicting—goals at the same time (*junyou biyi*). Probably the most frequent expression of this was the pairing of the beneficiaries' *guoji minsheng* (state finances and popular livelihoods).[10] Bao was a master of this

6. Bao, preface to *Anwu sizhong*, in *Quanji* (1997); Bao, "Du Tinglin yishu," in *Yizhou shuangji*, 2:1–4.

7. Bao, supplementary preface to *Zhongqu yishao*, in *Quanji* (1993), 8–10.

8. On shame, see especially preface to "Qimin sishu," in *Quanji* (1997), 159–61.

9. Ōtani, "Hō Seishin no jitsugaku shisō ni tsuite," 169–71.

10. Thomas A. Metzger, *The Internal Organization of Ch'ing Bureaucracy: Legal, Normative, and Communication Aspects* (Cambridge, MA: Harvard University Press, 1973), 55–56.

rhetoric, not least in his discussion of "profit." It was a basic premise of Bao's optimistic worldview that the "common interests" (*gongtong liyi*) of state and society might be advanced simultaneously, based on clear reasoning and a sound knowledge of empirical conditions. The fifth and final of the "Five Top Priorities" with which he concluded his 1801 manifesto *On Wealth* argued that any managerial strategy that did not profit the people (*bu li yu min*) could not, by definition, likewise profit the ruler (*bu li yu shang*). Variations of this formula—the expressed concern to simultaneously profit the people (*limin*) and profit the state (*liguo*)—remain a litany in Bao's prose for the subsequent half-century of his life.[11]

At this point we can return to two large questions that I raised conditionally in the introduction and that have informed my subsequent inquiry: what is Bao's position relative to social class, and what is his position relative to the polity? One way to approach this is to ask: what does he really mean by the "people" (*min*) and by the "state" (*guo*)?

Min is one of the most ubiquitous terms in Bao's writing, as it is in late imperial political-economic discourse more generally, and in both cases it covers a broad range of content. Bao uses it routinely to mean "society," or "private," or "nongovernmental," for example in the compounds *mincai* (private wealth or economic resources), *minli* (the financial capacity of the population for self-nurturance or to undertake infrastructural maintenance), and *mindi* (privately owned farmland). He also, as we saw in chapter 2, extrapolates from the last of these to designate the regime of private property ownership appropriately supported by the state (*minyou zhi*). In all of these, the bureaucratic state (*guan*) is the implied opposite, and at times in Bao's usage *min* is clearly a legal-administrative category. He speaks, for example of two types of fiscal arrears, those owed by the people to the state (*minqian*) versus those owed by one administrative unit to another (*guanqian*). *Min* as legal category is emphasized in Bao's discussion of grain tribute and salt administration reform, in which he lays out a variety of systems for procurement, delivery, and disposition in a series of four-character expressions dividing responsibility between private and bureaucratic personnel (*mincheng guandui* for grain, *minyun minshao* for salt, and so on). One of the most pregnant of such usages is the phrase, a favorite of "statecraft" literati and invoked on

11. Bao, *Shuochu*, 190; Bao, *Quanji* (1993), 8–10; Zhang Yan, "Bao Shichen," 134–36.

occasion by Bao, *cangfu yumin* (store wealth among the people), that is, avoid excessive government extraction in order to accumulate economic reserves in the hands of private households.[12]

The "people" in Bao's writings figure most often as a group whose profit, advantage, and convenience (*limin, bianmin*) is the principal goal of policy. They can and must be listened to. In the "Five Top Priorities" with which he concludes *On Wealth,* Bao stresses the need to recruit better officials who will truly understand popular sentiment (*minqing*); elsewhere, he argues that the essence of counterinsurgency military strategy may be summed up in three characters: *jin renqing* (get close to the real feelings of the people).[13] At the same time, however, the *min* are also a group to be guided by those, like Bao himself, with superior expertise and breadth of perspective. He is not above using condescending phrases such as *xiangli yumin*—effectively, "country bumpkins"—and referring to the responsibility of the lettered elite to exercise leadership over the general populace (*yiwei minchang*). The people are largely constrained by folkways (*minfeng*), which can be altered by policy.[14]

Most revealing, I think, is Bao's choice of the phrase *qimin* in the title of his 1844 collected essays on agriculture, social organization, law, and military affairs, *Qimin sishu. Qimin* can mean "the general population" or "ordinary people," and Bao does on occasion clearly use it in this sense.[15] But it is also a verb-object, as in the sentence from the *Analects* "put [the people] in order by means of ritual" (*qi zhi yi li*), which Bao in fact cites in the preface to his work.[16] It seems too much a stretch to credit the relatively humorless Bao Shichen with a pun here, but there may be a deliberate ambiguity intended, which hints at the author's awkward combination of plain-folk populism and elite paternalism.

The "people" for Bao is not a uniform category. There are divisions by native place or abode: local residents (*jumin*) versus sojourners (*kemin*)

12. For example see Bao, "Ti caobi," in *Huangchao jingshi wenbian,* 46:23–24. I discuss the meanings of this phrase in eighteenth-century official discourse in *Saving the World,* chap. 8.

13. Bao, *Shuochu,* 190; Hu Pu'an, *Nianpu,* 212–14. See also *Jingxian zhi,* 927; Shi Liye, "Bao Shichen 'Shuochu' chutan," 70.

14. Bao, "Ta zuzi Meng Kai shu," in *Quanji* (1997), 234–36.

15. Bao, *Shuochu,* 184.

16. Bao, "Yuyan" (Preface) to *Qimin sishu,* in *Quanji* (1997), 159–61.

versus dispossessed refugees (*yumin*). All three of these groups must be cared for—even the last, who, until or unless they turn into habitual vagrants (*liumang*), remain part of the "people." There are those who, he says, are our fellow countrymen (*guomin*), a sentiment to which I will return below. Among the people there are also moral categories, including rebels and criminals (*feimin*) and "traitors" (*jianmin*)—the latter for Bao less a sociological category than an all-purpose derogatory term applied to any group which engages in self-serving behavior (such as embezzlement or profiteering) at the expense of the good and law-abiding people (*liangmin*).[17] As much a champion of the agrarian population as Bao is, he is conscious that there are a select few who are habitually indolent (*duomin*), and whom local leaders are bound to prod or shame into productive activity.[18] Though the chief objects of his concern are cultivators, they are not alone. In his youthful *On Wealth* Bao lays out in orthodox fashion the various responsibilities of the classical four occupational groups (*simin*)—literati, farmers, artisans, and merchants—making clear that in his mind all comprise subsets of the "people."[19]

Bao was acutely aware of economic stratification, almost approaching class differentiation, among the people. Recall that as early as 1801 he proposed a system of classifying rural households according to their economic comfort level—with "poor households" (*pinhu*) and "destitute households" (*qionghu*) at the bottom—and of modest systematic redistribution of wealth based on these class labels.[20] In a letter of 1846 he acknowledges the distinction between the leisure class (*xianmin*) and those who derive their livelihood from their own labor or enterprise (*youye zhi min*), and the need to remain conscious of the differential effects policy changes might have on the two groups.[21] But the most routine term Bao employs to discuss the commoner class is "little people" (*xiaomin*), a word that seems to me roughly equivalent to the early

17. It is worthy of note that the *jianmin* (traitorous people) that is opposed to *liangmin* by Bao is never, to my knowledge, the other *jianmin* (debased people) that was so prominent in the discourse of a century earlier. For Bao, at least, by the early nineteenth century that particular set of concerns has been long laid to rest.

18. Bao, "Shuo baojia shiyi," in *Quanji* (1997), 271–82.

19. Bao, *Shuochu*, 133.

20. Bao, "Shuo baojia shiyi," in *Quanji* (1997), 271–82.

21. Bao, letter to Xu Taichang, in *Quanji* (1997), 237–39.

modern French *menu peuple*, albeit with a more rural valence.[22] When used as a paired category, *xiaomin* are most often opposed to *dahu* (great households), who "live in arrogant indolence," and are adept at shifting tax burdens to their poorer and less well-connected neighbors.[23]

It is worth noting that Bao never (that I have seen) invokes the common late imperial trope of *baofu* (preservation of private wealth) as a goal of economic policy, even though, in common with those who did so, he appreciated the role such wealth might play in relieving dearth or poverty. And whereas for other writers such as Tang Zhen (1630–1704) defense of profit seeking went hand in hand with a conception of wealth and luxury consumption as an engine of economic stimulation, Bao Shichen remained an emphatic champion of the classical virtue of personal and household frugality.[24]

Indeed, Bao is unequivocal that protecting and promoting the well-being of the *xiaomin* is the basic task of governance. The Duke of Zhou observed that if one is to do this, one must first understand how excruciatingly difficult their lives and labor are, and, as we saw in chapter 3, Bao describes this in detail. Writing at the height of the White Lotus uprising in 1801, Bao argues that the *xiaomin* are by nature good, and know right from wrong, but when immiserated they can easily be misled by traitorous elements into rebellion.[25] On the other hand, they are inherently wise or rational enough to follow "profitable" economic models when they are presented with them.[26] The ordinary burdens of the people are increasingly compounded in this contemporary age of crisis. Bao is not especially graphic in the language of exploitation, but he does decry the way the *min* are unnecessarily "exhausted" (*lao*) even by well-meaning but misguided government policies, and "oppressed" (*niu*) by evildoers.[27]

22. Less frequently he uses the still more patronizing *ximin* (trivial people).

23. Bao, "Haiyun shiyi," in *Quanji* (1993), 81–85; Ōtani, "Hō Seishin no jitsugaku shisō ni tsuite," 178.

24. Margherita Zanasi, "Frugality and Luxury: Morality, Market, and Consumption in Late Imperial China," *Frontiers of History in China* 10.3 (September 2015): 457–85.

25. *Shuochu*, 133.

26. Bao, *Quanji* (1993), 67–68.

27. Bao, *Shuochu*, 134; preface to supplement to *Zhongqu yishao*, in *Quanji* (1993), 8–10.

He is less reserved in identifying who these evildoers are: on the one hand, they are "thieving officials" (*taochen*), and on the other "evil gentry" (*liejin*), "traitorous grandees" (*haojian*), and "armed and wealthy degree holders" (*shenfu wuduan*) in rural society. It is the obligation of local administrators and the righteous local elite to shield the common people from predations such as these.[28]

Where does Bao situate himself in this diversity of humanity? How did he self-identify? He was, as we have seen, deeply proud that in his youth he had spent a short time actually practicing farm labor, and he was confident that this gave him a privileged understanding of both the techniques and the personal burdens of agriculture. But by no means did he see himself as a farmer or a "peasant." He protested that he was not a significant landholder, and thus his personal interests were not those of a presumed landlord class, but he accepted the fact that he was relatively leisured and comfortably well-to-do. At least once, revealingly, he refers to himself as part of "we Confucian literati" (*wuru*), a group whose role in life, he immediately adds, is to study and address questions of popular livelihood.[29]

Concern for the interests of popular well-being were considerably more central to Bao's thinking, Ōtani Toshio points out, than it was for Wei Yuan and other contemporary reformers.[30] They remind one more of mid-eighteenth-century statecraft officials such as Chen Hongmou, with one striking exception. For Chen and others of his era it was still possible to conceive of the pursuit of *minsheng* as a quest for genuine prosperity, even economic growth. For Bao, by contrast, "profiting the people" was more focused on the limited goal of alleviating popular immiseration (*minkun*). One clear example of his recognition of the reality of widespread destitution appears in his thinking on indigent family practice: whereas orthodox opinion held that wife selling was immoral and hence necessarily criminal, Bao argued that it was simply a rational response of households to economic desperation, and ought to be legal-

28. Bao, "Shuo koji shiyi" (On evaluating local officials), in *Quanji* (1997), 317–19.

29. Bao, "Yu Qin xueshi shu" (Letter to Subchancellor Qin), cited in Hu Qizhuang, *Zhongguo jingji sixiang shi*, 585.

30. Ōtani, "Hō Seishin no jitsugaku shisō ni tsuite," 182.

ized. Bao's optimism lay primarily in his faith that this far more modest goal—the relief of rural misery—was still attainable.[31]

Turning to the state side of the equation, we may ask to what extent Bao is a "statist," or indeed, as he is often depicted, a "nationalist"? It is striking at the outset that, in referring to the polity under which he lives and sometimes serves, Bao never once that I have seen uses the term "Qing," still less the court's favored "Daqing" (Great Qing). If called upon to name that polity his preferred usage seems to be "Zhonghua" (China?), clearly a reference to the millennial-old cultural entity that transcends individual imperial dynasties, either native or alien conquest.[32] On occasion he uses the modern toponym for China, "Zhongguo," but usually it is clearly opposed to *waifan*, that is, the portions of the empire that were not historically part of the Han domain but instead recently accreted by the Qing; in other cases he uses *neidi* (interior lands) with essentially the same meaning.[33] In all such instances, it is specifically the Zhongguo/*neidi*—not the empire as a whole—which is the object of Bao's own identification and sympathies.

As we have seen, Bao routinely uses the word *guo*, and almost as frequently the compound *guojia*. Both terms seem to me to refer not to the nation but to the polity, or the state, in contradistinction to the society or to outside forces. In at least one instance Bao uses *guojia* with the clear meaning of "dynasty," when he praises the "present *guojia*" for having maintained peace and prosperity for over 170 years.[34] The term's limited, administrative usage is underlined when Bao cites admiringly Gu Yanwu's dictum that *guo*s rise and fall, while the Tianxia (readable variously as the empire, the Chinese cultural ecumene, or civilization) has never been lost.[35]

Does this suggest an eagerness on Bao's part to distance himself subjectively from the Qing conquest regime? Not especially. In none of his work that I have read does Bao self-identify as "Han" (Chinese), and in-

31. Matthew H. Sommer, *Polyandry and Wife-Selling in Qing Dynasty China: Survival Strategies and Judicial Interventions* (Berkeley: University of California Press, 2015), 337–40.

32. For example, Bao, *Gengchen zazhu, er*, in *Quanji* (1997), 213.

33. Bao, *Gengchen zazhu, er*, in *Quanji* (1997), 213; *Shuochu*, 184–85.

34. Bao, "Gengchen zazhu, er," in *Quanji* (1997), 209.

35. Bao, "Du Gu Tinglin yishu," in *Yizhou quanji*, 2:1–4.

deed he only rarely uses the word "Han" at all; in one intriguing passage he refers to collaborators with the British as *hanjian* (traitors to the Han), but just a few sentences later replaces this term with *neijian* (traitors to their own domestic land).[36] He never uses the term "Man" or even "Qing" to refer to persons of Jurchen ancestry or identification; indeed, while he worked collegially and corresponded with a few high Manchu officials over the course of his career (Mingliang, Bailing, Yinghe), unlike other Han political activists he never seems to have numbered any Manchus among his active circle of friends. In sum, while Bao Shichen seems not to have harbored any active Han-chauvinist passions, he was largely indifferent to the realities of alien rule.

Even with Europeans, it was not racial antagonisms that seem to have motivated Bao. Like everyone else in his discursive universe, he referred to them as *yi* (somewhat misleadingly translated "barbarians"), and with good reason he increasingly hated them. But his deprecatory references to the British and others tended to concentrate on their puny numbers versus the vast Chinese populace, on their criminality (*taozei*), and on their generally "despicable" (*bi*) predatory conduct, rather than on an essentialized inferiority, either culturally or racially.

As we have seen, Bao Shichen was unembarrassed by his concern to "profit the state" (*liguo*), and saw this project as complementary rather than contrary to the need to "profit the people." It is likely not coincidental that his favored phrase for what scholars today translate as Qing "statecraft" thought was not the usual *jingshi* or "managing the world/society," but instead *jingguo*, or "managing the state."[37] Profiting the state meant several things—among them enforcing respect for its integrity and its laws (the body politic = *guoti*)—but it was financial interests that remained foremost in Bao's mind. At the very outset of his youthful *On Wealth* he argued that well-managed finances (*licai*) were the most crucial element in establishing and maintaining a successful polity (*liguo*), and he never wavered from this view throughout his life. As much as relieving the people's misery, stabilizing state budgets (*guoji*) was a cornerstone of his policy advice; his proposed salt reforms, perhaps

36. Bao, *Gengchen zazhu, er*, in *Quanji* (1997).

37. *Shuochu*, 134–35. Bao also used this phrase to describe the project of his role model Gu Yanwu, frequently portrayed as an antistatist.

above all, weré centrally designed to ensure that there will be no shortfalls in state revenues (*guoke buxu*).[38] Despite the success of many of his suggested reforms, however, he fretted to Meng Kai in 1846 that state budgets were running greater deficits every day (*rixu*). And it was not only a repair of alarming deficiencies, but also an active pursuit of state wealth and power that Bao sought.

Our conventional view of imperial Chinese political economy sees within it what Benjamin Schwartz identified as "two basic alternatives." One of these, "the main line of Confucian orthodoxy," saw the state as a moral agent, the "managerial and coercive functions" of which were minimalized, and which avoided as much as possible "military undertakings, ambitious public works, and the excessive luxuries of the ruling class" in order to keep the fiscal burdens on the people as low as possible. The second alternative, identified with Legalist thinkers of the Warring States period, frankly admitted the need for and desirability of state wealth and power. Although emperors and statesmen throughout imperial history in practice not infrequently acted in line with this statist alternative, even they tended to identify and announce themselves as "staunch Confucians" of the orthodox stripe. According to Schwartz, "the advocates of 'practical statesmanship' at the turn of the nineteenth century were firmly committed to the orthodox Confucian political-economic philosophy," and even the early Westernized reformers of the 1860s and 70s "essentially adhered to the same school." It was only in the final decades of the nineteenth century, under the direct influence of Western thought, that Chinese reformers "began to emphasize the old suspect motto 'wealth and power.' "[39]

The writings of Bao Shichen belie this familiar timeline. In his first significant work, the *On Wealth* of 1801, he sounded this theme proudly, and connected it with the new pressures of the post-"prosperous age" era: "Examining the current situation we see enfeebled troops and impoverished people, but these are but the raw materials out of which we can forge wealth and power [*fuqiang*]."[40] As passionate as he was about relieving fiscal and other burdens on the population, throughout his career span-

38. Bao, *Quanji* (1993), 162–69.

39. Benjamin I. Schwartz, *In Search of Wealth and Power: Yen Fu and the West* (Cambridge, MA: Harvard University Press, 1964), 10–18.

40. Bao, *Shuochu*, 134.

ning the first half of the nineteenth century Bao spoke unabashedly about pursuing goals of "state wealth" (*guofu*) and of "enriching the polity" (*fuguo*). Nor, of course, was Bao Shichen alone in this new orientation. Writing in some measure under Bao's influence, Wei Yuan observed that "Without wealth and power [*fuqiang*] there can be no *wangdao* [the Confucian model of moral/minimal rule]."[41] This theme in Bao's writing was only intensified as the terrible reality of the European threat, barely imagined in 1801, began to move ever more to the forefront of his consciousness.

To what extent is "Zhongguo" in Bao's writing at times translatable as "China," and *guomin* as "we Chinese"? To what extent is his frank concern for the interests, the wealth and power, of the *guo* or *guojia* capable of being read as at least a protonationalism? Bao's apparent lack of concern for racial categories seems to make the customary dismissive category "Han chauvinism" not usefully applicable in his case. He is certainly "patriotic," and *guojia* in his writing, if not fairly translatable as "the nation," is certainly at times equivalent to "the *patria*." But there are elements in his thinking that resonate closely with the unquestionably nationalistic thought of Chinese of several generations later.

Most immediately obvious is his economic protectionism. We have seen that he opposed the importation of Mongol salt as a means of alleviating problems in the domestic salt monopoly, on the grounds that this would effectively export the profits of the salt trade outside the confines of China proper (*neidi*). We have seen how, in his youthful *On Wealth*, he advocated for the total abolition of trade with Europeans, and the imposition of draconian punishments on those Chinese who participated in it. By the 1820s Bao had been reconciled to the existence of a certain limited degree of Western trade, but at the same time pioneered in the formulation of a mercantilist logic that opium imports were behind the empire's "silver famine," and advanced a sophisticated argument for the domestic immiseration caused by the consequent skewed silver-to-copper exchange rates. He observed with alarm in 1828 that the acceptance of foreign coin in domestic markets forced the empire's own coin to trade

41. Ōtani, "Hō Seishin no jitsugaku shisō ni tsuite," 168. See also Liu Guangjing, *Jingshi sixiang yu xinxing qiye* (Statecraft thought and modern enterprise) (Taibei: Lianjing, 1990), 2.

as a discount.[42] As we have seen, he was sympathetic to Wang Liu's arguments in the 1830s for the establishment of a national currency, even while he was perceptive enough to acknowledge that this alone would not rectify the imbalance of foreign trade that opium had precipitated. Most precociously "anti-imperialist" of all was Bao's complaint in 1846 that increased imports of foreign cotton cloth (*yangbu*) as a result of opening of the first treaty ports had reduced by more than half the sales of domestic cloth by Songjiang and Taichang merchants, and precipitated a depression in the village economy, which was dependent on spinning and weaving of handicraft cloth. This phenomenon, he insisted, was a clear loss of *li* (profit) to foreigners.[43] Bao himself may not have employed the term *liquan* (right to profits), articulated by Wang Liu in the 1830s and routinely used by Li Hongzhang and other "self-strengtheners" in the later nineteenth century as equivalent to the Western notion of economic "sovereignty," but he was a central party to the conversation in which such discursive formations first emerged.[44]

Bao Shichen's arguments against imperialism in the economic realm may be his most precocious theoretically, but his responses to Western territorial encroachment are impressive in another way: a man usually distinguished for his calm rationality, Bao here reveals a new dimension of his character, a radical intemperance. In 1828 he wrote to the incoming Guangdong provincial judge of his dire assessment of the British threat. The British, he says, sent two missions to the Qing court (those of Macartney and Amherst)—missions that failed due to British arrogance but that resulted nonetheless in their long progress from the north back to the south, during the course of which the "barbarians" had enjoyed the opportunity to gather much intelligence on local topographical and economic conditions. Now, supposedly limited to tightly regulated trade at Guangzhou, the British still managed to bring in opium and others of their imports at various ports along the coast, in some cases personally but more often in collusion with local magnates (*dahu*) and racketeers (*feimin*). Most distressing of all was that the British had now (since 1819)

42. Bao, "Zhi Guangdong ancha Yao Zhongcheng shu," in *Quanji* (1997), 486–88.

43. Bao, "Ta zuzi Meng Kai shu," in *Quanji* (1997), 234–36.

44. On the emerging Chinese notion of sovereignty, see work in progress by Anne Reinhardt.

managed to seize Singapore—an important outpost in the South China sea, which had long served as a lair for pirates and smugglers, and which now allowed the foreigners largely to overcome what had been their greatest strategic liability, the immense distance from China to their own home area.[45]

After his predicted (and sought) war with the British eventually broke out in 1839, the aging Bao observed with patriotic ire the gradual loss to foreign occupation of coastal territories such as Xiamen and Dinghai. He recommended to Qing commanders systematic consultation of maritime atlases in order to place these losses in broader geographic perspective.[46]

As it happened, Bao was residing in Nanjing when the British beseiged the former imperial capital in the spring of 1842 and the peace negotiations got under way. He was in no mood for conciliation. As he wrote, the barbarians' "contempt for China" (*miao Zhonghua*) was so offensive as to call for the most desperate measures. Deeply admiring the popular militia who at Sanyuanli and elsewhere had fought brave but ultimately doomed local defense efforts against the powerful foreigner, Bao worked late into the nights to develop his own plan to "annihilate the barbarian" (*jianyi*). His scheme involved redeploying many of the Qing forces operating in the lower Yangzi region, but its centerpiece was the recruitment of a corps of two hundred suicide bombers—"martyrs" (*sishi*)—who would board the several British warships tied up in Nanjing in the guise of bringing on supplies and explode them out of the water. With characteristic optimism, Bao wrote of the truth of the old saying that the deepest calamity—in this case the presence of the bulk

45. Bao, "Zhi Guangdong ancha Yao Zhongcheng shu" (To Guangdong Provincial Judge Yao), in *Quanji* (1997), 486–88. See also Waley, *The Opium War through Chinese Eyes*, 17; Matthew W. Mosca, *From Frontier Policy to Foreign Policy: The Question of India in the Transformation of Geopolitics in Qing China* (Stanford: Stanford University Press, 2013), 224–25.

46. Bao, "Zhisi tui wei Chen Junmen Jieping zuo," in *Quanji* (1997), 488–90. As Mosca argues (*From Frontier Policy to Foreign Policy*, 223), Bao was the first Chinese scholar-official to link the previously separate issue of coastal defense with a comprehensive geographic understanding of the overseas world.

of the British fleet at Nanjing itself—brings with it the possibility of good fortune.[47]

Bao Shichen was eyewitness to the long and deepening crisis of China's early nineteenth century. He began his career at the battlefront of a major domestic rebellion, the White Lotus, in the course of which he experienced firsthand the collapse of bureaucratic efficacy and morale inflicted by the Heshen corruption racket. He observed the heady optimism and gradual disillusionments of the "Jiaqing restoration," the dramatic reversal of the empire's long-standing favorable balance of trade, the multifaceted disaster of escalating opium imports, and the resulting (at least in his view) Daoguang depression of the 1820s. Despite his continued faith in the growth potential of the empire's agrarian economy, he lamented the intensifying immiseration of its farming population. He witnessed with alarm and wrath progressive encroachment on the part of his country's new and powerful maritime enemies, and was present in the city where the first of China's humiliating "unequal treaties" was assented to by Qing officials. He died in 1855, eighty years old and on the run from a new and unprecedentedly devastating civil war, that unleashed by the Taiping Heavenly Kingdom.[48]

Bao firmly believed that the basic problem underlying this crisis was not the empire's diminishing resource endowment nor its manifest population growth (which he applauded); nor was it the property regime and inequalities of wealth; nor was it even the imperial system, alien rule, or the basic structure of the Qing polity (*guoti*). Rather, it was a variety of specific institutional dysfunctions that led to wealth being siphoned off at an intermediate level (*zhongbao*) by self-interested parties (*jianmin*), depriving both the state and the people of the resources they needed to do their jobs. One concrete example came in Jiangxi in 1836, where he discovered that despite the Daoguang emperor's decree that all popular tax arrears from before the major flood of 1830 would be forgiven, these arrears were still being collected by local functionaries, in practice "immiserating the destitute while fattening up the clerks" (*lei gupin er fei shuyi*).[49] In

47. Bao, "Jianyi yi" (A plan to annihilate the barbarians), in *Quanji* (1997), 500–502: *Jingxian zhi*, 927; Chen Wenyu, "Aiguo chenmin," 48–49.

48. Hu Pu'an, *Nianpu*, 240; Mann, *Talented Women*, 118.

49. Letter to Chen Yusheng, 1836, in *Quanji* (1997), 256–60.

his 1846 letter to Meng Kai, Bao wrote that his entire career had been devoted to identifying and recapturing this sort of *zhongbao*, with the goal of returning it 30 percent to the state and 70 percent to the people.[50] This attack on *zhongbao* also informs the writings of Gu Yanwu, of course, but it achieved a new centrality in the thought of mid-nineteenth-century reformers such as Hu Linyi.[51] Bao Shichen seems thus somewhat precocious in his focus on this particular bogeyman.

Bao also believed that these dysfunctions were fully capable of correction by experts such as himself, who were clearsighted enough to identify the problems and courageous enough to propose major or minor systemic reforms (*gaizhi*, *bianfa*) and see them through to completion. He of course was not wrong about the latter, and in fact could and did contribute to some reform efforts that brought genuine relief. But did the crisis in fact run much deeper than even this highly perceptive man imagined?

What was really going on during the Jiaqing and Daoguang reigns that Bao Shichen missed, or was only barely aware of? There was major decay in the empire's infrastructure, which Bao periodically addressed in his proposals for hydraulic renovation (issues not looked at in this study) and which he implicitly acknowledged by advocating abandonment of the no-longer-viable Grand Canal for tribute grain transport. Related to this were new manifestations of long-term ecological decline, for example, greater propensity for flooding of the Yangzi River. One can debate about the particulars, but there were also major changes in the Qing empire's forces and relationships of economic production, as commercialization continued to intensify on every scale. And there were fundamental changes under way in the global economy, as the first implications of the industrial revolution in Western Europe began to affect distant markets such as the Qing empire.

We may conclude by suggesting some basic assumptions in Qing policy making that Bao Shichen embodies, and at least helped to bring about. One was a move away from Song-Ming *lixue* as the ideological grounding of public discourse; whereas even the most pragmatic reformers of the Yongzheng-Qianlong era had rooted their administrative

50. Letter to Meng Kai, 1846, in *Quanji* (1997), 237–39.
51. See, for example, Rowe, "Hu Lin-i."

activism in neo-Confucian rhetoric (and for many of these reformers, such as Chen Hongmou, this was also a matter of deep personal belief), Bao and other reformers of the Jiaqing and Daoguang reigns, while they still valued Confucian family ritual and other devices as contributors to public order, had moved well beyond *lixue* as a value system and legitimation for their public policy.[52] Along with this went a much greater acceptance of secular change as a reality of life. Bao may not have moved as far in this regard as Wei Yuan, Gong Zizhen, and other converts to new text or Gongyang studies, but he routinely prefaced his policy recommendations with an argument that there is no sense sticking to the way things once were done, because conditions have now fundamentally and irretrievably changed.

Bao's career also marks a significant, if not a singular, moment in the emergence of technical "expertise" as a valued personal and political asset. There is no question that the storied "amateur ideal" of the literatus-gentleman was still alive for some in his day, but this had already long been challenged by a growing professionalization of knowledge and careers. Charlotte Furth and her colleagues have explicated how over the late imperial period one particular method—the systematic analysis of case studies (*an*)—was employed in both the training and credentialing of specialist experts in the fields of medicine, law, Buddhist theology, and even Confucian moral and political thought.[53] Bao Shichen did not emphasize this method, but we have seen how regularly he deployed another technique, quantitative analysis, to demonstrate his superior expertise to that of *xiaoru*—"petty Confucians" or, here, perhaps better read as "armchair scholars" or "amateurs." Similarly, he brandished his use of field investigation and on-site interviews to report, for example, on the detailed organizational structure of salt transport and coastal shipping. He

52. Admittedly, a revival of Song *lixue* faith animated the thought of some, mostly Hunanese, activists of the mid-nineteenth century, such as Hu Linyi and Zeng Guofan. But as Mary Wright long ago pointed out, this was a rearguard movement that largely died out along with these individuals. The move away from Song *lixue* ideals that is evident in Bao, Wei Yuan, and others of their contemporaries would resurface as the ground of political reformism by the latter decades of the century.

53. Charlotte Furth, Judith T. Zeitlin, and Ping-chen Hsiung, eds., *Thinking with Cases: Specialist Knowledge in Chinese Cultural History* (Honolulu: University of Hawai'i Press, 2007). See especially Furth's "Introduction," 2–3 and 20–22.

did so, it appears to me, to a degree well in excess of the need to support his specific policy proposals, but rather as if to advertise that "I've been there and talked to these people, and you have not."

More than this, Bao relied heavily (and ostentatiously) in his argumentation on what Mary Poovey has called the "modern fact." According to Poovey, the advent of "political arithmetic," the insistence that policy making should be grounded in numbers and measurements, was a unique product of seventeenth-century England.[54] By contrast, throughout the nineteenth century Anglophone writers such as Samuel Wells Williams felt comfortable in dismissing the Qing empire as "a place without facts." As Tong Lam observes, it was not that late imperial China had no tradition of empirical reasoning—it did indeed have a rich one, as reflected for instance in both *kaozheng* philology and *jingshi* political economy—but that it lacked "the particular mode of knowledge production—the quantified 'fact' "—that the West proudly brandished as the necessary epistemological unit of sociopolitical discourse.[55] Here again, with his intense infatuation with numbers, Bao Shichen seems to anticipate by roughly half a century the emphases of "self-strengthening and new policies" reformers of the Qing's final decades.

Whether or not one chooses to see Bao Shichen as a Smithian economic "liberal" (and I have made it clear here that I do not), there can be no question that in his reforms to the grain tribute administration, the salt administration, and countless other smaller matters he evidenced a great openness to market forces. This was not new to the nineteenth century—it was common among high Qing administrators of a "practical studies" (*shixue*) or "statecraft" (*jingshi*) bent—but it would be hard to deny that Bao and others of his era such as Wei Yuan and Tao Zhu took their appreciation for the market and faith in the efficiencies of private commerce at least one step further.

54. Mary Poovey, *A History of the Modern Fact: Problems of Knowledge in the Sciences of Wealth and Society* (Chicago: University of Chicago Press, 1998). For a history of claims made for the superior persuasive power of quantification in the West, see also Theodore M. Porter, *Trust in Numbers: The Pursuit of Objectivity in Science and Public Life* (Princeton: Princeton University Press, 1995).

55. Tong Lam, *A Passion for Facts: Social Surveys and the Construction of the Chinese Nation-State, 1900–1949* (Berkeley: University of California Press, 2011), 12–23.

Central to all the above was Bao's single-minded focus on the pursuit of "profit" or "benefit," not only for the people but also for the polity. He was frank in his quest for "wealth and power" (*fuqiang*) for the state—for China—in a way that anticipates the new concerns of late Qing anti-imperialists and nationalists. It was not without reason that radical intellectuals like Kang Youwei and Liu Shipei saw him as one of their own, as indeed do patriotic Chinese historians of all political stripes today.

Glossary

aimin 愛民
an shangxin 安商心
Anwu sizhong 安吳四種

bachi 把持
bagu wen 八股文
Bailing 百齡
baishi 百世
baiwei feishi 百爲廢弛
baiwu 百物
bakao 罷考
Bao cun 包村
Bao Ganchen 包幹臣
Bao Junxue 包郡學
Bao Shichen 包世臣
Bao Shirong 包世榮
baochao 寶鈔
baodai hang 保戴行
baofu 保富
baoheng 暴横
baojia 保甲
baqi 八旗
bashi 罷市
benfu 本富
benmo xifu 本末習富
bi 弊
bianfa 變法
bingchuan 兵船
bingjia 兵家
bizheng 弊政
bu 步
bufen zhenyu 不分畛域
buhe zhi caiyuan 不涸之財源
bu jushou guren gezhe 佈拘守古人格轍
buli shangyuan 不立商垣
buru fa 不如法
buyou 不友

Cai Junbi 蔡君弼
Cai Shiying 蔡士英
Cai Zhiding 蔡之定
Cao Xibao 曹錫寶
caogui 漕規
caogun 漕棍
caomang yingxiong 草莽英雄
ceng 層
Changzhou 常州
Changzhou ershen 常州二申
chaochuan 鈔串
Chen Hongmou 陳宏謀
Chen Yusheng 陳玉生
Chen Zilong 陳子龍
Cheng Shishun 程世淳
cheng tianshi renshi 乘天時人事
chi 恥
chongjian chushe 崇儉黜奢

Chouban yiwu shimo 籌辦夷務始末
chuan 串
chuanzhu 船主
chuyang maoyi 出洋貿易
Chunqiu 春秋
congsheng daoshuai 從盛到衰

dabian 大變
dachao 大鈔
dahu 大户
Dai Quheng 戴衢亨
dan 石
dangshi 當事
daochen 盜臣
daochuan 島船
daozei 盜賊
daqian 大錢
Daqing 大清
Daqing huidian shili 大清會典事例
Daxue yanyi bu 大學衍議補
dayi 大益
dihuan 遞緩
dingjia 定價
dingyin gui tian 丁銀歸田
dongnan kaiyang 東南開洋
dongnan zhi huan 東南之患
dongnan zhi kun 東南之困
dongshi 董事
duifei 兑費
duomin 惰民

fajia 法家
Fang Bao 方苞
Fang Baoyan 方葆岩
Fang Dongshu 方東樹
fashenju 發審局
Fashishan 法式善
feimin 匪民
fei minjia siye 非民家私業
Feng Guifen 馮桂芬
foufei 浮費
fuguo 富國
fuhu 富户
fumin 富民
fuqiang 富強

gaizhi 改制
gang 綱
Ganyu 贛榆
Gaojia yan 高家堰
Gengchen zazhu 庚辰雜著
Gong Zizhen 龔自珍
gongfei 公費
gongran kaidian 公然開店
gongsi zhi liyi 公私之利益
gongtong liyi 共同利益
gongxiang 公項
gongyan 貢鹽
Gongyang 公羊
Gu Yanwu 顧炎武
guanbi minfan 官弊民反
guandian 官佃
guanggun 光棍
guanli 官力
guanqian 官欠
guanzheng guandui 官征官兑
gujin yiche 古今一車
guofu 國富
guoji dayu 國計大裕
guoji minsheng 國計民生
guojia 國家
guoke buxu 國課不虛
guomai 國脈
guomin 國民
guwen 古文

haiguo 海國
haiyun 海運
han 函
Hanjian 漢奸
Hanxue 漢學
Hanxue shangdui 漢學商兑
haojian 豪奸
haoshi 耗蝕
haozhe 耗折
He Changling 賀長齡
Heshen 和珅
Hong Liangji 洪良機
Hu Linyi 胡林益
Hu Pu'an 胡樸安
Huaibei 淮北

Huainan 淮南
Huaizhou 壞州
Huang Juezi 黄爵滋
Huangchao jingshi wenbian 皇朝經世文編
huiguan 會館
huipiao 會票
hunlan daohuan 昏爛倒換
huohao 火耗
huzhao 護照

jianmin 奸民
jianyou 簡優
Jiaqing xinzheng 嘉慶新政
jianyi 殲夷
jiesan yanjin 解散鹽禁
jin renqing 近人情
jincheng baowu 禁呈寶物
jingguo 經國
jingkong 京控
jingshi 經世
Jingxian 涇縣
jingxue 經學
jinri 今日
jinwen 今文
jiuqing 九卿
jixian 瘠縣
juanli 捐例
juanna 捐納
juansheng 捐生
jumin 居民
juncai 君財
junhuo biannong 均貨便農
junjichu 軍機處
junyou biyi 均有裨益
junzu 君足

kai taiping 開太平
kaifang 開放
kaiken 開墾
Kang Youwei 康有為
Kangwan 抗頑
kaozheng 考證
ke tan dingdi 課攤丁地
kemin 客民
kou'an 口岸
kuangtu 礦土

laohu tou 老虎頭
lei gupin er fei shuyi 累孤貧而肥書役
Lei Yixian 雷以諴
li (principle) 理
li (profit) 利
li (ritual) 禮
li (unit of distance) 里
Li Hongzhang 李洪章
Li Zhaoluo 李兆洛
liang 兩
Liang-Huai 兩淮
Liang Qichao 梁啓超
liangfa 良法
liangmin 良民
liangshang 良商
Liangyuan 兩淵
licai 理財
liejin 劣衿
liguo bianmin 利國便民
Lin Zexu 林則徐
lingshou 領首
liquan 利權
Liu Fenglu 劉逢祿
Liu Shipei 劉師培
Liu Xin 劉歆
Liu Yan 劉晏
Liu Zhihui 柳治徽
liumang 流氓
liutong 流通
lixue 理學
lizuo 力作
Longcheng 龍城
lougui 陋規
louru 陋孺
Lu Shiyi 陸世儀

maike 買客
meiyi 美意
Meng Kai 孟開
menpai 門牌
miao Zhonghua 藐中華

minbian 民變
mincai 民財
minchuan 民船
minfeng 民風
minghuan 名宦
Mingliang 明亮
mingnong 明農
minjuan guanban 民捐官辦
minjuan minban 民捐民辦
minkun 民困
minli 民力
minqian 民欠
minqing 民情
minsheng 民生
minshi 民食
minyou zhi 民有制
minyun minxiao 民運民銷
minzheng 敏政
minzheng guandui 民征官兑
minzheng mindui 民征民兑
minzu 民足
Miyun 密云
mofu 末富
moshi 沒世
mou 畝
mousheng 謀生
Mozi 墨子
muyou 幕友
Muzhanga 穆彰阿

neidi 內地
neijian 內奸
neiwufu 內務府
Ni Yuanlu 倪元璐
nongjia 農家
nongmin shenghuo 農民生活
nongshu 農書
Nongzheng 農政
nuemin 虐民

paigei 派給
piao 票
pingtiao 平糶
pinku gongzuo zhi jia
貧苦工作之家
pinhu 貧户
pinruo neifu 貧弱內府

Qi Yanhuai 齊彥槐
qi zhi yi li 齊之以禮
Qian Qianyi 錢謙益
Qianbi chuyan 錢幣芻言
qiangfu waifan 強富外藩
qiangu weiyou yu shi 千古未有於是
qianpiao 錢票
qianzhuang 錢莊
qimin 齊民
Qimin sishu 齊民四術
Qin Chengye 秦承業
qingcha ju 清查局
Qingjiang 清江
Qingkou 青口
Qingmou 清畝
Qingshi gao 清史稿
qinxin weiyuan 親信委員
qinzheng 勤政
qionghu 窮户
qisuan 起算
qiu er de 求而得
Qiu Jun 邱濬
Qiu Shutang 邱樹堂
quanli 權利
quannong 勸農
quanpai yanggei 勸派養給

raohu 饒户
raoxian 饒縣
renshi 人事
rixu 日虛
Rizhi lu 日知錄
Ruan Yuan 阮元

san da zheng 三大政
Sanyuanli 三元里
shachuan 沙船
shang liguo xia limin
上利國下利民
shanghu 上户
shenfu wuduan 紳富武斷
shengcai zhi dadao 生財之大道

shengshi 盛世
shenguanyuan 審官院
shengyuan 生員
shengzhe 生者
shi bubian 十不便
shidafu 士大夫
shidi xue 史地學
shimou 實畝
shixue 實學
shiye wulai 失業無賴
shizheng 實政
shoucheng 守成
shuaifu yipin 衰富益貧
shuili 水利
Shuochu 說儲
Shuowen 說文
shusheng yutan 書生迂談
shuishou 水手
siku quanshu 四庫全書
Sima Guang 司馬光
simin 四民
sishi 私士
sishi zhi li 司事之利
sishu 私書
sixiang wei cheng zhi genben 四鄉爲城之根本
Song Rong 宋熔
Songxue 宋學
suwang 素王

tan qianbi zhi quan 擅錢幣之權
Tang Zhen 唐甄
Tao Zhu 陶澍
tiandi zhi cang 天地之藏
tianxia 天下
Tianxia junguo libing shu 天下郡國利病書
tidu 提督
Tinglin yishu 亭林遺書
tizheng 體政
Tongcheng 桐城
tongju 銅局
tongshang 通商
tufeng 土風
tuntian 屯田

waifan 外藩
waiyang zhi ren 外洋之人
waiyi 外夷
Wang Anshi 王安石
Wang Ding 王鼎
Wang Liangsheng 王亮生
Wang Liu 王瑬
wangdao 王道
wanwu 萬物
Wei Yuan 魏源
weisuo 衛所
wen 文
Wenxuan 文選
wuru 吾孺
Wuxian 吳縣

xiahu 下户
xian (sharp) 銛
Xianfeng yiqian 咸豐以前
xiangli yumin 鄉里愚民
Xiangren li 鄉人禮
xiangxian 鄉賢
xianmin 閑民
xianyu weixin 咸與維新
xiaochao 小鈔
xiaomin 小民
xiaoru 小孺
xin (faith) 信
xingli chubi 興利除弊
Xinpu 新浦
Xinyu 新喻
Xu Guangqi 徐光啓
Xu Mei 訏楣
Xuannan 宣南
xunshi 訓示
Xunzi 荀子
xushang 恤商
xuzhong shiwai 虛中實外

yan li 言利
Yan Ruyi 嚴如熤
yanchai 鹽差
yangbu 洋布
Yanghu 洋湖
yangtong 洋銅

yanjin 嚴禁
yanke 鹽課
yanlu 言路
yanru caichu 鹽入財出
yantu 鹽徒
Yao Chengqian 姚承謙
Yao Fengnian 姚逢年
Yao Nai 姚鼐
yaren 牙人
yi (righteousness) 義
yihai daihe 以海代河
yihu 義户
yin 引
Yin Zhuangtu 尹壯圖
yindi zhili 因地致力
yinghao 英豪
Yinghe 英和
yingu choujin 引古籌今
yinhuang 銀荒
yinzhao 印照
yiren shengtian 以人勝天
yishang daiguan 以商代官
yizhen 義振
Yizhou shuangji 藝舟雙楫
yizui yin 議罪銀
yongzhi feian 壅滯廢閣
youhuo wushou 有貨無售
youmin 游民
youming yu shi 有名於世
youye zhi min 有業之民
youyong zhi xue 有用之學
Yu Damazi 余大麻子
yu min zheng li 於民爭利
yuan'e 元惡
yuanku ke sheng yan 冤苦可勝言
yuanqi 元氣
yufu 迂腐
yumin 淤民
yunsi 運司

zaoyi 皂役
Zeng Guofan 曾國藩
zettai kunshu 絶對君主
Zhang Qi 張琦
Zhang Tingyu 張廷玉
Zhang Yuanfu 張淵甫
zhaofu 招撫
Zhaolian 昭槤
zhengke 正課
zhengti 政體
zhidao 治道
zhiluan 治亂
zhiqian 制錢
zhishun 至順
zhizhao 執照
zhizhu zhi fei 紙硃之費
zhongbao 中飽
zhongchao 中鈔
zhongdi 重地
Zhongguo 中國
Zhongguo zhi chao 中國之鈔
Zhongguo zhi ren 中國之人
zhonghu 中户
Zhonghua 中華
Zhongjiang shuyuan 中江書院
zhongmai 中賣
Zhongqu yishao 中衢一勺
zhongshu 眾恕
Zhongwai yijia, shanggu liutong 中外一家商賈流通
Zhu Gui 朱珪
Zhuang Cunyu 莊存與
zhuquan 主權
zifei 自廢
zixingche 自行車
zixingren 自行人
zizhi 自止
Zizhi tongjian 資治通鑑
zouzhe 奏摺
zuixiao 朘削
zun guojia zhi titong 尊國家之體統
zuo'er 佐貳
zuoli 作力
Zuozhuan 左傳
zuzi 族子

Bibliography

Works by Bao Shichen

Note: Numerous editions of works by Bao Shichen have been published, beginning in his own lifetime and continuing today. I have chosen to rely for the most part on the "Complete Works" published in three volumes over the course of the 1990s by Huangshan shushe, in Hefei, Anhui, all of which, confusingly, bear the same title. Although this may or may not be a definitive edition of Bao's writings, it is certainly the most commonly available, and today the most frequently cited. While I have occasionally consulted other editions of Bao's individual works as needed, in this study I cite only the Guoxue baocun hui and Zhonghua shudian editions listed below.

Bao Shichen. *Bao Shichen quanji* (Complete works of Bao Shichen). Ed. Li Xing and Liu Changgui. Hefei: Huangshan shushe, 1991.
———. *Bao Shichen quanji* (Complete works of Bao Shichen). Ed. Li Xing. Hefei: Huangshan shushe, 1993.
———. *Bao Shichen quanji* (Complete works of Bao Shichen). Ed. Li Xing. Hefei: Huangshan shushe, 1997.
———. *Bao Shenbo Shuochu* (Bao Shichen's "Shuochu"). Shanghai: Guoxue baocun hui, 1906.
———. *Yizhou shuangji* (Two oars for the boat of art). Beijing: Zhonghua shudian, 1983.

Works by Other Authors

Bartlett, Beatrice S. *Monarchs and Ministers: The Grand Council in Mid-Ch'ing China, 1723–1820.* Berkeley: University of California Press, 1991.
Benedict, Carol. *Golden-Silk Smoke: A History of Tobacco in China, 1550–2010.* Berkeley: University of California Press, 2011.

Bernal, Martin. "Liu Shih-p'ei and National Essence." In *The Limits of Change: Essays on Conservative Alternatives in Republican China*, ed. Charlotte Furth, 57–87. Cambridge, MA: Harvard University Press, 1976.

Brewer, John. *The Sinews of Power: War, Money, and the English State, 1688–1783*. Cambridge, MA: Harvard University Press, 1988.

Chan, Wing-tsit. *A Sourcebook in Chinese Philosophy*. Princeton: Princeton University Press, 1963.

Chang, Hao. *Chinese Intellectuals in Crisis: Search for Order and Meaning, 1900–1911*. Berkeley: University of California Press, 1987.

Chen Weizhao. *Daixue de wange: Qingdai wenren de xintai shi* (Bloody requiem: the history of Qing literati mentality). Shijiazhuang: Hebei jiaoyu chubanshe, 2001.

Chen Wenyu. "Aiguo chenmin, lichang gaige de Bao Shichen" (Bao Shichen, a patriotic and populist reform leader). *Anhui shixue* 1994.1: 48–49.

Chen Zhaonan. *Yongzheng Qianlong nianjian de yinqian bijia biandong* (Changing relative prices of silver and copper in the Yongzheng and Qianlong reigns). Taibei: Zhongguo xueshu ju, 1966.

Cheung, Sui-wai. *The Price of Rice: Market Integration in Eighteenth-Century China*. Bellingham: Western Washington University Press, 2008.

Chinese People's University Institute of Qing History and Archives Department, comps. *Kang-Yong-Qian shiqi chengxiang renmin fankang douzheng ziliao* (Resistance struggles of urban and rural people in the mid-Qing). Beijing: Zhonghua shuju, 1979.

Chouban yiwu shimo (Complete record of foreign affairs management), Daoguang reign. Beijing: Palace Museum, 1929.

Ch'u, T'ung-tsu. *Local Government in China under the Ch'ing*. Stanford: Stanford University Press, 1962.

Collins, James B. "State Building in Early-Modern Europe: The Case of France." In *Beyond Binary Histories: Re-imagining Eurasia to c. 1830*, ed. Victor Lieberman. Ann Arbor: University of Michigan Press, 1997.

Dai, Yingcong. "Civilians Go into Battle: Hired Militias in the White Lotus Wars, 1795–1805." *Asia Major*, 3rd ser. 22.2 (December 2009): 145–78.

Dai Kan-Wa jiten (Great Chinese-Japanese dictionary). Ed. Morohashi Tetsuji. Tokyo: Taishūkan shoten, 1966.

DeBary, Wm. Theodore. *The Liberal Tradition in China*. New York: Columbia University Press, 1983.

DeBary, Wm. Theodore, and Richard Lufrano. *Sources of Chinese Tradition*. 2nd ed. New York: Columbia University Press, 2000.

Delury, John Patrick. "Depotism Above and Below: Gu Yanwu on Power, Money, and Mores." Ph.D. dissertation, Yale University, 2007.

Deng, Kent G. "Miracle or Mirage? Foreign Silver, China's Economy, and Globalization from the Sixteenth to the Nineteenth Centuries." *Pacific Economic Review* 13.3 (2008): 320–58.

Duan Zhao. *Tao Zhu yu Jia-Dao jingshi sixiang yanjiu* (Tao Zhu and Jiaqing-Daoguang statecraft thought). Beijing: Zhongguo shehui kexue chubanshe, 2001.

Dunstan, Helen. *State or Merchant? Political Economy and Political Process in 1740s China.* Cambridge, MA: Harvard University Asia Center, 2006.

Elman, Benjamin A. *Classicism, Politics, and Kinship: The Ch'ang-chou School of New Text Confucianism in Late Imperial China.* Berkeley: University of California Press, 1990.

Fang, Qiang. "Hot Potatoes: Chinese Complaint Systems from Early Times to the Late Qing (1898)." *Journal of Asian Studies* 8.4 (November 2009): 1105–36.

Faure, David. *Emperor and Ancestor: State and Lineage in South China.* Stanford: Stanford University Press, 2007.

Feng Tianyu. "Daoguang Xianfeng nianjian jingshi shixue" (Statecraft and substantive learning in the Daoguang and Xianfeng eras). *Lishi yanjiu* 1987.4: 138–51.

Folsom, Kenneth E. *Friends, Guests, and Colleagues: The Mu-fu System in the Late Ch'ing Period.* Berkeley: University of California Press, 1968.

Furth, Charlotte, Judith T. Zeitlin, and Ping-chen Hsiung, eds. *Thinking with Cases: Specialist Knowledge in Chinese Cultural History.* Honolulu: University of Hawai'i Press, 2007.

Gu Yanwu. "Junxian lun" (On bureaucratic local administration). In *Gu Tinglin shiwen ji*, 1:6–9. Beijing: Zhonghua shuju, 1959.

Guan Wenfa. *Jiaqing di* (The Jiaqing emperor). Changchun: Jilin wenshi chubanshe, 1993.

Guo Songyi. "Ming-Qing shiqi de liangshi shengchan yu nongmin shenghuo shuiping" (Grain production and rural standards of living in the Ming-Qing era). *Zhongguo shehui kexueyuan lishi yanjiusuo xuekan* 2001.1: 373–96.

Guy, R. Kent. *Qing Governors and Their Provinces: The Evolution of Territorial Administration in China, 1644–1796.* Seattle: University of Washington Press, 2010.

Hamashita Takeshi. *Chūgoku kindai keizaishi kenkyū* (Studies in modern Chinese economic history). Tokyo: University of Tokyo Press, 1989.

Han, Seunghyun. *After the Prosperous Age: State and Elites in Early Nineteenth-Century Suzhou.* Cambridge, MA: Harvard University Asia Center, 2016.

———. "Changing Roles of Local Elites from the 1720s to the 1830s." *Cambridge History of China*, vol. 9, *The Ch'ing Dynasty to 1800*, part 2, ed. Willard J. Peterson, 606–48. Cambridge: Cambridge University Press, 2016.

———. "The Punishment of Examination Riots in the Early to Mid-Qing Period." *Late Imperial China* 32.2 (December 2011): 133–65.

Hanyu da cidian (Great Chinese language dictionary). Ed. Luo Zhufeng. Shanghai: Hanyu da cidian chubanshe, 2001.

He Liping. "Yapien maoyi yu baiyin wailiu guanxi zhi cai jiantao" (Reexamining the relationship of the opium trade and silver outflows). *Shehui kexue zhanxian* 2007.1.

Helleiner, Eric. *The Making of National Money: Territorial Currencies in Historical Perspective.* Ithaca: Cornell University Press, 2003.

Hinton, Harold C. *The Grain Tribute System of China, 1845–1911.* Cambridge, MA: Harvard University, Chinese Economic and Political Studies, 1956.

Ho, Ping-ti. "The Salt Merchants of Yang-chou: A Study of Commercial Capitalism in Eighteenth-Century China." *Harvard Journal of Asiatic Studies* 17 (1954): 130–68.

———. *Studies on the Population of China, 1368–1968*. Cambridge, MA: Harvard University Press, 1969.

Horesh, Niv. "Printed in London, Disbursed on the Bund: The Hongkong Bank and Its Early Note Issue in Shanghai, 1865–1911." *Late Imperial China* 27.1 (June 2006): 109–40.

Hoshi Ayao. *Dai unga: Chūgoku no sōun* (The Grand Canal: grain tribute in China). Tokyo: Kondō shuppansha, 1971.

———. *The Ming Tribute Grain System*. Ed. and trans. Mark Elvin. Ann Arbor: University of Michigan, Center for Chinese Studies, 1969.

Hsiao, Kung-chuan. *Rural China: Imperial Control in the Nineteenth Century*. Seattle: University of Washington Press, 1960.

Hu Pu'an. "Bao Zhenbo xiansheng nianpu" (Chronological biography of Bao Shichen). In Bao, *Bao Shichen quanji* (1991), 105–240.

Hu Qizhuang. *Zhongguo jingji sixiang shi* (History of Chinese economic thought). Shanghai: Caijing Daxue chubanshe, 1998.

Hua Rende. "The History and Revival of Northern Wei Stele-Style Calligraphy." In *Character and Context in Chinese Calligraphy*, ed. Cary Y. Liu et al., 104–31. Princeton: Princeton University Art Museum, 1999.

Huangchao jingshi wenbian (Selected writings on statecraft from the ruling dynasty). Ed. He Changling and Wei Yuan. 1826.

Hucker, Charles O. *A Dictionary of Official Titles in Imperial China*. Stanford: Stanford University Press, 1985.

Hummel, Arthur, ed. *Eminent Chinese of the Ch'ing Period*. Washington, DC: U.S. Government Printing Office, 1943.

Hung, Ho-fung "Cultural Legitimacy, Capital Appeal, and Delayed State Breakdown in Qing China, 1805–1839." Unpublished paper, cited with permission.

Irigoin, Alejandra. "The End of a Silver Era: The Consequences of the Breakdown of the Spanish Peso Standard in China and the United States, 1780s–1850s." *Journal of World History* 20.2 (2009): 207–43.

Iwai Shigeki. "Chōkō to goshi: Hi 'chōkō taisei' ron no kokoromu" (Tribute and markets: a preliminary critique of the "tribute system" notion). http://www.hmm.bun.kyoto-u.ac.jp/asorder/meetings11-02.html.

Jingxian xu zhi (Continued gazetteer of Jing County). 1825.

Jingxian zhi (Gazetteer of Jing County). Beijing: Fangzhi chubanshe, 1996.

Jones, Susan Mann. "Finance in Ningpo: The 'Ch'ien Chuang,' 1750–1880." In *Economic Organization in Chinese Society*, ed. W. E. Willmott, 37–77. Stanford: Stanford University Press, 1972.

———. "Hung Liang-chi (1746–1809): The Perception and Articulation of Political Problems in Late Eighteenth Century China." Ph.D. dissertation, Stanford University, 1971.

Jones, Susan Mann, and Philip A. Kuhn. "Dynastic Decline and the Roots of Rebellion." In *Cambridge History of China*, vol. 10, *Late Ch'ing, 1800–1911*, part 1, ed. John King Fairbank, 107–62. Cambridge: Cambridge University Press, 1978.

Kaske, Elisabeth. "Fund-Raising Wars: Office Selling and Interprovincial Finance in Nineteenth-Century China." *Harvard Journal of Asiatic Studies* 71.1 (June 2011): 69–141.

Kishimoto, Mio. "New Studies on Statecraft in Mid- and Late-Qing China: Qing Intellectuals and Their Debates on Economic Policies." *International Journal of Asian Studies* 6.1 (2009): 87–102.

Kuhn, Philip A. "Local Self-Government under the Republic: Problems of Control, Autonomy, and Mobilization." In *Conflict and Control in Late Imperial China*, ed. Frederic Wakeman, Jr., and Carolyn Grant, 257–98. Berkeley: University of California Press, 1975.

———. *Origins of the Modern Chinese State*. Stanford: Stanford University Press, 2002.

———. *Rebellion and Its Enemies in Late Imperial China: Militarization and Social Structure, 1796–1864*. Cambridge, MA: Harvard University Press, 1970.

Kuroda Akinobu. "Kenryū no senki" (The inflation of copper cash in the Qianlong period). *Tōyōshi kenkyū* 45.4 (March 1987): 58–89.

———. "Shindai ginzen nikasei no kozo to sono hokai" (The structure and collapse of silver-copper bimetallism in the Qing). *Shakai keizai shigaku* 57.2 (1992): 93–125.

Kwass, Michael. *Contraband: Louis Mandrin and the Making of a Global Underground*. Cambridge, MA: Harvard University Press, 2014.

Lam, Tong. *A Passion for Facts: Social Surveys and the Construction of the Chinese Nation-State, 1900–1949*. Berkeley: University of California Press, 2011.

Lee, James Z., and Wang Feng. *One Quarter of Humanity: Malthusian Mythology and Chinese Realities*. Cambridge, MA: Harvard University Press, 1999.

Leonard, Jane Kate. *Controlling from Afar: The Daoguang Emperor's Management of the Grand Canal Crisis, 1824–1826*. Ann Arbor: University of Michigan, Center for Chinese Studies, 1996.

———. *Wei Yuan and China's Rediscovery of the Maritime World*. Cambridge, MA: Harvard University, Council on East Asian Studies, 1984.

Li, Bozhong. *Agricultural Development in Jiangnan, 1620–1850*. New York: St. Martin's Press, 1998.

Lin, Man-houng. *China Upside Down: Currency, Society, and Ideologies, 1808–1856*. Cambridge, MA: Harvard University Asia Center, 2006.

———. "A Time in Which the Grandsons Beat the Grandfathers: The Rise of Liberal Political-Economic Ideologies in China's Monetary Crisis, 1808–1854." *American Asian Review* 9.4 (December 1991): 1–28.

———. "Two Social Theories Revealed: Statecraft Controversies over China's Monetary Crisis, 1808–1854." *Late Imperial China* 12.2 (December 1991): 1–35.

Liu Guangjing [K. C. Liu]. "Jingshi ziqiang, xinxing qiye—Zhongguo xiandaihua de kaishi" (Statecraft, self-strengthening, and modern enterprise—the beginnings of China's modernization). In *Jingshi sixiang yu xinxing qiye* (Statecraft thought and modern enterprise), 1–22. Taibei: Lianjing, 1990.

———. "Shijiu shiji chuye Zhongguo zhishifenzi Bao Shichen yu Wei Yuan" (The early nineteenth-century Chinese intellectuals Bao Shichen and Wei Yuan). In *Zhongyang yanjiuyuan guoji Hanxue huiyi lunwenji* (Proceedings of the Academia Sinica International Conference on Chinese Studies), 995–1030. Taipei: Academia Sinica, 1980.

———. "Wei Yuan zhi zhexue yu jingshi sixiang" (Wei Yuan's philosophy and statecraft thought). In *Jindai Zhongguo jingshi sixiang yantaohui lunwen ji* (Papers from the conference on modern Chinese statecraft), comp. Institute of Modern History, 359–90. Taibei: Academia Sinica, 1984.

Liu, Lydia H. *The Clash of Empires: The Invention of China in Modern World Making.* Cambridge, MA: Harvard University Press, 2004.

Mann, Susan. *The Talented Women of the Zhang Family.* Berkeley: University of California Press, 2007.

Mao Haijian. *Tianchao de pengkui: Yaian zhanzheng cai yanjiu* (Imperial collapse: a revisionist study of the Opium War). Beijing: Sanlian shudian, 2005.

Mayers, William Frederick. *The Chinese Government.* Shanghai: Kelly and Walsh, 1897.

McMahon, Daniel. "Dynastic Decline, Heshen, and the Ideology of the Xianyu Reforms." *Tsing Hua Journal of Chinese Studies,* new ser. 38.2 (June 2008): 231–55.

Metzger, Thomas A. *The Internal Organization of Ch'ing Bureaucracy: Legal, Normative, and Communication Aspects.* Cambridge, MA: Harvard University Press, 1973.

———. "T'ao Chu's Reform of the Huaipei Salt Monopoly (1831–1833)." *Papers on China* 16 (1962): 1–39.

Momose, Hiromu. "Pao Shih-ch'en." In *Eminent Chinese of the Ch'ing Period,* ed. Arthur Hummel, 610–11. Washington: U.S. Government Printing Office, 1943.

Mosca, Matthew W. *From Frontier Policy to Foreign Policy: The Question of India in the Transformation of Geopolitics in Qing China.* Stanford: Stanford University Press, 2013.

Myers, Ramon H. *The Chinese Economy: Past and Present.* Belmont, CA: Wadsworth, 1980.

Naquin, Susan. *Millenarian Rebellion in China: The Eight Trigrams Uprising of 1813.* New Haven: Yale University Press, 1976.

Ni Yuping. "Daoguang liunian caoliang haiyun de jige wenti" (Some problems regarding the maritime shipment of tribute grain in 1826). *Qingshi yanjiu* 2002.3: 70–75.

———. *Qingchao Jia Dao caizheng yu shehui* (Financial administration and society in the Qing Jiaqing and Daoguang reigns). Beijing: Commercial Press, 2013.

Nivison, David S. "Ho-shen and His Accusers: Ideology and Political Behavior in the Eighteenth Century." In *Confucianism in Action,* ed. David S. Nivison and Arthur S. Wright, 209–43. Stanford: Stanford University Press, 1959.

Ocko, Jonathan K. "I'll Take It All the Way to Beijing: Capital Appeals in the Qing." *Journal of Asian Studies* 47.2 (May 1988): 291–315.

Ōtani Toshio. "Hō Seishin no jitsugaku shisō ni tsuite" (On Bao Shichen's "substantive studies" thought). *Tōyōshi kenkyū* 28.3 (December 1969): 162–95.

Peng Xinwei. *Zhongguo huobi shi* (Chinese monetary history). 1954. Reprinted Shanghai: Renmin chubanshe, 1965.

Peng Zeyi. "1853–1868 nian de Zhongguo tonghuo pengzhang" (China's currency inflation of 1853–1868). *Zhongguo shehui kexueyuan Jingji yanjiusuo jikan* 1 (1979).

———. "Qingdai qianqi shougongye de fazhan" (The development of handicrafts in the early Qing). *Zhongguo shi yanjiu* 1981.1.

———. "Yapien zhanzheng hou shinianjian yingui qianjian bodong xia Zhongguo jingji yu jieji guanxi" (The Chinese economy and class relations in the post-Opium War decade under the impact of rising silver-to-copper exchange rates). In *Shijiu shiji houbanqi de Zhongguo caizheng yu jingji* (Government finance and the economy in late nineteenth-century China), 24–71. Beijing: Renmin chubanshe, 1983.

Perdue, Peter C. *Exhausting the Earth: State and Peasant in Hunan, 1500–1850*. Cambridge, MA: Harvard University Press, 1987.

———. "Official Goals and Local Interests: Water Control in the Dongting Lake Region during the Ming and Qing Periods." *Journal of Asian Studies* 41.4 (August 1982): 747–65.

Platt, Stephen R. *Provincial Patriots: The Hunanese and Modern China*. Cambridge, MA: Harvard University Press, 2007.

Polachek, James M. *The Inner Opium War*. Cambridge, MA: Harvard University, Council on East Asian Studies, 1992.

Poovey, Mary. *A History of the Modern Fact: Problems of Knowledge in the Sciences of Wealth and Society*. Chicago: University of Chicago Press, 1998.

Porter, Theodore M. *Trust in Numbers: The Pursuit of Objectivity in Science and Public Life*. Princeton: Princeton University Press, 1995.

Qiu Jiasui. "Tongchao yi" (On copper certificates). In *Huangchao jingshi wenbian* (Compendium of statecraft writings of the present dynasty), ed. He Changling, 53:53–56. 1826. Reprinted Taipei: Guofeng chubanshe, 1963.

Rawski, Evelyn S. "Agricultural Development in the Han River Highlands." *Ch'ing-shih wen-t'i* 3.4 (1975): 63–81.

———. "The Qing Formation and the Early Modern Period." In *The Qing Formation in World-Historical Time*, ed. Lynn A. Struve, 207–41. Cambridge, MA: Harvard University Asia Center, 2004.

Richards, John F. "Early Modern India and World History." *Journal of World History* 8.2 (1997): 197–209.

Rowe, William T. *Crimson Rain: Seven Centuries of Violence in a Chinese County*. Stanford: Stanford University Press, 2007.

———. *Hankow: Commerce and Society in a Chinese City, 1796–1889*. Stanford: Stanford University Press, 1984.

———. "Hu Lin-i's Reform of the Grain Tribute System in Hupeh, 1855–58." *Ch'ing-shih wen-t'i* 4.10 (December 1983): 33–86.

———. "Provincial Monetary Practice in Eighteenth-Century China." In *Chinese Handicraft Regulations of the Qing Dynasty*, ed. Christine Möll-Murata, Song Jianze, and Hans Ulrich Vogel, 347–71. Munich: Iudicium, 2005.

———. *Saving the World: Chen Hongmou and Elite Consciousness in Eighteenth Century China*. Stanford: Stanford University Press, 2001.

———. "Urban Control in Late Imperial China: The *Pao-chia* System in Hankow." In *Perspectives on a Changing China*, ed. Joshua A. Fogel and William T. Rowe, 89–112. Boulder: Westview Press, 1979.

Saeki Tomi. "Chūgoku kinsei ni okeru zettai kunshu no keizai sei" (Absolutism in modern China). In *Chūgoku shi kenkyū* (Studies in Chinese history), 2.61–74. Kyoto: Tōyōshi kenkyūkai, 1971.

———. "Shindai Dōkō cho ni okeru Kainan ensei no kaikaku" (The reform of the Huainan salt administration during the Qing Daoguang reign). In *Chūgoku shi kenkyū* (Studies in Chinese history), 2.621–66. Kyoto: Tōyōshi kenkyūkai, 1971.

———. *Shindai ensei no kenkyū* (A study of the Qing salt administration). Kyoto: Tōyōshi kenkyūkai, 1956.

Schneider, Lawrence A. "National Essence and the New Intelligentsia." In *The Limits of Change: Essays on Conservative Alternatives in Republican China*, ed. Charlotte Furth, 90–112. Cambridge, MA: Harvard University Press, 1976.

Schwartz, Benjamin I. *In Search of Wealth and Power: Yen Fu and the West*. Cambridge, MA: Harvard University Press, 1964.

Shao Jing and Yi Menghong. *Zhongguo jindai jingji sixiang shi* (History of modern Chinese economic thought). Beijing: Zhonghua shuju, 1980.

Shi Liye. "Bao Shichen 'Shuochu' chutan" (A preliminary investigation of Bao Shichen's *Shuochu*). *Anhui daxue xuebao*, Philosophy and Social Science edition, 1997.6: 67–70.

Shimada Kenji. *Pioneer of the Chinese Revolution: Zhang Binglin and Confucianism*. Trans. Joshua A. Fogel. Stanford: Stanford University Press, 1990.

Sommer, Matthew H. *Polyandry and Wife-Selling in Qing Dynasty China: Survival Strategies and Judicial Interventions*. Berkeley: University of California Press, 2015.

———. *Sex, Law, and Society in Late Imperial China*. Stanford: Stanford University Press, 2000.

Sun, E-tu Zen. *Ch'ing Administrative Terms: A Translation of the Terminology of the Six Boards with Explanatory Notes*. Cambridge, MA: Harvard University Press, 1961.

Sun Guangde. "Gong Zizhen de jingshi sixiang" (Gong Zizhen's statecraft thought). In *Jindai Zhongguo jingshi sixiang yantaohui lunwen ji* (Papers from the conference on modern Chinese statecraft), comp. Institute of Modern History, 275–89. Taibei: Academia Sinica, 1984.

Sutton, Donald S. "Ethnicity and the Miao Frontier in the Eighteenth Century." In *Empire at the Margins: Culture, Ethnicity, and Frontier in Early Modern China*, ed. Pamela Kyle Crossley, Helen F. Siu, and Donald S. Sutton, 190–228. Berkeley: University of California Press, 2006.

Suzuki Chūsei. *Shinchō chūkishi kenkyū* (A study of the mid-Qing period). Toyohashi-shi: Aichi daigaku kokusai mondai kenkyūjo, 1952.

Telford, Ted A. "Family and State in Qing China: Marriage in the Tongcheng Lineages, 1650–1850." In *Jinshi jiazu yu zhengzhi bijiao lishi lunwen ji* (Modern family and political history), 921–42. Taibei: Institute of Modern History, 1992.

Thaxton, Ralph A., Jr. *Salt of the Earth: The Political Origins of Peasant Protest and Communist Revolution in China*. Berkeley: University of California Press, 1997.

Vogel, Hans Ulrich. "Chinese Central Monetary Policy, 1644–1800." *Late Imperial China* 8.2 (December 1987): 1–52.

Von Glahn, Richard. "Foreign Silver Coins in the Market Culture of Nineteenth-Century China." *International Journal of Asian Studies* 4.1 (2007): 51–78.

———. *Fountain of Fortune: Money and Monetary Policy in China, 1000–1700*. Berkeley: University of California Press, 1996.

Waley, Arthur. *The Opium War through Chinese Eyes*. Stanford: Stanford University Press, 1958.

Wang Hongbin. "Lin Zexu guanyu yingui qianjian de renzhi yu yinhuo" (Lin Zexu's understanding and suspicions regarding the high cost of silver). *Shixue yuekan* 2006.9: 35–41.

Wang Liu. *Huozhongyuan chugao* (Preliminary drafts from the Huozhong Garden) (1835). Reproduced photographically in Lin, *China Upside Down*, 150.

———. *Qianbi chuyan* (Modest proposals on coin and currency) (1837). In *Xuxiu Siku quanshu*, 838.599–653. Shanghai: Guji chubanshe, 1995.

Wang, Wensheng. *White Lotus Rebels and South China Pirates: Crisis and Reform in the Qing Empire*. Cambridge, MA: Harvard University Press, 2014.

Wang, Yeh-chien. *Land Taxation in Imperial China, 1750–1911*. Cambridge, MA: Harvard University Press, 1973.

Wei Xiumei. "He Changling de jingshi sixiang" (He Changling's statecraft thought). In *Jindai Zhongguo jingshi sixiang yantaohui lunwen ji* (Papers from the conference on modern Chinese statecraft), comp. Institute of Modern History, 393–408. Taibei: Academia Sinica, 1984.

Wei Yuan. "Junchu" (Military logistics), part 3. In *Shengwu ji*, 14:60–65. 1842; new ed. 1881.

Whitbeck, Judith. "From K'ao-cheng to Ching-shih: Kung Tzu-chen and the Redirections of Literati Commitment in Early Nineteenth Century China." In *Jindai Zhongguo jingshi sixiang yantaohui lunwen ji* (Papers from the conference on modern Chinese statecraft), comp. Institute of Modern History, 323–-40. Taibei: Academia Sinica, 1984.

Wilhelm, Hellmut. "The Background of Tseng Kuo-fan's Ideology." *Asiatisch Studien* 3–4 (1949): 90–100.

Wilkinson, Endymion P. *Studies in Chinese Price History*. New York: Garland Press, 1980.

Will, Pierre-Étienne. "Le contrôle de l'excès de pouvoir sous la dynastie des Ming." In *La Chine et la démocratie*, ed. Mireille Delmas-Marty and Pierre-Étienne Will, 116–25. Paris: Fayard, 2007.

———. "The 1744 Annual Audits of Magistrate Activity and Their Fate." *Late Imperial China* 18.2 (December 1997): 1–50.

———. "Un cycle hydraulique en Chine: la province du Hubei du 16ème au 19ème siècles." *Bulletin de l'école française d'extrême orient* 68 (1980): 261–87.

Xia Nai. "Taiping tianguo qian hou Changjiang gesheng zhi tianfu wenti" (The land tax problem in the Yangzi provinces before and after the Taiping rebellion). *Qinghua xuebao* 10.2 (April 1935): 409–74.

Xinyu xianzhi (Gazetteer of Xinyu county). 1849. Reprinted Taipei: Chengwen, 1988.

Xu Liwang. "Shiyi shibian: lun Bao Shichen yu Changzhou shiren di jiaowang ji jingshi sixiang de shanbian" (Conditions change over time: Bao Shichen's interactions with Changzhou scholars and the evolution of statecraft thought). *Anhui lixue* 2005.5.

Yen, Yuehping. *Calligraphy and Power in Contemporary Chinese Society*. London: Routledge, 2005.

Young, Arthur N. *China's Nation-Building Effort, 1927–1937: The Financial and Economic Record*. Stanford: Hoover Institution Press, 1971.

Zanasi, Margherita. "Frugality and Luxury: Morality, Market, and Consumption in Late Imperial China." *Frontiers of History in China* 10.3 (September 2015): 457–85.

Zarrow, Peter. "Anti-Despotism and 'Rights Talk': The Intellectual Origins of Modern Human Rights Thinking in the Late Qing." *Modern China* 34.2 (April 2008): 179–209.

Zhang Shiming and Feng Yongming. "Bao Shichen zhengyi de chengben" (The cost of Bao Shichen justice). *Qingshi yanjiu* 75.4 (November 2009): 1–34.

Zhang, Ting. "Penitence Silver and the Politics of Punishment in the Qianlong Reign, 1736–1796." *Late Imperial China* 31.2 (December 2010): 34–68.

Zhang Yan. "Bao Shichen yu jindai qianyue de 'haiyun nancao' gaige" (Bao Shichen and the sea transport of grain tribute on the eve of modernity). *Jindaishi yanjiu* 2000.1: 129–53.

Zhang Yufen. "Lun Jiaqing chunian de 'Xianyu weixin'" (On the "comprehensive reforms" of the early Jiaqing reign). *Qingshi yanjiu* 1992.4: 49–54.

Zhao Erxun, ed. *Qing shi gao lie zhuan* (Draft history of the Qing dynasty: biographies). Taipei: Mingwen shuju, 1983.

Zhao, Gang. "Reinventing China: Imperial Qing Ideology and the Rise of Modern Chinese National Identity in the Early Twentieth Century." *Modern China* 32.1 (January 2006): 3–30.

Zhao Gang. *The Qing Opening to the Ocean: Chinese Maritime Policies, 1684–1757*. Honolulu: University of Hawai'i Press, 2013.

Zheng Dahua. "Bao Shichen yu Jia-Dao nianjian de xuefeng quanbian" (Bao Shichen and intellectual change during the Jiaqing and Daoguang reigns). *Anhui shixue* 2006.4.

Zhongguo renming da zidian (Chinese biographical dictionary). Taipei: Taiwan shangwu yinhuaguan, 1990.

Zhou Bangjun. "Bao Shichen de bianji tudi liyong jixu sixiaang" (Bao Shichen's thought on techniques for utilizing marginal farmland). *Zhongguo nongshi* 21.4 (2002): 97–107.

Zhou Qirong. "Cong 'kuangyan' dao 'weiyan': lun Gong Zizhen de jingshi sixiang yu jingjin wenxue" (From "crazy words" to "trifling words": Gong Zizhen's statecraft thought and literature). In *Jindai Zhongguo jingshi sixiang yantaohui lunwen ji* (Papers from the conference on modern Chinese statecraft), comp. Institute of Modern History, 295–318. Taibei: Academia Sinica, 1984.

Index

Page numbers for tables and figures are in italics.

C

H

Harvard-Yenching Institute Monograph Series

(recent titles)

60. *Words Well Put: Visions of Poetic Competence in the Chinese Tradition*, by Graham Sanders
61. *Householders: The Reizei Family in Japanese History*, by Steven D. Carter
62. *The Divine Nature of Power: Chinese Ritual Architecture at the Sacred Site of Jinci*, by Tracy Miller
63. *Beacon Fire and Shooting Star: The Literary Culture of the Liang (502–557)*, by Xiaofei Tian
64. *Lost Soul: "Confucianism" in Contemporary Chinese Academic Discourse*, by John Makeham
65. *The Sage Learning of Liu Zhi: Islamic Thought in Confucian Terms*, by Sachiko Murata, William C. Chittick, and Tu Weiming
66. *Through a Forest of Chancellors: Fugitive Histories in Liu Yuan's* Lingyan ge, *an Illustrated Book from Seventeenth-Century Suzhou*, by Anne Burkus-Chasson
67. *Empire of Texts in Motion: Chinese, Korean, and Taiwanese Transculturations of Japanese Literature*, by Karen Laura Thornber
68. *Empire's Twilight: Northeast Asia Under the Mongols*, by David M. Robinson
69. *Ancestors, Virgins, and Friars: Christianity as a Local Religion in Late Imperial China*, by Eugenio Menegon
70. *Manifest in Words, Written on Paper: Producing and Circulating Poetry in Tang Dynasty China*, by Christopher M. B. Nugent
71. *The Poetics of Sovereignty: On Emperor Taizong of the Tang Dynasty*, by Jack W. Chen
72. *Ancestral Memory in Early China*, by K. E. Brashier
73. *'Dividing the Realm in Order to Govern': The Spatial Organization of the Song State*, by Ruth Mostern
74. *The Dynamics of Masters Literature: Early Chinese Thought from Confucius to Han Feizi*, by Wiebke Denecke
75. *Songs of Contentment and Transgression: Discharged Officials and Literati Communities in Sixteenth-Century North China*, by Tian Yuan Tan
76. *Ten Thousand Scrolls: Reading and Writing in the Poetics of Huang Tingjian and the Late Northern Song*, by Yugen Wang
77. *A Northern Alternative: Xue Xuan (1389-1464) and the Hedong School*, by Khee Heong Koh
78. *Visionary Journeys: Travel Writings from Early Medieval and Nineteenth-Century China*, by Xiaofei Tian
79. *Making Personas: Transnational Film Stardom in Modern Japan*, by Hideaki Fujiki
80. *Strange Eventful Histories: Identity, Performance, and Xu Wei's* Four Cries of a Gibbon, by Shiamin Kwa
81. *Critics and Commentators: The* Book of Poems *as Classic and Literature*, by Bruce Rusk
82. *Home and the World: Editing the Glorious Ming in Woodblock-Printed Books of the Sixteenth and Seventeenth Centuries*, by Yuming He
83. *Courtesans, Concubines, and the Cult of Female Fidelity*, by Beverly Bossler
84. *Chinese History: A New Manual, Third Edition*, by Endymion Wilkinson
85. *A Comprehensive Manchu-English Dictionary*, by Jerry Norman

86. *Drifting among Rivers and Lakes: Southern Song Dynasty Poetry and the Problem of Literary History*, by Michael Fuller
87. *Martial Spectacles of the Ming Court*, by David M. Robinson
88. *Modern Archaics: Continuity and Innovation in the Chinese Lyric Tradition, 1900-1937*, by Shengqing Wu
89. *Cherishing Antiquity: The Cultural Construction of an Ancient Chinese Kingdom*, by Olivia Milburn
90. *The Burden of Female Talent: The Poet Li Qingzhao and Her History in China*, by Ronald Egan
91. *Public Memory in Early China*, by K. E. Brashier
92. *Women and National Trauma in Late Imperial Chinese Literature,* by Wai-yee Li
93. *The Destruction of the Medieval Chinese Aristocracy,* by Nicolas Tackett
94. *Savage Exchange: Han Imperialism, Chinese Literary Style, and the Economic Imagination*, by Tamara T. Chin
95. *Shifting Stories: History, Gossip, and Lore in Narratives from Tang Dynasty China,* by Sarah M. Allen
96. *One Who Knows Me: Friendship and Literary Culture in Mid-Tang China,* by Anna Shields
97. *Materializing Magic Power: Chinese Popular Religion in Villages and Cities,* by Wei-Ping Lin
98. *Traces of Grand Peace: Classics and State Activism in Imperial China,* by Jaeyoon Song
99. *Fiction's Family: Zhan Xi, Zhan Kai, and the Business of Women in Late-Qing China,* by Ellen Widmer
100. *Chinese History: A New Manual, Fourth Edition,* by Endymion Wilkinson
101. *After the Prosperous Age: State and Elites in Early Nineteenth-Century Suzhou,* by Seunghyun Han
102. *Celestial Masters: History and Ritual in Early Daoist Communities,* by Terry F. Kleeman
103. *Transgressive Typologies: Constructions of Gender and Power in Early Tang China*, by Rebecca Doran
104. *Li Mengyang, the North-South Divide, and Literati Learning in Ming China*, by Chang Woei Ong
105 *Bannermen Tales (Zidishu): Manchu Storytelling and Cultural Hybridity in the Qing Dynasty*, by Elena Suet-Ying Chiu
106. *Upriver Journeys: Diaspora and Empire in Southern China, 1570-1850*, by Steven B. Miles
107. *Ancestors, Kings, and the Dao*, by Constance A. Cook
108. *Restoring the Broken Halberd: Jian'an and the Three Kingdoms*, by Xiaofei Tian
109. *Speaking of Profit: Bao Shichen and Reform in Nineteenth-Century China,* by William T. Rowe
110. *Building for Oil: Daqing and the Formation of the Chinese Socialist State,* by Hou Li
111. *Reading Philosophy, Writing Poetry: Intertextual Modes of Making Meaning in Early Medieval China,* by Wendy Swartz
112. *Writing for Print: Publishing and the Making of Textual Authority in Late Imperial China,* by Suyoung Son